Entrepreneurial Economics

Entrepreneurial Economics

Keith S. Glancey

and

Ronald W. McQuaid

Consultant Editor: Jo Campling

338.04
G54e

First published in Great Britain 2000 by
MACMILLAN PRESS LTD
Houndmills, Basingstoke, Hampshire RG21 6XS and London
Companies and representatives throughout the world

A catalogue record for this book is available from the British Library.

ISBN 0–333–73645–1

First published in the United States of America 2000 by
ST. MARTIN'S PRESS, INC.,
Scholarly and Reference Division,
175 Fifth Avenue, New York, N.Y. 10010

ISBN 0–312–23227–6

Library of Congress Cataloging-in-Publication Data
Glancey, Keith.
Entrepreneurial economics / Keith S. Glancey, Ronald W. McQuaid.
p.   cm.
Includes bibliographical references and index.
ISBN 0–312–23227–6 (cloth)
1. Entrepreneurship. 2. Economic history. I. McQuaid, Ronald, 1955– II. Title.

HB615 .G57   2000
338'.04–dc21
                                                                99–056266

This book is printed on paper suitable for recycling and made from fully managed and sustained forest sources.

10   9   8   7   6   5   4   3   2   1
09   08   07   06   05   04   03   02   01   00

Printed and bound in Great Britain by
Antony Rowe Ltd, Chippenham, Wiltshire

For Susan and Gillian
Carpe diem

Contents

List of Tables and Figure

Acknowledgements

Throughout this project we have been fortunate to have had the support and encouragement of many people. We would like to thank the academics, entrepreneurs and policymakers who have given generously of their time in sharing their experiences and views of entrepreneurship. In particular, Professor Mark Brownrigg, Pamela Siler, Ian Brackall, Derek Gavin and Tom Macdonald provided comments which were of great assistance on earlier drafts. Thanks are also due to Jo Campling for her invaluable advice and support, to Cathy Craig for providing excellent secretarial back-up, and to *Scotland on Sunday* for allowing us to use an article on Richard Branson as the basis for a case-study. Finally, our wives Susan and Gillian, and our families, have displayed considerable patience in tolerating our obsession with the project and the many late nights it entailed. Without their support and encouragement we could not have grasped the opportunity to write this book.

Part I
What is Entrepreneurship?

1
Introduction to Entrepreneurship

Introduction

Entrepreneurial Economics considers the role of entrepreneurship and entrepreneurs in economic theory. Economic theory helps to provide insights into the wide variety of behaviour of different producers, consumers and markets, and how each of these changes over time. A key component of these is the role of entrepreneurship. As the economist William Baumol has argued, much of traditional neoclassical economics considered the three key factors of production in economic theory to be land, labour and capital, but this neglected the role of the individual and of entrepreneurship in the economy and in the competitiveness of organizations. Earlier classical economists, such as Adam Smith, had also recognized the importance of entrepreneurship and many economists now add a fourth factor of production, entrepreneurship – the focus of this book.

The aims of this book are:

- to describe, analyse and compare how different economic theories have incorporated entrepreneurship;
- to assess the contributions of sociological, psychological and management perspectives towards understanding entrepreneurship and to compare them to economic perspectives;
- to analyse public policies promoting entrepreneurship;
- to increase the understanding of entrepreneurship across the economy and society.

The term entrepreneurship has been used to mean different things by different writers. So this chapter starts by giving a broad introduction to the main perspectives on what is meant by the terms entrepreneurship and entrepreneurs. In later chapters of the book the use of these perspectives in different theories is considered in more depth. The second part of this chapter provides an outline of the book and how the different chapters fit together. First let us discuss entrepreneurship and the entrepreneurs that practice it.

What is entrepreneurship?

There is little dispute that people who have started and developed major companies are entrepreneurs. Examples might include Bill Gates of Microsoft who became arguably the world's wealthiest person, Richard Branson founder of the Virgin Group who started a series of businesses from record companies to airlines, Ted Turner the founder of Turner Broadcasting System including the CNN News company and Henry Ford, the founder of Ford Motors. The infamous robber barons of the last century were also entrepreneurs. They were renowned for their much criticised business practices and monopoly power in fast growing industries, but they did introduce new mass market products and new production processes, such as John D. Rockerfeller's Standard Oil helping to bring cheap kerosene, and later oil, to American households, Ford giving mobility to working-class people and Andrew Carnegie helping to replace poor quality iron products with the new steel products. They also brought their entrepreneurial persistence and clear vision to philanthropy, setting up fabulously resourced charitable foundations. Indeed Carnegie said 'the man who dies thus rich dies disgraced' and by 1919 he had given over $350 million, worth many billions today, to charity.

Some writers have focused upon entrepreneurship as the setting up and owning a new small business or being the owner-manager of a business. However, others focus upon their opportunistic and innovative behaviour and include as entrepreneurs those who transform an existing company or organization rather than setting it up – people who focus on what can be done rather than just what is currently done. For instance, Rey Kroc took the McDonalds hamburger restaurant and created new ways of producing food in an efficient and standardized way, and of organizing and marketing the company. This resulted in the giant corporation we know today. Even though Kroc did not own or start the firm, he was certainly entrepreneurial. So entrepreneurship is not simply owning and managing a business – otherwise someone who simply opened and ran the seventh hamburger restaurant in a street, and did not develop it, would be called an entrepreneur but Kroc would not.

The Concise Oxford Dictionary defines an entrepreneur as: 'a person who undertakes an enterprise or business with the chance of profit or loss; a contractor acting as an intermediary; the person taking effective control of a commercial undertaking...from the French entreprende, to undertake'. This set of definitions points towards an entrepreneur as someone looking for rewards but taking some risk (potentially suffering a profit or loss), someone who links different people and resources for commercial reasons (a contractor), or someone in control of a business. The dictionary definition can be broader and even includes 'a person who organizes entertainment especially musical shows' – the musical entrepreneur!

However, many writers on entrepreneurship and the economy bring in the notion of creating new things or innovation, and do not restrict the role of the entrepreneur to that of commercial businesses. For instance, Hisrich and Peters (1998, p. 9) define entrepreneurship as 'the process of creating something new with value by devoting the necessary time and effort, assuming accompanying financial, psychic, and social risks, and receiving the resulting rewards of monetary and personal satisfaction and independence'.

This suggests that the entrepreneur creates something of value to someone or improves economic efficiency – perhaps a new way of selling insurance, or a new way of organizing emergency admissions to a hospital. The entrepreneur invests resources (which are not necessarily financial) and assumes the risk of doing this, such as loss of money, self belief, time or status. The rewards may be independence (perhaps controlling your own firm or being allowed to significantly influence what you do if you work in a large organization), and psychic and/or financial benefits. Hence, entrepreneurs may be present in any type of private, public or third-sector organization.

In the literature there are five broad sets of views or perspectives for considering who entrepreneurs are. The first set looks at the role or function of entrepreneurs in the economy. The second considers that entrepreneurs are those who exhibit particular forms of behaviour. The third set focuses upon the characteristics of entrepreneurs and the fourth set links entrepreneurship to particular events, such as the creation of a new firm or organization. The fifth perspective, is that of an entrepreneur as an owner-manager of a (usually small) business. However, as shall be seen these are more generally described as small business people rather than entrepreneurs.

There is a large degree of overlap between these differing perspectives, but each can help us to understand various aspects of the entrepreneurship process and entrepreneurs. Now let us consider these five broad sets of views in turn.

Entrepreneurship as an economic function

Entrepreneurs have a number of functions in the development of economies. These include acting as risk takers, resource allocators and innovators.

(i) Entrepreneur as risk taker

One of the earliest uses of the term 'entrepreneur' was by the French writer Richard Cantillon around a quarter of a millennium ago in 1755. He saw the entrepreneur as someone who bought at certain prices but sold at uncertain prices (as when they purchased the goods at a given price they could not be sure what price they would sell them for). So he or she bore the risk and uncertainty of a venture but kept the surplus after the contractual payments had been made. The profit resulted from the entrepreneur accepting uncertainty, and the function of the entrepreneur was to carry out these 'risky' ventures. It should be noted that in economics it is usual to distinguish risk (where you can assign a probability to an outcome) from uncertainty (where a probability of the event occurring cannot be assigned) but here the term 'risky' includes both as is discussed in Chapter 3.

Hence, entrepreneurship may be viewed as requiring the taking of calculated risks, and bearing the uncertainty in return for potential benefits, such as large profits. So a key entrepreneurial skill is calculating, managing and minimising this risk, including perhaps transferring some of the risk to others. As one entrepreneur is reputed to have said: 'I get others to take the risk, but I keep the rewards' suggesting that he sought to minimize his own risk.

According to Knight (1921) (who is discussed more fully in Chapter 3) an entrepreneur is someone who calculates and then takes those risks and has to manage the uncertainties, and take responsibility for both good and bad outcomes. Hence as risk takers, entrepreneurs play an important role in the economy in ensuring that identified risky opportunities are taken up. This may thus develop and improve the economic efficiency of the economy.

(ii) Entrepreneur as resource allocator

Another famous French philosopher, Jean-Baptiste Say (1821) thought of the 'entrepreneur' as an organizer of factors of production. She or he shifted economic resources (labourers, skills, education and capital) from areas of lower to areas of higher productivity and greater yield. As with Cantillon this co-ordinating function also carried an element of risk although the entrepreneur did not necessarily provide the finance or the capital for the venture. So Say stressed the function of entrepreneurship as bringing together and co-ordinating resources. To take a musical example, it was the blend of different musical skills and personalities that helped make the Rolling Stones or the Beatles so successful, as individually they would not have been so popular at the time.

Mark Casson (1990) argues that the skill of an entrepreneur is to make judgmental decisions about the best allocation and use of resources and to co-ordinate scarce resources (see Chapter 5). He suggests that the entrepreneur must control the resources, usually through having capital to purchase them. This entrepreneur is a co-ordinator of resources, a deal-maker and a successful risk taker. Changes in the external environment (for example, the state of technology, markets and so on) provide opportunities, and the entrepreneur will then make judgements on whether or not to take these opportunities, based upon the rewards, risks and uncertainty. In a small firm, it is usually the owner-manager who is the economic agent who makes strategic decisions about resources and so is the entrepreneur.

Another view is that while the availability of resources is crucial to realizing ideas, an entrepreneur is someone who pursues opportunities, on their own or inside an organization, without regard to the resources they currently control. So an entrepreneur tries for those things that others think cannot be achieved (for instance, as the others do not believe that there are enough resources). This need not contradict Say's or Casson's views, as a key skill of the entrepreneur will be to find somehow to actually assemble the necessary resources to achieve their vision, such as through convincing potential backers.

Overlapping the other functions of entrepreneurs is that of being a middleman. Kirzner (whose views are discussed in Chapter 4) argues that the entrepreneur is alert to and sees opportunities in the economy and uses his or her knowledge of them to gain a profit. This knowledge is available to everyone, so the entrepreneur is not special, except perhaps in them actually 'grasping' the opportunities. He or she is a 'middleman' in the market.

Some, however, argue that this knowledge may often be restricted to certain people, hence social contacts through school, membership of clubs and so on, may provide special information (hence representing perhaps a failure of the free market). Such contacts also offer the opportunity to test out information the entrepreneur gains on other knowledgeable and supportive people. In other cases such knowledge may be restricted to those with certain technical expertise, such as specialist scientists or engineers.

(iii) Entrepreneur as innovator

While the opportunistic and risk bearing roles of entrepreneurs are important in helping the economy to adjust to its ceaseless changes, other writers see entrepreneurs as causing rather than responding to these changes. Joseph Schumpeter (1943) saw entrepreneurs as innovators, that is, those who wish to change things or do things differently.

He defined the entrepreneur as someone who implements 'new combinations of means of production'. This can be done through: introducing new economic goods or products; introducing a new method of production or production processes; opening a new market; gaining a new source of raw materials or inputs (including finance); or changing the organization of an individual organization or an industry. Clearly this could occur in not-for-profit as well as in for-profit organizations. While innovation is an important component of Schumpeter's entrepreneur, it must include implementation of the new idea or activity and not just generating a new idea as an inventor might do.

So entrepreneurship is seen as the source of change and dynamism in society and the economy. Schumpeter's innovations create new activities and markets and so also 'destroy' or supersede the old markets, hence its role in the economy is both creative and destructive (see Chapter 4 for further discussion). This suggests that entrepreneurship is temporary and if she or he ceases to develop new products or services or develop or expand the business then they join the ranks of small business owners and managers rather than entrepreneurs. Some, such as Curran (1986), argue that the 'hallowed' term entrepreneur should be reserved for those small business owners who are innovative and opportunistic in deploying resources or providing new products and services in pursuit of profit. Others who are not innovative and simply provide established products and services to existing markets (such as franchises) are simply small business owners.

Innovation may involve the new application of inventions made by others. Peter Mathias (1983, p. 141) argues that relatively few of the 'new' entrepreneurs of the industrial revolution in nineteenth-century Britain were the pioneers of major innovations or inventions in their own right, rather they had knowledge of the new techniques and could apply them effectively to meet changing market needs. In those days the entrepreneurs tended to buy and transport raw materials themselves and adapted their production to the new mass markets, so an important role for them was to assemble and manage diverse resources. In that era access to capital was limited, and this was often a fundamental characteristic of entrepreneurs. So it is possible to see how the various approaches to defining entrepreneurs often relate to the economic and social environment of the time they were developed.

However, how do we determine which organizations are truly innovative and which are imitators? Steve Jobs and the Apple Corporation can claim to have developed the first commercially viable personal computer as a tool for ordinary people and businesses, but most developments since then have not represented such a quantum leap. If innovation implies being first to do something, such as entering a new market, then is there only one innovative personal computer manufacturer among the hundreds such as Dell, Apple, IBM, Compaq, ACT and so on? However, each may claim to be innovative in the sense that their products, even if only for a few months, may be significantly new or their process or organization may be innovative. In general however, the personal computer and now the internet continue to be sources of innovation and change both in the way products are produced and also the products themselves. Similarly the biotechnology industry may be a source of entrepreneurs for both new and existing products and markets, although large firms are often dominant.

Closely related to innovation is the idea of entrepreneurship as a creative force, whereby the entrepreneur is someone who imagines and creates new opportunities or solves problems in a new way, rather than just identifying existing opportunities. For instance, Shackle (see Chapter 3) argues that an entrepreneur is imaginative, original and creative. Creativity must also be linked to the realization of the idea, often through the stages of invention, then innovation and design to create a workable prototype and finally the development of the desired product.

Estée Lauder started developing new cosmetic products while still at school, apparently experimenting in her family kitchen to make various types of cosmetics and face creams which were then (in the 1920s) becoming popular. She was also innovative in introducing new marketing techniques, which resulted in her products being displayed in prominent positions in major department stores world-wide. This led to her company becoming a dominant player in the various niches of the cosmetics business. Another example of creativity and innovation was the idea for a small portable tape player which came to its inventor before the technical issues were fully understood and the engineering expertise was harnessed to solve them. The Sony Walkman was the result of this idea. Once this product was available lots of other firms took the opportunity to fill gaps in this new market with their own 'Walkman' or to extend the idea from tape to CD players.

Who judges whether something or someone is creative or imaginative? For an artist it may be the views of friends and others in 'the industry', such as fellow artists or critics. The judgement of whether or not a mathematician is creative is much less subjective – their solution to a problem must be novel but also must stand up to rigorous proof. An engineer may design an elegant bridge or new product using creative materials or new engineering concepts, but here the proof comes when it is seen if the bridge stands or the product works. For the entrepreneur in business the test will be whether the product or service serves its function, like the bridge, but also whether it is profitable. The 'Walkman' passed these tests and was both a marvel of design and engineering and created a whole new market at the time for Sony and those following. This would also pass Drucker's (1985) narrow definition of an entrepreneur as one who 'drastically upgrades the yield from resources and creates a new market and a new customer'. Although Drucker goes on to give a wider perspective on entrepreneurs (see below).

Hence the entrepreneur can be seen as someone with a specific role in the economy. However, a second perspective, which is now considered, is that of the entrepreneur as someone who exhibits a particular form of behaviour.

Illustration – Anita Roddick

The successful international chain Body Shop International started out in the 1970s as a single shop in a small southern English town selling cosmetics and related products based on natural ingredients. A key characteristic of the firm has been the importance of integrity in dealings with customers, staff and suppliers and a strong environmental ethos. Its founder, Anita Roddick, has said that what distinguished the Body Shop when it was set up was her lack of business experience, telling the truth, and re-using or recycling everything they could (partly due to lack of money). She has said she tried to keep the firm daring, brave and fun, partly by protecting the firm from 'big business'.

The firm is well known for its campaigning and education roles covering issues such as environmentalism and human rights. These are based partly on the wider values, vision and goals of the firm which they have claimed go beyond profit and loss and gross national product. This helped motive staff, customers and others and also distinguished them from many of their competitors. There have been some controversies about maintaining their high ethical stance on occasion, but the firm grew into a profitable international chain in just over a decade.

Entrepreneurship as a form of behaviour

This second perspective considers that entrepreneurs should be defined by their behaviour, that is, what they do, rather than who they are (or their personal characteristics). Stevenson and Sahlman (1989) believe that 'entrepreneurship is most fruitfully defined as the relentless pursuit of opportunity without regard to resources currently controlled'. They also argue that the process of entrepreneurship starts with identifying opportunity and ends with the achievement of one's goals and gaining the rewards from one's endeavours.

Entrepreneurship is not a simple behavioural characteristic but rather a range of behaviour. In particular the entrepreneur behaves differently from a manager, administrator, or small business owner in terms of being strategically oriented and pursuing opportunities, rather than being preoccupied with and restricted to the resources they currently control. The manager concentrates on using the resources most efficiently while the entrepreneur concentrates on doing things differently and getting the resources to do it. The opportunities will vary according to the person's age, experience, resources and even their social circumstances – that is, opportunity is relativistic. So to buy the rights for a film script for $2 million may be a cheap opportunity for Steven Spielberg, but it is hardly an opportunity for a budding producer who is still a media studies student. It is worth noting that Stevenson and Sahlman argue that the entrepreneur does receive the main compensation from identifying and realizing the opportunity although they may not have to have ownership of the resources.

Peter Drucker (1985) also argues that entrepreneurship is a form of behaviour, and it can be learnt (that is, we are not 'born' entrepreneurs). So entrepreneurship results primarily from nurture (life experiences and learning) not nature (the basic personality we were born with). His entrepreneur is someone who 'always searches for change, responds to it, and exploits it as an opportunity' (p. 25). Change in the economy or wider environment is normal and provides new opportunities. Hence the Latin saying *carpe diem* (seize the day/grasp your opportunities) should perhaps be the motto of entrepreneurs. Drucker argues that entrepreneurs must learn to practise systematic innovation, which 'consists in the purposeful and organised search for changes, and in the systematic analysis of the opportunities such changes might offer for economic or social innovation' (p. 49).

Entrepreneurship is about doing things differently (hopefully, although not necessarily, better), about seeking change and taking opportunities. Drucker goes on to argue that the characteristics of entrepreneurship go beyond size, newness or growth of business, so large existing firms (such as 3M, IBM or Marks and Spencers) can be entrepreneurial. Indeed, some firms support employees acting as intrapreneurs – that is, 'entrepreneurs' within their own organizations, through developing innovative ideas and transforming them into profitable or high value added activities within the organization. According to Pinchott (1985) for intrapreneurs to succeed in larger organizations they need the opportunity to develop their innovations and ideas, the freedom to see them through to the end, and a toleration within the organization of risk taking and mistakes.

So firms in, for example, fast changing 'high tech' sectors such as e-commerce or biotechnology should be based upon purposeful innovation – purposefully seeking to identify and open new opportunities. Drucker also argues that entrepreneurs may therefore be in any part of the economy or society – in local government or charities as well as in the latest software start-up company, in hospitals as well as in General Motors. Also the key is 'doing' things differently, as Schumpeter said, so entrepreneurship may involve making a new product, or reorganizing how the product is made, or how the organization itself operates.

A major behavioural characteristic of entrepreneurs is to think and act strategically. Taylor (1988) studied a number of outstandingly successful women entrepreneurs, such as Estée Lauder, and claimed that entrepreneurs had five principles in common for formulating successful strategies. These were that successful entrepreneurs: get business experience in their youth; are market focused and seek out and identify 'niche' opportunities; demand high standards of themselves and build strong teams of similarly talented, ambitious and hard-working associates around themselves and whose strengths complement the entrepreneur's weaknesses; form strong and good relations with key suppliers and bankers; and they learn to understand accounts and financial statements. So each of these forms of behaviour may be linked to entrepreneurship.

Entrepreneur as a type of personality

In 1859 Samuel Smiles' book *Self Help* described many of the most famous Victorian entrepreneurs. These included Josiah Wedgewood who after 30 years 'by his energy, skill and genius, ... established the (porcelain pottery) trade upon a new and solid foundation' thus providing employment and good wages to many thousands of families (pp. 53–6), and Richard Arkwright who founded the first cotton mills in the industrial revolution. According to Smiles, the key psychological traits of an entrepreneur were integrity, self-learning, courage, conscientiousness, patience, perseverance, self-discipline and self-respect. Within a decade or two this became one of the most influential and popular foreign books in Japan.

More recent psychological and sociological approaches to entrepreneurship have concentrated upon why some people start firms, while under similar circumstances others do not. Much research then has focused on who these entrepreneurs are and what their particular qualities or motivations are. As is discussed in Chapter 7, some argue that, compared to non-entrepreneurs, entrepreneurs have a greater need for achievement or to control their working environment, or they have different approaches to risk taking, or different values or life and work experiences.

This approach of looking at the characteristics of entrepreneurs has been criticized for sometimes providing long lists of traits that when taken together would result in the description of a sort of generic 'Everyman'. Further criticisms are that access to resources is often crucial as there are limits to resources an entrepreneur may gather particularly when faced by discrimination. Also an entrepreneur usually operates with a team and the experiences, characteristics and interrelations of the strategic team of top managers in an organization may be more important than those of one particular individual, even if that individual is in overall control. However the study of characteristics can be useful in helping identify important questions. Why are certain groups or types of people over or under represented among entrepreneurs? It has, for instance, been argued that some groups such as women or some minorities have in the past been held back by institutional forces including not being able to so easily access appropriate finance or information. More recently the number of new firms set up by women has increased dramatically, especially in the US, so why is this? Other questions include how certain characteristics, such as an entrepreneur's network of social relationships influence the manifestation and success of entrepreneurial behaviour.

Learning is important to how individuals respond in different circumstances, so while personality may be important, it is only one of many factors that may influence entrepreneurial behaviour. It should not be ignored but, by itself it is not an adequate explanation of entrepreneurship or of the role of entrepreneurship in the economy.

Entrepreneurship as an event – the creation of new organizations

The fourth perspective on entrepreneurship is to consider it as the process leading to the event of creating new organizations. Gartner (1988) suggests that 'who is an entrepreneur?' is the wrong question. Rather entrepreneurship is to do with creating new business ventures, regardless of whether they are high growth orientated or not. The focus is upon looking at the process of creating the organization rather than on the individual person who created an organization in the past. Much of the literature that equates starting a small firm with being an entrepreneur follows this approach. This may suggest that the entrepreneurial role ends once a new organization has been created.

One common modification of this view is that an entrepreneur is one of the rare 'self made' people who start-up and grow a giant organization. It can be argued also that entrepreneurial behaviour continues after the firm has been created rather than ending once the new organization has been started. The organization itself still keeps going, perhaps to growth, maturity and possibly to decline, but the original entrepreneur takes on different roles in each stage. For instance, their role may change from being an innovator, to being a small business owner, manager, or becoming a vice-president of a division of the firm when it becomes large. So the behaviour of someone who is a manager running an organization will be different from that when they were an entrepreneur (that is, when they were starting the organization), even though it is the same person carrying out each role.

There are some empirical difficulties in deciding if a new organization has been created or exactly when the creation stage ends. Is someone who takes over an existing small firm that is 'going nowhere' and sets it off on a new growth and development path acting entrepreneurially? Perhaps they are if the regenerated firm is considered as a 'new' organization, but in practice it can be difficult to differentiate such a firm from an ordinary developing small business. So this 'event' perspective suggests that in order to determine what is entrepreneurial behaviour (what does it involve, what are its distinguishing characteristics and how does it vary?), they need to be observed as they actually create new organizations.

Entrepreneurship as being an owner-manager

Sometimes the term entrepreneur is applied to anyone who owns and manages a business. This covers most small businesses, but could exclude those who create a fast growth firm and sell its shares to investors, so the founder no longer owns a majority of the shares.

If we think the person setting up the seventh hamburger restaurant in the street (in the example given earlier) should be termed a small business person but not an entrepreneur, then in addition to creating a new economic entity (such as the firm or restaurant) or owning and managing one, there needs to be something more. This additional factor may be the creation of an innovative or novel product or service or new way of production which is significantly different from other services and products or production processes offered elsewhere in the market. So most of the theories discussed in this book do not treat those that are simply owner-managers as entrepreneurs.

This brief review has shown some of the broad ways in which entrepreneurship has been studied and the reader will come across each of these different overlapping perspectives in various chapters. Roughly, new and small businesses will be discussed in Chapter 2, the role of risk taker and the approach of neoclassical economics in Chapter 3, innovation in Chapter 4, resource allocation, organizational and socio-economic factors in Chapters 5 and 6, sociological, psychological, management and more general approaches, in Chapter 7, and entrepreneurship as a form of behaviour in Chapter 8. Now we move on to a more detailed overview of the rest of the book.

Outline of the book

The book is made up of three parts: what is entrepreneurship, theories of entrepreneurship and entrepreneurship in the wider society. Part I sets the overall context for the book. It includes the present chapter which considers different perspectives and definitions of entrepreneurship and Chapter 2 which provides a brief overview of the importance, and characteristics, of small and new firms in the European Union, US and UK economies.

Part II describes the main theories of entrepreneurship in Chapters 3 to 7. It is not possible to discuss every aspect of each theory covered, so attention is concentrated upon the key general characteristics of each model and the differences between the models. Chapter 3 introduces the theoretical perspectives which have been developed by economists in exploring the function of entrepreneurship in the economy. It reviews the nature and scope of traditional neoclassical economic thought, including Knight's view of the entrepreneur as a bearer of uncertainty and an explanation of the equilibrium approach to analysing economic systems. The discussion identifies the limited role of a specific entrepreneurial function in traditional economic thought.

Chapter 4 moves on to discuss alternative economic approaches to explaining entrepreneurship, in particular the work of Kirzner and Schumpeter. They both identify a role for entrepreneurship in the process of market dynamics which determines economic equilibrium. However, they develop conflicting theories. To help understand the work of Kirzner, we consider the wider context within which he developed his theories (that is, the methodology of the Austrian school of economics).

Chapter 5 continues the discussion of economic theories by examining Casson's theory of entrepreneurship, which synthesizes elements from the theories reviewed previously and introduces the importance of recognizing societal influences on entrepreneurship. Following this the focus of the discussion shifts away from role of entrepreneurship in influencing economic equilibrium, to considering the role played by entrepreneurs in the evolution of economies. First of all attention is directed to Etzioni's socio-economic analysis of entrepreneurship and then to the evolutionary approach of Nelson and Winter. These theories are considered in the context of Casson's comprehensive equilibrium-related theory.

The evolutionary theme is then further developed in Chapter 6. This builds on earlier chapters by considering one of the major contemporary topic areas in economics and its related disciplines, that of the changing patterns of industrial evolution in response to the increasing globalization of markets. In doing so, the roles of entrepreneurship in equilibrium and evolutionary economic theory are brought together in the context of the methodological approaches of contractarian economics and social networks theory. Thus a wide range of economic approaches are developed and pulled together in addressing the key issue of industrial evolution, and the influence of entrepreneurs in determining the patterns of production in economies at a local, national and global level. This discussion serves to illustrate the need to consider a much wider range of economic perspectives than conventional neoclassical economics, when analysing entrepreneurship.

Moving on to 'non-economic' approaches to entrepreneurship, Chapter 7 considers the major sociological, psychological and management approaches to analysing entrepreneurial activity. Sociological approaches include the social marginality thesis, the life-cycle theory and the ideal type models of entrepreneurs. The psychological approaches reviewed include the psychodynamic model and personality trait approaches. Management theorists in particular cover the forms of entrepreneurial management behaviour adopted in developing successful businesses. These approaches are compared with that of economics and their implications for economists attempting to understand the concept are discussed. The development of a multi-disciplinary 'entrepreneurship paradigm' is then considered in terms of its theoretical and methodological implications for an emerging 'entrepreneurial science'. The chapter concludes with a review of the main themes and points which have been discussed in Part II.

Part III considers the connections between entrepreneurship and the wider society. Chapter 8 continues to consider some of the issues covered in Part II by relating entrepreneurship to business organizations which have predominantly social objectives. In particular it considers the notion of the social entrepreneur in the not-for-profit sector or third sector, and also covers entrepreneurship in 'alternative' business structures, such as co-operatives and community businesses. In Chapter 9 policies to promote entrepreneurship, such as assisting start-up and small businesses and wider entrepreneurial development, are considered. The rationale for government support is also analysed.

The Conclusion summarizes the main themes which have been explored, and draws out some of the main implications of the material for entrepreneurs, the performance of economies, and policymakers concerned with encouraging the development of entrepreneurial activity.

Finally, when an entrepreneur decides whether or not to go ahead with a new project or business, he or she must consider both the specific characteristics of the business and the influences of forces in the wider economy. The Appendix provides an outline of the components of a business plan for a new or expanding business. This identifies and helps us understand some of the key practical issues faced by entrepreneurs as they seek to turn ideas into action in the economy. The book will be useful for those on advanced undergraduate or postgraduate courses as well as researchers in the broad area of entrepreneurship. Each chapter contains illustrations of how entrepreneurs develop opportunities and create or adapt to market changes. These illustrate the theories and models of entrepreneurship and firm performance by applying them to 'real life'. Many also show the personal characteristics and backgrounds of the individuals involved, their motivations for undertaking entrepreneurial activity, their business objectives and their managerial practices. Each chapter also contains references and recommended reading to aid more in-depth analysis of specific points.

Conclusion

The entrepreneur has an important role in helping the economy to deal with innovation and change and the associated risks and uncertainty. This chapter discussed a variety of approaches to what is meant by the term entrepreneurship. Many writers argue that entrepreneurship, in its widest sense, is not simply concerned with business but rather can encompass all parts of society, private, public or third sector. Five overlapping broad perspectives for considering entrepreneurs and entrepreneurship were described.

First entrepreneurship as an economic function considered the various roles of an entrepreneur within the economy, especially those of risk taking, resource allocation, innovation and as 'middleman'. Second, entrepreneurship was viewed as a form of behaviour, where people can learn to behave as entrepreneurs. Third, entrepreneurs were discussed in terms of their individual characteristics or personality. Fourth, entrepreneurship was viewed as an event, such as the creation of a new firm or organization. Aspects of these will be considered in more depth in later chapters. Finally, the idea of an owner-manager was considered to be an inadequate concept for an entrepreneur.

Therefore entrepreneurship results from a combination of: the socioeconomic environment such as the opportunities in the economy and the social context they live in (for example, are entrepreneurs encouraged or frowned upon in our society); the personality of the entrepreneur; the learning and use of necessary skills and attitudes; and actually using purposeful insights to do something about the opportunities identified. So the two-way interactions between the entrepreneur and the environment within which they operate are significant.

What is important to remember is that the different theories reflect different views of what entrepreneurship is and its role in society and the economy. Many disciplines (such as economics, management, psychology and sociology) can help us to better understand their role and behaviour. The primary concern of this book though, is with the economic basis of entrepreneurial activity. Non-economic perspectives are considered in the context of their value in helping to understand more fully the economic impact of entrepreneurial activity. However, by considering different views a better general understanding can be obtained.

Finally, a purpose of the entrepreneur in the economy can be seen as to create wealth and add value to society. Hence illegal drug traffickers may act entrepreneurially in some ways, but the wider effects of their activities mean that they detract rather than add value to society, so we would not include them as entrepreneurs. While the main focus of this book is on wealth creation through the development and building of new business ventures, other types of entrepreneurs, including social entrepreneurs who are primarily seeking to add value to society in other ways, are also briefly considered. The final element of entrepreneurship is concrete achievement – they actually make things happen.

References and further reading

Baumol, W.J. (1987) 'Entrepreneurship in Economic Theory', *American Economic Review (Papers and Proceedings)*, Vol. 58, pp. 64–71.

Casson, M. (1990) *Entrepreneurship*, Aldershot, Edward Elgar.

Curran, J. (1986) *Bolton Fifteen Years On: a Review and Analysis of Small Business Research in Britain 1971–1986*, London, Small Business Research Trust.

Deakins, D. (1999) *Entrepreneurship and Small Firms*, 2nd edn, London, McGraw-Hill.

Drucker, P.F. (1985) *Entrepreneurship and Innovation*, London, Heinemann.

Gartner, W.B. (1988) 'Who is an Entrepreneur? is the wrong question', *Entrepreneurship Theory and Practice*, Spring, Vol. 12, pp. 47–67.

Hisrich, R.D. and M.P. Peters (1998) *Entrepreneurship*, 4th edn, New York, Irwin/McGraw-Hill.

Mathias, P. (1983) *The First Industrial Nation. An Economic History of Britain 1700–1914*, 2nd edn, London, Methuen.

Pinchott, C. (1985) *Intrapreneuring*, New York, Harper Row.

Schumpeter, J.A. (1943) *Capitalism, Socialism and Democracy*, London, Allen and Unwin.

Smiles, S. (1859) *Self Help, with Illustrations of Character and Conduct*, London, John Murray (republished in 1996, London, IEA).

Stevenson, H.H. and W.A. Sahlman (1989) 'The entrepreneurial process', in P. Burns and J. Dewhurst (eds) *Small Business and Entrepreneurship*, pp. 94–157, Basingstoke, Macmillan.

Storey, D.J. (1994) *Understanding the Small Business Sector*, London, Routledge.

Taylor, R.R. (1988) *Exceptional Entrepreneurial Women, Strategies for Success*, New York, Quorum Books.

2
Entrepreneurship in the Economy

Introduction

In recent decades entrepreneurs have been particularly important for the economy because of their contribution to new jobs, innovation and flexibility. Each of the concepts of entrepreneurship considered in the previous chapter provides differing perspectives of the importance of entrepreneurs in the economy. Now the significance of small firms is considered, reflecting on the entrepreneur as an owner-manager of a business. Also the importance of new, and small, firms in a dynamic economy is discussed, reflecting entrepreneurship as the event of creating an organization, as a source of innovation and as a form of behaviour.

This chapter starts by looking at different definitions of small firms (most but not all of whom are owner-managed) and how they have been applied in the European Union (EU), the US and the UK. It then reviews the number, employment and turnover of small firms, in order to understand their importance in these places. Next the significance of new and small firms in generating jobs and wealth is considered. Some of the reasons for the growth in small and new firms are discussed. Together these give a brief general overview of the importance of small and new firms and wider entrepreneurship within the economy.

Definitions of small firms

In analysing small firms in the economy we need to start by identifying some workable definitions. There are two main approaches to defining a small business – the quantitative and the qualitative approaches. Often, as we will see, both quantitative and qualitative measures are combined within a single definition.

The first approach is to provide a quantitative definition based upon criteria such as employment, turnover, asset size and similar characteristics. There are many different quantitative definitions which vary across time, the industry involved, location and the purposes the definition is used for. For instance, what may be seen as small in one industry (for example, a window cleaning business) may be totally different in scale to what is considered small in another industry (for example, a petrochemical firm). Similarly a firm considered relatively small in one country or region may be considered large in another.

The second approach to defining small businesses uses qualitative factors such as the ownership or the control of the business. For instance, a branch of a large global firm can hardly be termed a small enterprise even if it employs only a few people and has a low turnover. So a definition of small firms should include those firms that are largely independent and not mostly owned or directly controlled by larger firms. However, there is no exact measure of where the boundary lies between being controlled by a larger firm and being largely independent. As we will see from theoretical perspectives in later chapters, the boundaries between firms (and indeed of a firm itself) are often 'fuzzy'.

A further development of the qualitative approach to defining small firms is to try to capture the meanings, beliefs and behaviour aspects, including issues facing managers, that distinguish small businesses from large firms (Curran and Blackburn, 1994). This assumes that small firms face different issues from those facing large firms. Such a type of definition is 'grounded' in the views of those actually involved in the particular industry (for example, owner managers, Trade Associations and so on) and is determined through the researcher asking them what they think a small, medium or large firm is in their industry. However, there may be disagreement among those providing views, in terms of both what the key issues distinguishing firms of different size are, and on which firms should be categorized according to each issue.

Looking now at actual operational definitions of small firms we will consider three examples in the UK, EU and US. It is useful to start with the definition developed by the Bolton Report of the Committee of Inquiry on Small Firms (1971) which illustrates the various components of such a definition. This committee was set up by the government to investigate the problems of small firms in the UK. It argued that greater attention should be paid to the needs of small firms as they were important to the competitiveness of the national economy and it recommended that legislation which at the time favoured large firms be changed. The Report put forward a number of bases for defining small firms in different industries, and set the limits at: under 200 employees for small manufacturing firms; an annual turnover of £50 000 or less for retailing (around £1 million in today's money); and 25 employees or less in construction. Clearly all of these employment size limits were somewhat arbitrary, and as shown, for different purposes different limits were sometimes used.

The Bolton Report also discussed a more qualitative aspect of their definition covering issues of market share, control, ownership and type of management. They considered a small firm as 'one that has a relatively small share of the market... is managed by its owners or part-owners in a personalized way, and not through the medium of a formalised management structure..., is also independent in the sense that it does not form part of a larger enterprise and its owner-managers should be free from outside control in taking their principal decisions' (Bolton Report, 1971, p. 1).

Second, in the European Union the definition of small and medium-sized enterprises (SMEs) includes those with fewer than 250 employees (CEC, 1996). This group is further disaggregated into micro enterprises (with fewer than 10 employees), small enterprises (with 10–49 employees) and medium-sized enterprises (with 50–249 employees). Micro enterprises would include self-employed people working for themselves with no employees (see below). Sometimes the term small, medium and micro-sized enterprises (SMMEs) is used rather than SMEs.

Many firms subcontract much of their work and so have relatively few employees, but have a large turnover and so on, so employment by itself is not always an adequate basis for defining SMEs. Hence turnover, assets and ownership are also included in the EU definition. When considering state aid to SMEs (such as grants or other government support) the European Union definition of SMEs stipulates that generally firms must have under 250 employees and either their annual turnover must not exceed ECU 40 million (roughly $40 million) or the annual balance sheet total should not exceed ECU 27 million (see Table 2.1). Small and micro-sized enterprises are defined as having 0–50 employees and either a turnover of not more than ECU 7 million or a balance sheet not exceeding ECU 5 million. These turnover and asset figures are normally to be adjusted every four years to reflect changing economic circumstances such as inflation or the productivity of enterprises.

Added to these quantitative size based definitions of the SMEs, the EU include a more qualitative dimension based upon ownership.

Table 2.1 European Commission Definition of Small and Medium-Sized Enterprises

	Micro-enterprise	*Small*	*Medium-sized*
Number of employees	0–9	10–49	50–249
Maximum turnover (in million ECU)	–	7	40
Maximum balance-sheet total (in million ECU)	–	5	27

Note: To be classed as an SME or a micro-enterprise, an enterprise has to satisfy the criteria for the number of employees and one of the two financial criteria, that is, either the turnover total or the balance sheet total. In addition, it must be independent, which means less than 25 per cent owned by one enterprise (or jointly by several enterprises) falling outside the definition of an SME or a micro-enterprise, whichever may apply. The thresholds for the turnover and the balance sheet total are to be adjusted regularly, to take account of changing economic circumstances in Europe (normally every four years).
Source: Commission of the European Communities (1996) – 'Commission Recommendation concerning the definition of small and medium-sized enterprises', C(96) 261 final, adopted (Official Journal L107 of 30.4.96, p. 4).

This ownership measure states that not more than 25 per cent of the enterprise's capital or voting rights are to be owned by one enterprise (or jointly by several enterprises) that are not an SME themselves, except where ownership is held by public investment corporations, venture capital companies or institutional investors (provided no control is exercised by them). So a firm with a large venture capital investment in it may still be counted as small.

The third example of a definition is from the United States. There the Small Business Act also uses a combined quantitative and qualitative definition of small business. This states that they are independently owned and operated and, a possibly more qualitative measure, that they are not dominant in their field of operation. A quantitative maximum number of employees or turnover is also set for those businesses eligible for support such as government loans from the Small Business Administration. This maximum varies from industry to industry. Generally in wholesale industries firms must have no more than 100 employees while most manufacturing firms must have no more than 500 employees, although in some industries such as petroleum refining this limit rises to as many as 1500 employees. In retail and service industries, as well as construction and agriculture, the maximum size is measured in dollars of turnover. Currently this normally ranges from around $3.5 million, for instance in dry cleaning plants, up to $21.5 million for motion picture and video tape production or distribution firms.

Self-employment definitions

A large share of small businesses is comprised of self-employed people. The self-employed can be defined as those who, in their main employment, work on their own account, whether or not they have employees. In some cases self employed people are considered to be entrepreneurs, although as discussed earlier, many self-employed may not act entrepreneurially in terms of innovation or behaviour.

The definition of self-employment varies from country to country (the definition above is used in the UK). The OECD (1992) argue that two types of self-employment can be distinguished. There are firstly, 'persons who are leading a business which is not legally incorporated. They gain no salary, but the enterprises profits from their income. They personally have full liability for the conduct of business.'

The second type of self-employed people also gain a salary and are 'owner managers who gain profits as well as a salary as a managing director of an unincorporated business. This type of entrepreneur (sic) only runs a risk equal to his share of the paid-up capital of the business.' In some EU countries the first group only are considered self-employed (France, the Netherlands and the UK), while in other countries (Belgium, Denmark, Germany, Ireland, Italy, Luxembourg, Portugal and Spain) both definitions are used as owner-managers of unincorporated businesses are included. In Greece the legal position is not clear (ENSR, 1993, p. 165).

Small and new firms in the economy

The vast majority of businesses in most developed and developing economies each employ only a few people. However, in aggregate, small firms, including new start-up firms, provide a substantial share of total non-government jobs in most economies and have generally been increasing their share of jobs. International comparisons are often difficult due to the lack of comparable data, and small firm employment in the US, European Union and the UK are now considered in turn.

Small and new firms in the US

US Bureau of Census figures (1998) show that around 74 per cent of the 6.6 million US business establishments (excluding self-employed people) employ under 10 people, 87 per cent employ under 20 and 98 per cent of them employ under 100 people. However, only 26 per cent of employees (around 26 million) work in establishments of under 20 employees (15 per cent work in establishments of under 10 employees), while a further 29 per cent work in establishments with 20–99 employees. So large establishments remain an important source of employment with 45 per cent of employees working in firms of 100 or more. Indeed, the less than 1 per cent of firms with over 500 employees employ 20 per cent of all employees.

Some 62 per cent of all new jobs created in the US during 1994 were in small businesses according to the Small Business Administration figures with some 13 per cent of US employees in 1995 working for firms that did not exist five years earlier, which indicates the enormous changes occuring in the economy. The composition of small businesses and start-ups is not homogeneous and varies by time, sector, demographic make-up and location. During 1997 there were 166 740 business start-ups, compared to 83 384 business failures, so the flow in and out of businesses each year is large. Earlier, during most of the 1980s, the number of starts had been much larger (249 770 in 1985), and the number of failures lower, with only 57 078 failures in 1985, although the business cycle influences the figures and also new business incorporations rose after the 1980s (US Bureau of Census, 1998).

Different industrial sectors contributed various numbers of new start-up firms. In 1997 out of 166 740 business starts only 8 per cent of new starts were in manufacturing, while 22 per cent were in retailing, 9 per cent in wholesaling, 30 per cent in services, 11 per cent in construction, 7 per cent in finance, insurance and real estate (FIRE), 5 per cent in transport and public utilities, and the remaining 7 per cent in primary industries or unclassified (the figures do not add up to 100 per cent due to rounding). In terms of jobs the distribution was slightly different. Out of a total 738 606 new jobs in these firms, 13 per cent were in manufacturing due to their larger average size, while 22 per cent were in retailing, 8 per cent in wholesaling, 32 per cent in services, 9 per cent in construction, 8 per cent in FIRE, 6 per cent in transport and utilities and 2 per cent elsewhere. So services and retailing were by far the largest new employers, although these particular industries often have high rates of part-time jobs, and also new firms may frequently displace trade and jobs from others nearby.

The demographic make-up of those starting up new businesses is also changing. In 1972 fewer than 5 per cent of US businesses were owned by women. Between 1975 and 1990 there was a doubling of the number of self-employed women and it is estimated that roughly 40 per cent of new businesses are now run by women (SBA, 1994). The number of minority owned businesses is also rising rapidly, although from a low base. The rate of ownership of small firms remains low for some ethnic groups with only around 3 per cent of businesses being run by Afro-Americans who make up 12 per cent of the population.

Geographically, some regions appear to have superior infrastructure, access to markets, attractiveness for living or attitudes towards new business creation. There appear to be 'entrepreneurial subcultures' often linked to advanced technology in areas such as Route 128 around Boston, Silicon Valley, the North Carolina Triangle, Los Angeles, Denver, Cleveland, Austin and Minneapolis/St Paul. The South Atlantic Census division, including Florida and eight other states, had the greatest number of business start-ups in 1997 (30 528), closely followed by the Mid-Atlantic area of New York, New Jersey and Pennsylvania (28 381), and the Pacific (27 557). The state with by far the greatest number of start-ups was California (with 22 497) and although this is expected as it is also the most populous state, it had a relatively high per capita rate of start-ups.

Small and new firms in the European union

In the last decade in the European Union most (99 per cent) of the 18 million enterprises were small, with fewer than 50 paid workers. Of these around 93 per cent were micro-enterprises with under 10 employees. However, these small and micro-firms employed an average of around 2 people, and so their share of total private employment was only 52 per cent in 1996 (Eurostat, 1997; ENSR, 1997). A further 14 per cent of employment was in medium-sized firms (50–249 employees) and 34 per cent in large firms. The share of employment in small and micro-firms varied by country ranging in the early 1990s from 40 per cent in Germany to 65 per cent in Italy (Eurostat, 1994).

The importance of small firms also varied by industry. Service and construction industries had the highest proportions of employment in small enterprises, while manufacturing had the lowest. In all the EU countries more than 50 per cent of service employment was in small firms, with the exception of the UK (with 47.3 per cent). The small firm share of turnover was even lower than their employment share, ranging from 37 per cent in Germany to almost 55 per cent in Italy, with an average of ECU 325 000 across the EU. Productivity was greater in larger firms with turnover per person of ECU 99 000 for small enterprises, ECU 149 000 for medium-sized enterprises (50–249 employees) and ECU 150 000 for larger firms. Value added per employee also generally followed this pattern although data were only available in three countries (Denmark, France and Italy). The pattern of higher turnover per person in larger firms was particularly marked in manufacturing and energy industries with average figures of ECU 93 000, 114 000 and 164 000 for small, medium and large enterprises respectively.

As is discussed below, it has been said that new firms have been a major source of new jobs in the EU in the last two decades. The birth rate of new firms varies across the EU with the annual number of new firms per 10 000 population around 1990 estimated at 144 in Italy and 118 in France, but only 55 in Germany and around 70–80 in the UK (Eurostat, 1994). Business birth rates have also varied over time. In Germany they rose rapidly during the last quarter of the twentieth century, partly as more females and young graduates started up businesses, with annual start-ups doubling between 1978 and 1988, although relatively stabilizing since then.

Small and new firms in the UK

The position of small firms in the UK is generally similar to that in the US and EU. There was a long-term decline in employment in and the number of small firms until the 1960s. Since then the number of small businesses has increased, rising from 2.4 million in 1980 to 3.8 million in 1990. However, during the 1990s the share generally fluctuated around this level (falling to 3.5 million in 1993, but rising back to 3.7 million in 1998), so it is uncertain to what extent the sharp rise in new firm creation in the 1980s reflected specific circumstances, such as the widespread contraction of large employers, and how the position may change in the early decades of the current century.

As is the case in the EU, over 99 per cent of all businesses are small. Approaching two-thirds (64 per cent) of the UK's 3.7 million businesses have no employees and a further 35 per cent have under 50 employees (Labour Market Trends, 1999). However together these provided less than half (45 per cent) of non-government jobs, only slightly more than the share of all jobs (43 per cent) provided by the largest firms (those with over 250 employees), with just over a tenth of jobs (12 per cent) provided by medium sized firms in 1998.

Industries also have different size profiles. A number of industries have high shares of employment in small firms with zero or under 50 employees, include construction (78 per cent of all construction employment), education (69 per cent), real estate, renting and business activities (58 per cent), hotels and restaurants (50 per cent) and other community, social and personal services (67 per cent). On the other hand in the financial intermediation industry, 77 per cent of employees were in firms employing 250 people or more and only 16 per cent in firms with under 50 employees.

Small firms account for around 38 per cent of turnover (excluding the financial sector which is dominated by large firms), with medium firms (50–249 employees) accounting for 14 per cent and large firms 48 per cent. This indicates that generally small firms, especially those with no employees, have overall lower productivity in terms of turnover per employee. This, however, can be somewhat misleading as firms employing 1–49 people had higher productivity than large firms in some industries such as transport or wholesale, retail and repair or real estate, renting and business services. Indeed, if we consider only companies or public corporations (20 per cent of all businesses, but 70 per cent and 85 per cent shares of employment and turnover respectively), then small businesses employing 1–49 people have a turnover per employee 18 to 37 per cent greater than that for medium and large companies. Sole traders and partnerships with no employees tend to have relatively low turnover per job (that is, per proprietor). Value added per employee may differ but this suggests that within small sized businesses some are more productive and probably more entrepreneurial than others and so it can sometimes be misleading to combine all small firms together.

Geographically, the number of new firms per 10 000 of the civilian labour force is highest in the more prosperous South-East (including London) and the East Anglia and South-West regions. The regional development agency Scottish Enterprise estimated that if Scotland had achieved the same business start-up rate per capita as the South-East, then it would have 86 per cent more businesses. Such information helped to lead to a policy initiative called the 'Business Birthrate Strategy' to increase the number of new start-up firms (see Chapter 9 for a discussion of policies).

So all sizes of businesses are important to the economy, although small firms increasingly have been a major source of employment and have provided part of the 'seed corn' for future major businesses. Their importance varies by industry and location. In aggregate their productivity is usually lower than larger firms, although this appears to vary considerably between industries and types of small firms.

New and small firms and job generation

A number of studies have emphasized the importance of small firms for job (and wealth) creation in the economy. In particular a major study by David Birch (1979) found that over 60 per cent of US jobs in the 1970s were created by firms employing under 20 people and later work has shown the continued importance of small firms in job creation. In the European Union SMEs have also had a significant role in job generation, however, this was mainly due to restructuring and downsizing of larger firms, and while SMEs create relatively more jobs they also lose more jobs, so employment growth is almost the same for enterprises of different sizes (ENSR, 1997). It is important, however, to distinguish 'newness' from size, as many of the currently large firms may only be a few years old (for instance, Microsoft), and may have been 'small firms' for only a short period of their lives.

The changes in employment patterns depend to a large extent upon the characteristics of individual industries. Where an industry is in decline, those made redundant may be able to undercut existing firms by using cheaper accommodation and second-hand equipment. This may displace employment in competitors, so resulting in few extra jobs in the industry. However, growing industries, such as information technology or financial services in recent decades, can support many new small firms, some of which may expand rapidly. So new firms may be particularly important in new fast growing industries or niches within industries, which is also crucial for wealth creation. Overall the evidence is inconclusive and varies as an industry matures or the business cycle improves. However, a complacent mature industry may always be attacked by new competitive industries or firms. Such evolution of the mode of production in different industries is considered in Chapters 5 and 6.

Most new firms do not grow significantly. Storey (1994) argues that only 4 per cent of new firms create half of the employment generated during their first decade. Of the companies started in Massachusetts in 1978 only 2.8 per cent employed more than 50 people by 1990. Others argue that while these 'high flying' or 'gazelle' fast growth firms are important, the scale of their contribution to new jobs may have been exaggerated. For instance Daly *et al.* (1991) claim that half the net job generation comes from moderate growth firms with under five employees expanding to having under ten employees. These differences between types of new firms has clear implications for policy, as discussed in Chapter 9.

An interesting illustration of the fine line between enormous growth and business failure is shown by GO Corporation (Kaplan, 1995). Jerry Kaplan had a doctorate in artificial intelligence and considerable business experience with Lotus when he tried to revolutionise personal computers by creating a pen-based computer. After discussing his ideas with Mitchell Kapor, the founder of Lotus, he decided to set up his own firm. He kept a detailed diary of his seven-year struggle to make it an industry leader. Strong opposition from the industry giants IBM and Microsoft and from Apple's 'Newton' pen computer led to many adjustments to his own company goals and a continuous search for more venture capital in order to bring his idea to market. Eventually the company failed, perhaps illustrating Schumpeter's 'creative destruction' of capitalism at work (see Chapter 4).

Some criticisms of studies of the role of small firms in employment creation

In order to more accurately assess the importance of small firms in employment creation it is worthwhile considering a number of potential criticisms of some such studies. These suggest that the importance of small firms may sometimes have been exaggerated. The first criticism is that internationally not all countries have seen an increase in self-employment or a reduction in the average size of firms (for example, Japan). Next, there are often significant problems obtaining appropriate data. Some studies have been criticized for a number of methodological reasons, such as data being based upon samples that may not be fully representative of the small firm population. The availability of good quality comprehensive data is a common problem. The use of national data sources such as sales or value added tax (VAT) returns also has problems as they do not capture smaller firms that are below the VAT threshold. There are also methodological criticisms based upon the size distribution fallacy. This is outlined in the annex at the end of the chapter. A further data issue is that studies looking at job generation often do not fully take account of the type and quality of jobs (in terms of pay, conditions and training) which may be relatively poorer in some small firms.

Another issue is that it is estimated generally that over half of businesses fail in the first five years and the net job creation from new firms is therefore lower than implied by the gross number of new firms. In the UK, the Department of Trade and Industry estimates that only 40 per cent of firms registered for VAT remain registered five years later (based on 1988–95), although some may have deregistered due to their turnover falling below the registration level. Their estimates suggest that up to 60 per cent of new firms (including non-VAT registered ones) cease trading within five years. If business birth rates rose it was assumed that the death rate would be relatively constant, so net job growth would occur. However, it has been argued that changes in the business death rate is more important for increasing employment than simple business birth rates.

Davis *et al.* (1996) have argued that while small firms (with under 20 employees) create a disproportionate share of gross new jobs in the US, they also lose a disproportionate number due to their high closure and shrinkage rates, so their net contribution is sometimes lower than that of other types of firms. Their data also suggest that different firms, industrial sectors and sizes of firms react differently to the business cycle. So the relative contribution of small firms to new jobs varies during different time periods and stages of the business cycle. During a recession there is faster industrial restructuring, and while gross job creation rates do not change greatly compared to 'boom times' the job destruction rate rises, so there is a net decline in jobs. So the importance of small firms to job creation varies according to the time period studied. While no clear pattern emerges, they argue that middle-sized firms (50–99 employees) have often contributed large numbers of net new jobs in manufacturing. Interestingly they also found that two-thirds of job creation and job destruction takes place in plants where there are expansions or contractions of at least 25 per cent in 12 months – suggesting that perhaps much of the creation is concentrated in a relatively few entrepreneurial firms with huge growth rates. However, the study did focus upon manufacturing firms at the plant level and the situation may differ in other sectors such as service industries.

Even if small firms are generating most new jobs, then most of the jobs come from a small minority of fast growth firms, together with a larger group of moderate growth firms also exhibiting more entrepreneurial behaviour. So most small firms contribute relatively little employment. All of these criticisms of studies of small firm employment creation do not mean that small and new firms are unimportant. Clearly they are extremely important for job creation and other reasons such as flexibility and innovation, but the criticisms do suggest that entrepreneurship within existing larger organizations is also crucial for the economy, and their organizations, to respond to changes and opportunities effectively and efficiently. Hence it is important to consider entrepreneurial behaviour in larger as well as smaller or new organizations.

Reasons for the growth of new businesses

There are a number of reasons for the relative rise of employment in new and small firms in recent decades. These can be divided into four broad overlapping groups: changing demand and production opportunities; a more supportive environment for entrepreneurship; a greater supply of potential business creators; and organizational changes in firms, including relative decline of employment in larger organizations. The first set of reasons include greater opportunities such as the changing nature of market demand for goods and services that can be provided effectively by small businesses together with the speed, flexibility and efficiency of new or small firms to respond to them. Much of the increased demand is linked to rising incomes leading to an expansion of markets for products with high income elasticity of demand, for example, niche markets, customized or fashion goods, financial services and health care, in some of which small or new firms may have a competitive advantage. Demographic changes, such as the ageing population in many developed countries, and changing government policies including reforming pensions, have also created opportunities that have been taken up by the self-employed or small firms directly or by them acting as agents on behalf of larger companies.

Linked to increased opportunities in some sectors have been the many technological and knowledge changes which make it easier for small firms to take opportunities by quickly providing new or more appropriate products. Technological changes have also allowed them to run small-scale production processes and administration of the business more efficiently. In particular information and other technology and the development of the internet have allowed many opportunities to be exploited by small firms by reducing the minimum efficient scale of production and the effects of economies of scale, hence lowering the level of barriers of entry to the market.

A second set of reasons for an increase in small firms is improved support or facilitating factors. These include the greater availability and appropriateness of finance (including venture capital), premises, advice and access to market opportunities. Government policies in these areas and in areas such as regulation and taxation are also important and are discussed in Chapter 9. Of importance may be the changing attitudes of people towards entrepreneurship, with starting a business being seen as a more attractive career option nowadays. This is reinforced by the increasing number of careers that people have during their lifetime. Many people previously had one major career during their lifetime, but now they may have several with starting a business being seen as one of these possible 'careers'. The growth in 'management buyouts' has also created many new business owners as a result of the entrepreneurial behaviour of the managers.

A third set of factors behind the growth in new firms is the increase in the potential supply of entrepreneurs due to demographic changes (including the large number of people in the 'baby boom' generation who have reached an age when they are more likely to start-up a business), better general education, and greater knowledge of and education in entrepreneurship. Also important are higher incomes and two income households (so providing more finance for start-ups and greater security if the business fails so allowing greater risks to be taken). The general large rise in house prices and investments since the middle of the twentieth century has also provided some people with substantial capital for starting a new business and lowering the personal risk if the business fails. Better management education and training for existing employees may also increase their expertise and confidence related to starting and running their own business.

A further issue likely to increase the supply of entrepreneurs is redundancy or the threat of job loss, where many people move into self-employment or starting up a small firm as a result (Storey, 1982). This and more general recessionary pressures in the economy can therefore lead to 'push' factors where skilled workers and management set up firms in preference to training or looking for another job as an employee, especially due to a lack of alternative jobs, job insecurity, lack of promotion prospects or unemployment. This would suggest that self-employment may rise during recessionary periods, but then business failures of the self-employed may also rise.

A fourth set of factors is the changing structure of organizational relationships within and between firms in recent decades, particularly their reduction in direct employment by large firms and organizations (including the public sector), and hence their share of jobs in the economy. The trend for larger firms to sub-contract or 'outsource' functions previously carried out internally within the large firm results in an apparent growth in small firm employment and declining large firm employment. However this activity has often only been shifted between firms and considerable effective control is still maintained by the large firm which may be the new firm's prime customer. So functionally there is still a direct link with the larger firm. The scale of these changes has been large, particularly in the 1980s with the Fortune 500 companies losing some 4–6 million jobs in the first few years of that decade alone in the US with a continuing decline in jobs in large public and private organizations during much of the 1990s.

Such 'outsourcing' may involve the firm subcontracting a function or encouraging a management buyout with former managers starting a business and selling their services back to the employer. This has resulted in many opportunities for new or small firms. It offers the original employer a number of advantages, including fewer overhead costs (in terms of savings in pensions, office costs, holiday pay and so on), greater flexibility to meet changing requirements, and the ability to reduce costs through bringing in competition to keep prices down after the initial contract period. Hence a number of costs and risks are transferred from the original employer to the former employee who is now the owner of the start-up business. The advantages for the former employee may include the ability to achieve economies of scale by servicing a number of additional customers, tax advantages, financial gain where expenses previously paid by the employer are now absorbed by the former employee at a reduced cost (for example, having lower quality office space or by using their house for an office), and greater control and flexibility of how work is organized. Also there may be greater incentives to work harder (as any extra profit is retained) so their productivity may rise. However, there can be dangers of 'outsourcing' for the original firm, such as losing direct contact with customers and getting less customer feedback and information.

Indeed, with continued structural changes and 'outsourcing' by larger organizations the largest global firms could reduce employment while keeping a strong hold on product marketing, distribution and development. In many cases small suppliers could hardly be described as fully independent as they may be largely dependent upon the larger firms. Also the competitive pressures between the global firms could be different than those between the smaller supplier firms, so market structure and behaviour may differ between the various markets. There has even been the suggestion that this could lead to the possibility of 'virtual' utility companies which would be contracted to provide utilities such as electricity, gas and water, but would sub-contract virtually all the actual administration and supply work. On the other hand such relationships do, however, offer opportunities for the small firm to develop wider markets. The wider issues of network and contractual links between firms is considered in greater detail in Chapter 6.

Hence there is a range of inter-related reasons for the relative growth of employment in small firms, but such factors do not necessarily mean a continuation of this trend. Future employment trends will depend upon which factors continue, how they operate and what new factors emerge.

Conclusion

New business formation and small businesses have played an important role in helping many economies to adapt to fundamental economic changes over recent decades. The vast majority of businesses in an economy are very small, so if entrepreneurs are considered as owner-managers then entrepreneurship is important in most economies. Small firms have generally been increasing their share of total employment although large firms are still very significant in terms of total employment and output, so entrepreneurial behaviour in larger firms remains important. Small and new firms have been extremely important for job generation in many countries, however, most jobs and wealth have come from a tiny minority of very rapid growth new or small firms, that is those which have shown most entrepreneurial behaviour and innovation, in risk taking and resource allocation rather than simply being owner-managed firms. This has important implications for public policies (as will be seen in Chapter 9).

The growing importance of small and new firms has been the result of a number of inter-related sets of factors, as will be considered in later chapters. These include changes in the general socio-economic and technological environments leading to greater opportunities for new firms, a more supportive environment for entrepreneurship, a greater supply of potential business creators together with the restructuring of employment in large organizations. How these factors will change in the future is however, uncertain.

Annex to Chapter 2 – Small firms and employment change: some methodological issues

Great care needs to be taken when trying to estimate the importance of small firms to job creation within the economy. Some problems include the precise definitions of firm sizes, the stage of the business cycle that the data cover, and the problems of identifying and measuring the number of firms.

The size and distribution fallacy, as described by Davis *et al.* (1996), is a further methodological problem that is sometimes found in small business literature. To illustrate this fallacy, assume that a small business is defined as one that employs less than 50 people. Let us assume that in an economy in year 1 there are three firms: firm A employing 30 people, firm B with 55 and firm C with 65 employees (Table 2.2). Hence in year 1 there are 30 people employed in small firms of under 50 employees and 120 people in large firms. Now in year 2 firm A reduces its number of employees from 30 to 5 and firm B from 55 to 35, while firm C actually increases its jobs from 65 to 110. If we just add up all the jobs in firms that are classified as being small (employing under 50 people) in year 2 we now get 40, a rise of 10 over year 1.

Table 2.2   Size Distribution Fallacy

| | Firm | | | Total small firms | Total large firms | Total all firms |
	A	B	C			
Year 1	30	55	65	30	120	150
Year 2	5	35	110	40	110	150
Net Change	−25	−20	+55	+10	−10	0

Note: Small firms employ less than 50.

Meanwhile large firms (employing 50 or over) have seen a supposed drop from 120 to 110 total employment. Clearly the small firm (firm A) has not contributed any employment growth. However, if we just look at the total columns in the table then we would think that small firms had grown by a third, from 30 to 40 and large firms had shrunk by 10. We might incorrectly conclude that all new jobs had come from small firms! So it is important to be very careful when comparing aggregate data over different time periods.

There are also problems when analysing longitudinal studies of relationships between job creation and firm size, that is, where changes in individual firms are tracked over a number of years. For example a researcher might run a multiple regression to try to explain employment change in firms. One of the dependant variables might be the size of the firm, and others may be the industrial sector and so on. However, the results of such a regression using firm size as a variable may be biased due to transitory fluctuations in the size of firms being observed. For example if the employment size of a firm is allocated according to size in a specific base year (for example, the year 2000) and then one year it crosses the size boundaries (for example, from the small to the large firm size band) and then recrosses it again another year (from the large back to the small firm size band), then the regression results obtained can be meaningless. These transitory fluctuations may be the result of real changes or of measurement error (this is called the regression fallacy by Davis *et al.*) So it is always worth carefully considering the assumptions behind any data or statistics that you come across.

References and further reading

Birch, D. (1979) *The Job Generation Process*, Cambridge, Mass., MIT Program on Neighbourhood and Regional Change.
Bolton Report (1971) Report of the Committee of Inquiry on Small Firms, Cmnd-4811, London, HMSO.

CEC (Commission of the European Communities) (1995) *The European Employment Strategy: Recent Progress and Prospects for the Future*, COM (95) 465 Final, Luxembourg, Office for Official Publications of the European Communities.

CEC (1999) *Enterprises in Europe* 5th Report, Luxembourg, OOPEC.

Curran, J. and R. Blackburn (1994) *Small Firms and Local Economic Networks: the Death of the Local Economy*, London, Paul Chapman.

Daly, M., M. Campbell, G. Robson and C. Gallacher (1991) 'Job generation 1987–89: the contributions of small and large firms', *Employment Gazette*, November, pp. 589–94.

Davis, S.T., J.C. Haltiwanger and S. Schuh (1996) *Job Creation and Destruction*, London, MIT Press.

Department of Trade and Industry (DTI) (1995) *Small Firms in Britain 1995*, London, HMSO.

ENSR (1997) *The European Observatory for SMEs, Fifth Report*, Brussels, European Network for SME Research.

Eurostat (1994) *Enterprises in Europe*, 3rd Report Vol. 1, Luxembourg, OOPEC.

Eurostat (1997) *Eurostat Yearbook*, 3rd edn, 1997, Luxembourg, OOPEC.

Harrison, J. and B. Taylor (1996) *Supergrowth Companies, Entrepreneurs in Action*, Oxford, Butterworth-Heinemann.

Kaplan, J. (1995) *Startup: A Silicon Valley Adventure*, New York, Penguin.

Labour Market Trends (1999) 'Small and medium enterprises: their role in the economy', *Labour Market Trends*, October, pp. 543–50.

Moore, D.P. and E.H. Buttner (1997) *Women Entrepreneurs*, London, Sage.

OECD (1992) *Employment Outlook*, July 1992, Paris, OECD.

Small Business Administration (SBA) (1994) *Handbook of Small Business Data*, Washington D.C. Government Printing Office.

Storey, D.J. (1982) *Entrepreneurship and the New Firm*, London, Croom Helm.

Storey, D.J. (1994) *Understanding the Small Business Sector*, London, Routledge.

Storey D.J., K. Keasey, R. Watson and P. Wynarczyk (1987) *The Performance of Small Firms: Profits, Jobs and Failures*, London, Croom Helm.

US Bureau of Census (1998) *Statistical Abstract of the United States 1998*, Washington D.C., Government Printing Office.

Part II
Theories of Entrepreneurship

3
Entrepreneurship in Neoclassical Economics

Introduction

In Part II of this book the concern is with theoretical treatment of entrepreneurs and the activities that constitute 'entrepreneurship'. In Chapter 1 it is demonstrated that while there is by no means a consensus in academic thought regarding the definitions of 'entrepreneur' and 'entrepreneurship', there are common themes, of which the acts of creating and developing innovative new business ventures are the foremost. Another issue to emerge from the discussion of small businesses in Chapter 2 is the fact that few small businesses ever grow to a significant extent, although in aggregate the sheer number and diversity of small business activity makes this an important sector in both advanced and developing contemporary market economies. The concept of entrepreneurship in practical terms is commonly linked to small business activity, with the 'ideal' model of business success being the growth of a small business into a corporate giant.

However, it is shown during the course of Part II that while this model can explain some entrepreneurial activity in the small business sector, entrepreneurship in theoretical terms has been viewed from a much wider range of perspectives by the mainstream social sciences of economics, sociology and psychology, and a substantial body of multidisciplinary literature. In examining the major ways in which entrepreneurship has been considered in academic thought it is shown that there are commonalities which can be derived from both economic and non-economic thought on the subject. This is despite the diversity of theoretical views regarding the activities which constitute entrepreneurship and the types of people who can be regarded as entrepreneurs. It is important to gain a good understanding of the range of theoretical perspectives as a basis for analysing the economic and social impact of entrepreneurship, and the policy initiatives which many governments have implemented in promoting entrepreneurial activity. Throughout Part II, the importance of the theoretical perspectives used to give a full understanding of the impact of entrepreneurial activity is demonstrated using real world illustrations.

In Chapter 3, the foundations for considering theories of entrepreneurship are laid by examining the ways the concept has been analysed in 'neoclassical' economics. The discussion begins by considering the nature and scope of neoclassical economics within the historical context in which it has developed. Then the methodology of neoclassical economics is examined and the major ways in which entrepreneurship has been analysed by neoclassical economics are considered. The historical and methodological review is intended to help place the development of neoclassical methodology in context and thus enhance the reader's understanding of this methodology as a precursor to examining alternative economic theoretical approaches. The discussion serves to outline the strengths and limitations of the neoclassical approach and provides departure points for the theoretical treatment of entrepreneurship by alternative economic viewpoints.

What is neoclassical economics?

Quite simply, neoclassical economics has been the conventional mode of economic theory and research since the latter part of the nineteenth century when its principles were developed. The term 'neoclassical' refers to the body of thought which followed that developed by the 'classical' economists who pioneered the subject of economics in the eighteenth and early nineteenth centuries, such as Adam Smith and David Ricardo, and who laid the foundations for the development of contemporary economic thought and identified its key concerns. These concerns include the efficient operations of the market economy, the role of markets in economic development and the role of governments in helping the market economy to achieve economic and social equity, for example, through progressive taxation. The body of thought developed by economists such as Smith and Ricardo was generally termed 'political economy', a term which reflected its normative, prescriptive nature and its underpinnings in social philosophy.

This state of affairs changed however, when the subject was transformed methodologically into 'positive economics' in the latter half of the nineteenth century, when the concern of economists changed from making subjective statements of value to objective statements of fact. This reflected the general scientific mood of the times, in which rapid advances in the development of scientific thought in the natural and physical sciences set the scene for the development of the 'social sciences', including economics. Economic science, or neoclassical economics, became the orthodoxy in the subject, where the rigorously objective methodology of the natural sciences was replicated as far as possible to analyse the economic activities of humans, without making any judgement about what is right or wrong in economic terms. The concern of economic science is to explain the operations of economies and the behaviour of economic 'actors', of whom some of the key ones are entrepreneurs. This describes the activities of humans in playing their part in resolving the central economic problem, which is the allocation of scarce resources in the production of goods and services in order to satisfy the demands of consumers.

This issue has always been the central concern of economics, including political economy, but it was the way in which neoclassical economics set about tackling this problem that distinguished it clearly from the approach of classical economics and it is this approach that has remained the orthodoxy in economics subsequently. In the next section, the methodology developed and adopted by neoclassical economists is considered in detail, but before that it is helpful in gaining a broad understanding of this approach to consider the historical development of the major theoretical models familiar to any leader who has studied elementary economic theory. Here a concise look at the rationale underpinning the development of these models helps to place the methodological overview in the following section in the context of the manner in which neoclassical theory has developed.

The central principle of neoclassical economics is that the economy can be modelled as a system in which equilibrium is attainable. The preferred type of economic system in neoclassical economics is the decentralized market economy, rather than the centralized command economy in which it is the government that makes decisions regarding resource allocation. In examining the operations of the market economy, particular emphasis is placed on understanding the co-ordinating role of prices in the system. However, because of the complexities of reality, an approach is adopted which is aimed at simplifying the market economy into readily identifiable units of analysis, namely consumers and producers, and using deductive reasoning to make predictions about their behaviour in the system in directing the flow of scarce resources to achieve a state of equilibrium. This approach was pioneered by economists such as Walras (1874) in *Elements of Pure Economics*, and Marshall (1919) in *Principles of Economics*, key works which laid the foundations for conventional economic analysis.

The major analytical tools of supply and demand analysis, cost curve analysis and perfect competition were developed by early neoclassical economists, and still help us understand some of the basics of markets. Those following in their footsteps, for example Robinson (1933) and Chamberlin (1933), developed this further in elaborating a 'theory of the firm' in which imperfect and monopolistic competition were developed as an alternative viewpoint to perfect competition, and hence as an alternative economic context within which entrepreneurs might operate. In the model of perfect competition, the firm as a decisionmaking unit with a degree of control over price and output decisions does not exist. A prime concern of perfect competition is to predict the profit maximizing price and output decisions of the producers of standardized goods in response to changes in external factors such as consumer preferences and technology. Here production is merely regarded as the transformation of inputs into outputs, and the productive unit is seen as a 'black box' through which this process occurs. In imperfect and monopolistic competition the firm has a degree of discretion over its price and output decisions by virtue of product differentiation.

At the same time another body of neoclassical work was being developed which sought to analyse the decisionmaking operations of the modern corporate firm, in which ownership and control are separated between shareholders and professional managers. Previously, when the 'firm' was analysed as a unit of analysis, it was regarded as an owner controlled, single product entity. Two major bodies of neoclassical thought emerged subsequently, which sought to examine the price and output decisions of large corporate firms. The first concentrated on the oligopolistic market environments in which corporate firms typically operate, where there is an interdependency of behaviour between firms. Here, the analytical models of pricing theory (Hall and Hitch, 1939) and game theory (von Neumann and Morgenstern, 1944) were developed in order to predict the price and quantity decisions of oligopolistic competitors.

The second body of thought formed the 'managerial theories of the firm', which were developed in order to predict the price and output decisions of corporate firms where controlling managers have a degree of discretion in pursuing their own objectives at the expense of shareholders' objectives (Baumol, 1959; Williamson, 1964; Marris,

1964). Thus while oligopoly theory recognizes the external influences on decisionmaking in large corporations, managerial theory concentrates on the internal influences. Both, however, still focus on the central concern of neoclassical economics, which is to analyse the role of the producers of goods and services within the economic system, in determining equilibrium.

While this short guide to the major developments in neoclassical economics is by no means exhaustive, it does provide a context to the major theoretical models. It is essential that the nature and purpose of its methodology is understood fully, in order to reach a judgement about the ability of neoclassical economics to deal with the concept of entrepreneurship, which as Chapter 1 demonstrated, is commonly associated with dynamic and charismatic individuals. The discussion which follows builds upon these issues, in elaborating more fully on the methodology of neoclassical economics.

The methodology of neoclassical economics

The concept of 'natural' forces leading to equilibrium in the economic system is at the heart of neoclassical economics. Just as there are laws in the natural world which allow it to function and develop, for example, the laws of physics, it is assumed that there are similar laws which govern the economic activities of humans. The key features of such a system are that it is self contained and there is a natural point of equilibrium where the components of the system behave and interact in such a way so as not to disturb this equilibrium. The only ways in which equilibrium can be disturbed are: (a) if there is a shock to the system caused by some external influence; (b) if some component within the systems begins to behave in a disruptive manner. Thus the survival and development of any system depends upon the system's components and the co-ordination mechanisms through which they interact being able to adapt to change, whether these changes are caused by an exogenous 'shock' or an endogenous disruption. A distinction can be made between the static equilibrium of a system at a point in time, and the dynamic process through which equilibrium is restored after the system is thrown into disequilibrium because of exogenous or endogenous change.

It is important to understand the operations of systems in order to appreciate economic theories of entrepreneurship. It is therefore worth pursuing this line of enquiry further here by using a simplified example from the natural world, before considering neoclassical analyses of the market economy as an economic system. A suitable example of a natural system is a food chain made up of a number of carnivorous animals in which there is a hierarchy of natural predators, with possibly a herbivorous animal at the bottom of the hierarchy. The balance between the population numbers of each part of the chain is maintained by the fact that there are natural laws which govern the animal's behaviour and interaction. For example, most animals will normally only kill each other in line with their survival instinct, and the 'fittest' animals will only reproduce at certain times of the year in line with their mating instinct.

If behavioural 'rules' are followed by all animals, and the climate remains constant, so that the vegetation upon which the herbivorous animals feed can grow, the system will reach a natural point of equilibrium. This equilibrium can be disturbed by an exogenous factor, such as a dramatic climate change, or by an endogenous factor, such as the carnivores at the top of the chain choosing to become vegetarian. The latter possibility is unlikely to happen because it can be assumed that in the natural world, animal behaviour is not a matter of purposeful choice, rather it is determined by instincts and responses to environmental stimuli which develop through repetition of experience. In the case of either exogenous or endogenous change the balance between the numbers of animals at each stage of the food chain would be disturbed and eventually the chain would collapse if it did not adapt to take account of the new circumstances. It may be assumed that in this case the process of evolution would determine 'the best way' in which the chain could adapt.

It will become apparent that within this crude analogy of a natural system lie most of the key elements which are necessary to understand economic theories of entrepreneurship. The first concern though, is with the way in which neoclassical economists have applied the systems approach to understanding the economic world, and in particular the operations of market economies in addressing the central economic problem of allocating scarce resources to optimal effect. Two broad approaches to the analysis of the economic system can be identified within neoclassical thought: first, general equilibrium analysis, and second, partial equilibrium analysis. The distinction between these modes of analysis is defined in terms of their level of abstraction. General equilibrium analysis was originally developed by Walras and is concerned with analysing how equilibrium can be achieved in the whole economy, taking account of the interrelationships between markets. Partial equilibrium analysis was originally developed by Marshall and represents a more disaggregate view of the market economy, focusing on the operations of particular markets and the firm as a decisionmaking unit.

It is important to note, however, that while general equilibrium analysis represents an aggregate view of the market economy, it is not the same type of analysis as Keynesian macroeconomics (Keynes, 1936). While Keynesian analysis is concerned with analysing the ways in which governments can intervene in market economies to alleviate problems such as inflation and unemployment, neoclassical general equilibrium analysis assumes that a free market economy is capable of allocating resources to optimal effect without any help from governments. On the contrary, government intervention is deemed to be undesirable. Besides influencing the macroeconomic environment it is claimed to affect the efficient operation of markets through the 'natural' forces of supply and demand and the co-ordinating role of prices, which direct the flow of resources in the production of goods demanded by consumers. Thus in general equilibrium analysis, the economy is perceived as a series of interrelated markets connected through the price mechanism. It is theoretically possible that at a point in time all markets are in equilibrium, where the quantity of a product demanded by consumers equals the quantity supplied by producers. At this point, the markets for the factors used in the production process (land, labour and capital) are also in equilibrium.

There are certain conditions which must be met in this theoretical framework before a general equilibrium is possible. The first of these conditions is that it must be assumed that individual consumers and producers act rationally in the sense that they will make decisions which will maximize their utility (satisfaction). For producers this relates to profit maximization because of the second of the conditions underlying general equilibrium theory, that of the existence of perfectly competitive markets. Perfect competition exists in a market full of small, atomistic competitors, each of whom produces an identical product and therefore faces a perfectly elastic demand curve for their output. There are no barriers to entry or exit so that producers can enter or leave the market without incurring any costs.

All of these features of the market environment mean that individual producers have no control over the price they can charge, this is determined by the level of market demand. Producers must seek to maximize profits in order to survive. The arithmetic calculation of profits is made easy for producers because it is assumed that there exists perfect knowledge in the economy. That is, producers know all consumer preferences and the prices, costs and optimal modes of producing all goods. This is not to say that all knowledge is ready at hand at every point in time, it may be that some search activity is required. The point is that all the relevant knowledge required to make an optimal decision can be accessed by all decisionmakers. It is therefore little problem for producers to decide which goods to produce, and how best to produce them.

Therefore it could be claimed that the firm as a decisionmaking unit does not really exist in perfect competition because it is no more than a production process transforming inputs into outputs as efficiently as possible. The perfectly competitive nature of the market environment renders production decisions as no more than arithmetic calculations in order to produce the profit maximizing level of output, at the price determined by the market. Decisionmaking by producers is purely reactive to changes in the consumer preferences and production technologies. The cause of change, and the process through which equilibrium is restored in order to accommodate change, is not generally explored at all. Furthermore, in equilibrium, no individual producer earns profits over and above any other. All firms operate at the level of output where they break even in economic terms, in that there is no better opportunity to earn a higher level of profit using their particular set of productive resources. All producers are doing the best they can in order to survive and there is no scope to earn an element of monopoly profit when the economy is in equilibrium.

The assumption of perfect knowledge is particularly contentious although it is essential to general equilibrium analysis as a tool of predicting the price and output combinations of all goods and factors of production in an economy at a point in time. General equilibrium can only exist for a given set of consumer preferences and production technologies. If either of these change a new equilibrium will be reached once the change has been accommodated by producers, in which a different set of price and output combinations will prevail. The theory is therefore a static analysis of an economy at one point in time compared with another. The problems of time and uncertainty can be dealt with by assuming that there exists a complete set of futures and insurance markets (Arrow and Debrue, 1959). Thus consumers and producers can determine their consumption and production plans in the present, with complete knowledge of all future prices, and they can insure themselves against any foreseeable risk.

General equilibrium analysis is an abstract theoretical treatment of the market economy as a system of resource allocation. It is often criticized on the basis that it is too 'unrealistic' to be of any use as a model of how actual economies operate. However, neoclassical economists do not claim that a general equilibrium model is representative of any actual economy. It shows in a robust, scientific manner what conditions are needed for the market economy to work to optimal effect. While perfect competition may not exist in reality, it nonetheless provides a yardstick against which the operations of actual markets can be compared and their deficiencies analysed. The emphasis of the neoclassical approach is what may be termed 'theoretical elegance' rather than attempting to explain practically, all of the operations of a dynamic and turbulent economy. It would be impossible to incorporate all of the complexities of reality into a mathematical model, no matter how complex, so that simplifying assumptions are necessary in order to allow such a feat to be attempted in the first place. Neoclassical analysis must therefore be judged within these parameters.

Aside from the theoretical purpose of neoclassical methodology, some prominent contemporary neoclassical economists such as Friedman and Lucas have defended its underlying assumptions by pointing out that there have been periods of relative stability in advanced market economies, where consumers and producers can develop decision rules which will tend to persist until change occurs. While such circumstances do not represent general equilibrium in a pure mathematical form, there is an equilibrium in the sense that the behaviour of decisionmakers can be anticipated by others, with some degree of accuracy. Furthermore, the accumulated experience of decisionmakers means that even if they have never encountered a situation before, past experience of broadly similar situations can provide guidelines on how to react. On the other hand, other prominent economists such as Shackle and Kaldor have criticized the methodology of neoclassical economics. They argue that human behaviour is inherently unpredictable. Thus the components of an economic system are not like animals in a biological system, they are unpredictable human beings whose decisionmaking processes cannot be as objective as neoclassical economics assumes. It is argued by these critics of neoclassical methodology that it is impossible to predict how the 'average' person will behave in any situation, whether they have previous experience or not, and it is therefore impossible to determine theoretically what constitutes rational economic behaviour.

Entrepreneurship in neoclassical economics

In a general equilibrium system, in which there is perfect knowledge and decisionmaking is routine and determined by the environment, there is little scope for entrepreneurship. In early general equilibrium models entrepreneurship was assumed to be a rather intangible fourth factor of production, along with land, labour and capital. Entrepreneurs are regarded as manager co-ordinators of the other three factors, charged with the task of calculating the profit maximizing level of output for a given set of consumer preferences and available technologies. This function is best described as one of 'superintendence' of the production process.

The need to react to a change in exogenous factors in order to survive is forced upon entrepreneurs by the competitiveness of the market environment. In equilibrium there is no need for entrepreneurship defined in these terms because all resources are deployed efficiently. It is important to note here that while the function of entrepreneurship is defined as one of adjustment to new circumstances, this process is nothing more than a mechanical arithmetic calculation, the outcome of which is determined by the environment and not the entrepreneur. There is no scope for proactive and dynamic behaviour of the type that is commonly associated with entrepreneurs.

In the partial equilibrium approach developed by Marshall, there is also little mention of entrepreneurship, although again an entrepreneurial function can be identified implicitly. Marshall differed from his neoclassical contemporaries in that he was more concerned with incorporating an element of realism into his analysis. In point of fact, Marshall's main concern was with economic development, in other words, how an economy evolves through time. The problem of time is assumed away in general equilibrium analysis so that economic evolution is no concern of general equilibrium models. In developing partial equilibrium models of producer behaviour in order to predict price and output levels, Marshall attempted to incorporate the feature of change occurring through time, acknowledging that firms and markets are dynamic entities which are subject to uncertainty.

The assumptions underlying Marshall's analysis are that change is slow and gradual and subsequently economic evolution is a predictable incremental process. Marshall's partial equilibrium analysis of producer behaviour can be thought of in terms of cartoon animation. The characters move but their movement is comprised of a large number of static frames being shown quickly one after the other in a predictable order. Change is organic, it occurs from within the economic system, and it is contributed to by all producers who must constantly test out new ideas in the marketplace in the search for profit opportunities. Thus change occurs in the supply side of the economy.

In order for their firms to develop, business managers must use their accumulated knowledge acquired through experience, to improve productivity and develop new products. Marshall, however, does not draw any distinction between managers and entrepreneurs and there is no specific function attributed to entrepreneurship. The process of the 'natural selection' of the best production techniques and products is contributed to by all managers. Furthermore, the accumulated body of knowledge in an industry is available to all business managers. Knowledge is 'in the air' and all firms can potentially benefit from the actions of their rivals in implementing new and better ideas. In common with the evolutionary basis of his theory, Marshall perceives the process of natural selection in markets as being one in which new, small firms with the best ideas, grow into large firms through becoming more efficient as they accumulate experience. At some point in their life cycle, however, the ability of a firm to learn and improve diminishes. Managers' motivations decline and their ideas become less well suited to market conditions. These firms decline or fail and new dynamic firms take their place.

This rather limited treatment of entrepreneurship is not all that neoclassical economics has to say about the concept. Other economists within the neoclassical school have identified a more explicit entrepreneurial function, albeit within the parameters of static equilibrium analysis.

Knight – risk and uncertainty

The first economist to explicitly identify a specific entrepreneurship function within a general equilibrium system, other than one of passive superintendence, was Knight (1921). Knight sought to address the deficiencies of early general equilibrium models in overcoming the problem of uncertainty by assuming perfect knowledge. Here the term uncertainty needs to be clarified in order to appreciate the basis of Knight's analysis of entrepreneurship. Typically most business decisions are such that the costs of implementing the decision are borne immediately or within a short period of time, whereas the benefits may or may not accrue at some uncertain time in the future.

Furthermore, many business decisions are not repeated in exactly the same form, so that it is difficult to develop decision rules which can be tried and tested over and over again. Uncertainty of outcome is therefore a pervasive fact of everyday business life. Knight makes an important distinction between pure uncertainty and predictable risk. While risk can be quantified and measured against some statistical distribution of the probability of alternative outcomes to any one decision, uncertainty cannot be treated in this manner because the probability of outcomes are themselves unknown. It is important to note that at least some of the possible outcomes can be identified but the likelihood of their occurrence cannot be predicted. Thus risk can be insured against but uncertainty cannot. The question arises of how a general equilibrium system can function with the prevalence of uncertainty? In this context, Knight defines the function of entrepreneurship as uncertainty-bearing so that it is entrepreneurs, and no other economic actors, who make the sort of decisions that require judgement to be exercised in the face of uncertainty.

The distinctive ability entrepreneurs possess which permits them to make such decisions is foresight. Some individuals have a greater degree of foresight than others and it is those with the greatest amount of foresight that achieve high level decisionmaking posts in businesses. These individuals are entrepreneurs and they are not merely managers of routine administrative tasks. Entrepreneurs are strategic decision-makers who generate profits by their actions in deploying resources to optimal effect in an uncertain economic environment. Furthermore, entrepreneurs are capable of making 'good' strategic decisions (that is, those which generate profits) repeatedly. The distinction between entrepreneurs and managers is thus based on Knight's conception of uncertainty.

An important point to note here is that in this analysis capitalists do not bear uncertainty, although they benefit from the actions of entrepreneurs. This does not exclude the possibility that entrepreneurs can be also be capitalists if they self-finance their business ventures. Furthermore, entrepreneurs may exist in new and small businesses and in large corporate businesses. Knight assumes that the choice between self-employment and paid employment is determined by the relative income which can be earned from each activity. So he assumes that entrepreneurs are motivated to earn the highest level of income possible.

Knight argues that large corporations are essentially 'pools' of entrepreneurs with large-scale capital at their disposal so that uncertainty is reduced overall by the law of averages. The best entrepreneurs get to the top in large firms through sheer proof of their ability and active competition. The reward entrepreneurs receive for undertaking the function of uncertainty-bearing in the economic system is a residual income taken from profits generated by their actions after all costs have been borne by the firm, including the salaries of non-entrepreneurial managers. Entrepreneurial income is pure 'profit' and this is not a contractual income in the same way as a manager's salary. In this respect entrepreneurship entails an element of monopoly. Firms that consistently earn profits over and above the average level in their markets do so because they have better entrepreneurs. This element of monopoly is beneficial to the economy because without it there could be no economic equilibrium as uncertainty would prevail. Profit is therefore created by uncertainty.

Production function approaches

More recent neoclassical approaches have also been concerned with identifying a specific entrepreneurial function within a general equilibrium system. These approaches are based on the notion that the decision to become an entrepreneur, as opposed to a worker, is a voluntary choice which requires that individuals assess their abilities to become an entrepreneur. Here the individual is faced with a choice of earning an uncertain income, which is residual profit generated by undertaking entrepreneurial activity, or a certain contractual income from undertaking paid employment. It is assumed that an equilibrium wage rate is determined by a perfectly competitive labour market. This wage is therefore the opportunity cost of choosing to undertake entrepreneurial activity, and thus individuals must be sure that they can earn an income from residual entrepreneurial profit in excess of this wage. If this is the case, then it is a rational choice to choose entrepreneurship over paid employment. This decision depends upon the entrepreneur's self assessment of the extent to which they possess certain abilities which are assumed to be required to undertake successful entrepreneurial activity.

The rational decision to become an entrepreneur is therefore assumed to be based solely on the fact that the expected income will be higher than that from waged employment. If the wage rate falls the opportunity cost of entrepreneurship will become lower and less able entrepreneurs will be attracted into entrepreneurship. Implicit in this analysis is the assumption that individuals will always choose entrepreneurship if they can earn more income from this activity than from paid employment.

The theoretical basis of neoclassical economics requires that the components of a general equilibrium system behave in a rational manner if equilibrium is to be achieved. Thus it is possible to predict that in equilibrium there will be no entrepreneurs active in the economy.

If this situation changes because of changing preferences or technologies, a new equilibrium will be found by the number of active entrepreneurs adjusting to a level which is required to achieve equilibrium in the new set of economic data. The question is, therefore, what specific ability is required to be an entrepreneur? Three approaches have developed in this field of study. These are Kihlstrom and Laffont (1979), Lucas (1978) and Oi (1983), all of which have identified different abilities which entrepreneurs must possess.

Kihlstrom and Laffont (1979) follow Knight and identify this ability as being the willingness to bear risk, which they take to mean uncertainty in common with Knight's distinction. Entrepreneurs play a key role in the general equilibrium system of bearing uncertainty but their reward is specifically associated with their entrepreneurial ability and not with the function of uncertainty-bearing *per se* as in Knight's analysis. All individuals in the economy are assumed to be risk averse but entrepreneurs are less risk averse than workers. There is some critical level of entrepreneurial ability which partitions the set of economic agents in the production process in any static equilibrium. If circumstances change, the critical level of this ability will change and the numbers of active entrepreneurs will adjust accordingly, creating a new point of static equilibrium.

Lucas (1978) identifies the ability as being one of managerial co-ordination. While this has commonalities with the early general equilibrium models in terms of the function of entrepreneurship, here the ability to undertake entrepreneurship is specifically associated with an income generated through entrepreneurial activity when the economy is in equilibrium. This is not the case in early general equilibrium models, when there is no need for entrepreneurs, when the economy is in a state of equilibrium. Lucas argues that there is a random distribution of managerial ability in the set of economic actors and that more able managers can manage larger production processes. If there is an improvement in technology which causes workers' productivity to increase, the critical level of managerial ability required to earn an income over and above that from waged employment will change. Less able entrepreneurs will become workers, thus raising the average level of ability of the remaining entrepreneurs. While all producers are efficient in that they must be cost minimizers and profit maximizers, firm size is directly related to the entrepreneur's managerial ability. Larger firms are managed by more able entrepreneurs who earn higher incomes for their superior levels of managerial ability. In this analysis, there is no distinction between entrepreneurs and managers, as there is in Knight's analysis.

The last of these approaches (Oi, 1983) identifies the ability to manage time effectively as being the critical ability required to be an entrepreneur. More specifically it is the ability to use effectively the residual time available after monitoring the workforce, assuming that the stock of capital assets is inanimate and does not need monitoring. As in the previous two production function approaches there is a critical level of this ability which determines the number of active entrepreneurs when the economy is in equilibrium. Larger firms are again associated with more capable entrepreneurs who can use residual time effectively in raising the productivity of their workforce and increase the level of output from the production process. Better entrepreneurs are associated with more productive workers. In this analysis entrepreneurship represents an input into the production process rather than managerial co-ordination of the production process *per se*, as in Lucas's analysis.

Conclusion

This review of the ways in which entrepreneurship has been treated in conventional neoclassical economic thought concludes with some general comments. The first point to note is that the methodology of neoclassical economics is aimed at predicting the price and output combinations in all markets that make up a general equilibrium economic system. The concern generally is with the end point of equilibrium at a point in time rather than the process through which equilibrium is achieved if change occurs. In this static analytical approach there is little scope for analysing entrepreneurship outside very narrow parameters. These parameters are set by the need to specify the rational behaviour of economic actors. Entrepreneurs are a component in the system with their behaviour being directed by exogenous forces.

In early general equilibrium models there is no scope for entrepreneurship when the economy is in equilibrium. In later general equilibrium models that identify a specific function for entrepreneurship in equilibrium, this function is narrowly defined in terms of management of a production process in some respect, and the motivation for undertaking entrepreneurial activity is income generated from residual profits. However, this approach can suggest a wider view of people following their own rational self interest. Self interest can mean more than simply generating income or profits, as an individual's preferences may be for other things (such as enjoying their family or making a positive contribution to their community and so on). Also being rational does not mean that they do not make mistakes, rather it implies that they do not make the same mistake time and again, that is, they do not make systematic mistakes.

In the Marshallian partial equilibrium approach, it is suggested that while all business managers have to be 'enterprising' in order to survive and develop, there is no specific group of economic actors who may be defined as entrepreneurs rather than business managers. An important aspect of Marshall's analysis, however, is the concern with economic evolution rather than the purely static approach of general equilibrium theory which largely ignores time. Of all the approaches considered in this chapter, only Knight makes a clear distinction between entrepreneurs and managers, this being expressed in terms of entrepreneurs possessing the ability to make strategic decisions which generate profits for their firms. Administrative managers cannot do this as they do not have sufficient foresight. In general then, the role of entrepreneurs in neoclassical theory is often very limited.

References and further reading

Arrow, K.J. and G. Debrue (1959) *Theory of Value*, New Haven, Yale University Press.

Baumol, W.J. (1959) *Business Behaviour, Value and Growth*, New York, Macmillan.

Chamberlin, E.H. (1933) *The Theory of Monopolistic Competition*, Cambridge, Mass., Harvard University Press.

Hall, R.L. and C.J. Hitch (1939) 'Price theory and business behaviour', *Oxford Economic Papers*, Vol. 2, pp. 12–45.

Keynes, J.M. (1936) *The General Theory of Employment, Interest and Money*, London, Macmillan.

Kihlstrom, R.E. and J.J. Laffont (1979) 'A general equilibrium entrepreneurial theory of firm formation based on risk aversion', *Journal of Political Economy*, Vol. 87, pp. 719–48.

Knight, F.H. (1921) *Risk, Uncertainty and Profit*, New York, Houghton Mifflin.

Lucas, R.E. (1978) 'On the size distribution of business firms', *Bell Journal of Economics*, Vol. 9, pp. 508–23.

Marris, R. (1964) *The Economic Theory Of Managerial Capitalism*, London, Macmillan.

Marshall, A. (1919) *Principles of Economics*, London, Macmillan.

von Neumann, J. and O. Morgenstern (1944) *Theory of Games and Economic Behaviour*, Princeton, NJ, Princeton UP.

Oi, W.Y. (1983) 'Heterogeneous firms and the organisation of production', *Economic Inquiry*, Vol. 21, pp. 141–71.

Robinson, J. (1933) *The Economics of Imperfect Competition*, London, Macmillan.

Walras, L. (1954, 1874) *Elements of Pure Economics*, translated by W. Jaffe, London, Allen and Unwin.

Williamson, O.E. (1964) *Economics of Discretionary Behaviour: Managerial Objectives in a Theory of the Firm*, Englewood-Cliffs, NJ, Prentice-Hall.

4
Entrepreneurship and Market Dynamics

Introduction

The concern of this chapter is with the economic theories of entrepreneurship developed by Kirzner and Schumpeter. Both of these theorists identify an explicit function for entrepreneurship within an equilibrium approach to analysing the operations of a market economy, but do so from entirely different perspectives from each other and from that of neoclassical economics. Both Kirzner and Schumpeter relate entrepreneurial activity to the process through which the market economy adjusts in response to factors which create disequilibrium. In Chapter 3 it was shown that changing consumer preferences and production technologies are the major causes of disequilibrium but that neoclassical economics is not concerned with explaining why these factors should change in the first place.

The neoclassical concern is with the end point of equilibrium once the economy has adjusted to change and not the process through which adjustment occurs. In considering the theories of Kirzner and Schumpeter, these deficiencies of the neoclassical approach are addressed. In doing so it is demonstrated that in order to examine market processes a different economic perspective has to be adopted, such as that of the Austrian school of economic thought. In contrast to the neoclassical school the Austrian school is concerned with the dynamic nature of the operations of market economies. The theoretical basis of the Austrian school is fundamental to Kirzner's theory and to a lesser extent Schumpeter's theory. In Schumpeter's theory the notion of economic evolution is also incorporated although in a substantially different way to that of the Marshallian approach considered in Chapter 3. Kirzner and Schumpeter both identify entrepreneurial behaviour as being proactive and purposeful, in contrast to the passive role played by entrepreneurs in neoclassical theory. Both theorists also have more to say about the abilities required to be an entrepreneur.

The chapter is structured in the following way. First, the methodology of the Austrian school of economics is considered briefly to provide a rigorous basis for analysing the theories of Kirzner and Schumpeter. Kirzner's theory is then examined, in which entrepreneurship is related to the concepts of disequilibrium and arbitrage. Following this an illustration which represents the key elements of Kirznerian entrepreneurship is provided. Attention is then directed to Schumpeter's theory, in which entrepreneurship is related to the concepts of disequilibrium and 'creative destruction'. An illustration which represents Schumpeterian entrepreneurship is then provided. Following this, a comparative critique of the two theories is undertaken. Finally, the chapter concludes with a summary of the key elements from the discussion of these theories.

Austrian economics

Contemporary Austrian economics was developed in the mid-twentieth century principally by Hayek and Mises, from the earlier work in the late nineteenth century in the 'subjectivist tradition' pioneered by Menger, Boehm-Bawerk and Wieser. The development of this earlier variant of Austrian economics paralleled that of neoclassical economics. Both had a mutual concern with demonstrating that the free market is the best way of allocating scarce resources and that there are natural forces which co-ordinate the market economy. The fundamental difference, however, concerned the nature of human behaviour, with the subjectivist tradition rejecting the rational economic behaviour model of neoclassical economics.

More fundamental differences between Austrian and neoclassical economics developed in the 1930s with the direction in which Hayek and Mises took the Austrian school. Austrian economics became explicitly different from that of neoclassical microeconomics in that it rejected the idea of static equilibrium based on the assumption of perfect knowledge. Austrian economics became concerned with the market economy as a system in flux, in which the problems of time and change and the process through which market economies adjust, are fundamental.

The most crucial aspect of Austrian economics is the way in which it deals with problem of imperfect knowledge. Here it is recognized that no individual can possibly have all of the 'correct' information necessary to make an optimal decision. While consumers may know their preferences they may not know all of the products they could possibly purchase; and while producers may know the costs of current production processes they may not know all of the alternative methods. Imperfect knowledge in this sense entails a complete ignorance of at least some of the knowledge that exists in the economy. Decisionmakers act in the belief that they are making the best choices with the information they have and they are unaware that better choices may be available. They may, however, be 'surprised' to find out later that they have made a mistake and they will learn from this experience and alter any subsequent decisions.

In common with the subjectivist tradition, Austrian economics perceives decisionmaking as a spontaneous and creative act and views human behaviour as being inherently unpredictable. The market economy is therefore viewed as a complex system in which vast amounts of information must be processed continually in response to an ever changing environment. Given these complexities Austrian economics rejects the notion of static equilibrium, which is a practical impossibility, and places emphasis on the processes through which equilibrium may be achieved. Given that equilibrium in any market can never actually be achieved, however, these processes are merely stabilizing forces which restore some sort of order to the operations of the whole economy. It is important to realize that this approach still assumes that the underlying knowledge which could theoretically lead to a general equilibrium still exists in the economy but the nature of the distribution of knowledge prevents the theoretical possibility of general equilibrium from actually occurring.

The problems addressed are therefore how can an economy operate effectively with imperfect knowledge?; and what are the equilibrating forces which prevent complete chaos in the economic system? In addressing the first of these problems Hayek argued that only a market economy could operate effectively in the presence of imperfect knowledge and not socialist or command economies. Hayek saw the market as a process in which imperfect knowledge is discovered through the exchange of products, that is through people's actions. Imperfect knowledge is a problem only as long as it is unknown and is in private ownership, rather than publicly revealed through people's actions in buying and selling on the market.

In addressing the second of the problems, that of the equilibrating forces that exist in market economies, Mises developed the notion of the market as an entrepreneurially driven process in which the actions of consumers and producers alone cannot create a situation where markets tend towards equilibrium. It is only by the actions of an intermediary that this can occur and this is the function of entrepreneurship. In this sense entrepreneurs are perceived as being profit seeking speculators who are 'middle men' in the exchange process and whose actions ultimately co-ordinate the process of market adjustment. The ideas of Hayek and Mises can therefore be combined in perceiving the market economy as a system which is co-ordinated through an entrepreneurial discovery process. This concept is the basis of Kirzner's theory of entrepreneurship.

In closing this brief overview of Austrian economics it must be pointed out that the idea of the market as an entrepreneurial discovery process is by no means accepted by all economists in the Austrian tradition. For example, Lachmann (1991) has argued that markets are so dynamic that there is no certainty that equilibrating forces will outweigh disequilibriating forces and thus there is no certainty that market economies will tend towards equilibrium at any time. The notion of equilibrium is therefore questioned as a valid basis for economic enquiry, in common with the contemporary radical subjectivist approach of Shackle (1972), who is one of the principal opponents of the equilibrium approach in economic thought. Similar to the Austrian approach, Shackle places great importance on uncertainty and the spontaneity of human decisionmaking and fundamental to his work is an emphasis on the prevalence of true uncertainty as opposed to insurable risk.

Shackle proposes an alternative treatment of uncertainty based on the concepts of possibility and potential surprise. Even though an individual may not be able to attach a probability to an event because they have no prior experience, they may be able to 'guestimate' the probability of its occurrence and the level of surprise they would experience if it were to occur. Shackle therefore equates 'perception' to the imagination of future possibilities so that decisionmaking cannot be a rational choice based on prior experience as in neoclassical analysis. Rather, it is based on expectations of future experiences. For example, many people imagine the pleasure associated with a date with a film star and would undoubtedly choose this event if it were a realistic possibility, despite having no prior knowledge on which to base this choice. The implications of this view of human decisionmaking are such that equilibrium in an economy could not possibly exist if opportunities are figments of peoples' imaginations.

However, the central purpose of Shackle's analysis is not to provide a theory of business behaviour but a theory of individual choice. Every individual faces choices, and in choosing, exercises entrepreneurial imagination. If the equilibrium paradigm is rejected there can be no explicit function for entrepreneurship in the economic system. It is interesting to note that both the extremely 'objective' Walrasian general equilibrium model and the extremely 'subjective' approaches of Lachmann and Shackle both fail to identify an explicit economic function for entrepreneurship.

Kirzner – entrepreneurship, disequilibrium and arbitrage

Kirzner (1973, 1985, 1997) is the key writer in the Austrian tradition on the role of entrepreneurship. Kirzner builds his analysis of entrepreneurship on the notion of the market as an entrepreneurially driven discovery process, in a world where knowledge is unevenly dispersed between market participants and where there exists genuine ignorance on the part of some individuals. Some choices are essentially mistakes, where a different choice would have been made if the individual had been aware of other knowledge at the time the decision was made. It is important to realise that not all individuals are ignorant at the same time, rather some are better informed than others and can therefore exploit their superior knowledge in the pursuit of their own self interest. In doing so, however, their actions must be made public and thus others are made aware of this knowledge. People learn from their mistakes and adapt their behaviour accordingly.

Against this backdrop, Kirzner is concerned with the problem, identified by Hayek and Mises, of how the market economy can operate effectively in allocating scarce resources. More specifically, he focuses on the processes which lead to the discovery of knowledge and the adjustment of markets towards equilibrium following a disequilibriating change in consumer preferences or technology. In elaborating on the ways in which entrepreneurs play a key role in helping to 'solve' this problem, it is important to note that Kirzner provides no explanation for the causes of exogenous change in common with neoclassical economics. Furthermore, while Kirzner associates entrepreneurial activity specifically with periods of disequilibrium following exogenous change, this is not the starting point of his analysis. In common with Hayek and Mises, Kirzner is fundamentally concerned with developing the notion of the market as a discovery process in which entrepreneurs perform a key function.

The mechanism through which entrepreneurial activity brings about a tendency towards equilibrium following an exogenous change involves the concept of arbitrage. This entails the exploitation of price differentials. Assuming that a market has been thrown into disequilibrium following a change in exogenous circumstances, how then does entrepreneurial arbitrage operate in order to help restore the market back toward equilibrium? In disequilibrium it must be the case that there is no equilibrium price and that it is possible that some people are paying too much for the product and others are paying too little. In neoclassical theory it would be assumed that the 'price mechanism' would adjust automatically to restore equilibrium through the 'invisible hand' of the market.

Kirzner, however, finds a more purposeful human function in the adjustment of prices back toward equilibrium levels. In disequilibrium, imperfect knowledge must exist in the sense that some individuals are better informed than others and some are ignorant of at least some of the knowledge associated with this change in market circumstances. All individuals continue to make what they perceive to be correct choices given the information they have and therefore some individuals must be making incorrect choices, although they are unaware of this fact. In practical terms, some people are therefore paying a higher price than they would if they had other information available while others are paying too low a price. In these circumstances there is an opportunity for profitable exchange in order to exploit this price differential. Kirzner argues that it is entrepreneurs who perform this function by buying low and selling high. Entrepreneurs are therefore traders who possess superior knowledge and benefit profitably through the ignorance of others.

In order to perform this function entrepreneurs must possess certain abilities which allow them to acquire this superior knowledge. Kirzner views these abilities as being greater perception and alertness to new opportunities. Entrepreneurs are more perceptive and alert than other individuals. More specifically, entrepreneurs are alert to the fact that identical or equivalent products are being sold at different prices. Their alertness, however, has nothing to do with searching for information about profit opportunities, these opportunities are obvious to entrepreneurs without any effort being expended on their part in looking for them. While it is essential to his theory that entrepreneurs have this ability, Kirzner is not really concerned with explaining how they possess it. He does, however, suggest that in many cases 'outsiders' to a situation may have a fresh perspective and notice opportunities which are lost on those who are familiar with the situation.

By virtue of their greater alertness entrepreneurs notice price differentials and exploit these opportunities to reap pure profit. In acting upon an opportunity, however, entrepreneurs must signal the opportunity to other entrepreneurs who were not sufficiently alert in the first instance. These entrepreneurs follow in the footsteps of the prime mover and compete away the profit opportunity by rapidly adjusting the levels of supply and demand in the market. In acting on the opportunity they were first to notice, an entrepreneur destroys their own profit potential by invoking competition with other entrepreneurs. It is this entrepreneurial competition which speeds up the equilibrating adjustment process. The fact that profit seems certain in the first instance, however, is enough to cause entrepreneurs to act, and through their actions they turn private knowledge into public knowledge. Thus the pursuit of their own self interest serves the public good. The dynamic nature of the market economy ensures that there will always be some markets tending towards disequilibrium and there will always be new profit opportunities for entrepreneurs to exploit.

It is important to realize that in this theoretical framework, entrepreneurs are primarily traders and not producers. If a profit opportunity entails production of a good, entrepreneurs can arrange a contract with a producer and then sell the product on the market themselves. Gaining access to finance is no problem as profit seems certain in the first instance and a capitalist who is willing to finance the venture can always be found. Kirzner argues that entrepreneurs need not actually own any resources in order to exploit profit opportunities. Entrepreneurs are purely intermediaries between the product and factor markets, buying at a lower price and selling at a higher price in return for a certain profit.

This is not to say, however, that all entrepreneurial ventures are successful, some may fail if entrepreneur's initial perceptions are faulty. This may occur if the profit opportunity is not based upon the discovery of past error but from uncertainty about the 'knowable' future. In the latter case Kirzner extends the model of basic arbitrage to one which involves arbitrage across time, where there is a discrepancy between present and future prices. The identification of intertemporal opportunities of this nature must entail entrepreneurial abilities such as imagination and foresight, rather than mere alertness in the present. Following in the subjectivist tradition of Austrian economics, Kirzner would not wish to predict how individuals would possess such abilities. There is a conceptual difficulty in the notion of arbitrage through time, however, in that Kirzner does not attempt to explain what causes changes in preferences or technologies. This raises the issue of how entrepreneurs can possibly know what will happen in order to cause changes in these exogenous factors which in turn lead to a price differential between the present and the future. If human decisionmaking is inherently unpredictable, as the Austrian approach stresses, how can the unpredictable be imagined or foreseen?

Kirzner purposively limits his analysis to explaining entrepreneurial activity in terms of arbitrage and therefore does not find a wider role for entrepreneurs outside that of price adjustment. Entrepreneurs like all individuals, however, will learn from their mistakes in the event of a venture failing. Furthermore, other entrepreneurs will not have followed their lead in such cases so that their resources will not have been misallocated. Kirzner's approach is one of sequential decisionmaking and only correct decisions which are proved to be successful in the marketplace will be replicated by others.

In summary, Kirzner identifies a key role for entrepreneurship in market economies in which disequilibrium is prolific. In the chaos created by imperfect knowledge entrepreneurs, by virtue of their superior abilities to spot profit opportunities created by price differentials, act in their own self interest. In doing so they invoke an equilibrating force which restores order, at least partially, to the system. Entrepreneurship is thus a countervailing force in a world of disequilibrium.

Illustration

Arbitrage and entrepreneurship: George Soros

George Soros, the billionaire fund manager, currency speculator and international philanthropist, earned the title of 'The man who broke the Bank of England'. In an act which he later apparently indicated was primarily aimed at gaining him political influence with the US and British governments, whom he did not believe were doing enough to promote reforms in the former communist countries of Eastern Europe, Soros took on the British pound on 16 September 1992, a day which was to become legendary in the financial markets. At the time, sterling was in the European Exchange Rate mechanism (ERM), a semi-fixed exchange rate regime where currencies were only allowed to move against each other within quite tight bands. The system was intended to facilitate economic convergence among the member states of the European Union as a precursor to full monetary union.

The ERM threatened to become unstable following the dramatic events leading to the reunification of West and East Germany and the costly burden of financing this reunion for the German government. As Germany was the largest and most influential economy in the EU, the German Deutschmark had been the peg upon which all other currencies hung. Any difficulties experienced by the German economy could therefore destabilize the ERM and have adverse consequences for all the economies of EU members. A public remark made to this effect by the President of the German Bundesbank led to this potential instability being drawn to the attention of George Soros. At the time, it was also widely thought in Britain that sterling had gone into the ERM at too high a value in relation to the underlying performance of the British economy and that this value was unsustainable in the long term. British interest rates were high in order to help maintain the value of sterling by attracting financial investors and this was damaging the British domestic economy. Many economic commentators were calling for a withdrawal from the ERM in order to take the 'squeeze' off the domestic economy and to allow sterling to fall to its true market level in a floating exchange rate regime.

Against this background George Soros had earlier 'taken on' the Italian lira, one of the weaker currencies in the ERM and won, short-selling the lira against other ERM currencies which soon led to the lira's collapse and withdrawal from the regime. It seemed inconceivable that a major currency like sterling could suffer the same fate, although Soros bet that the pound would not be able to hold its value against the other ERM currencies. He began short-selling sterling, pitting the might of his billions of dollars worth of funds against the Bank of England, which had to fight to maintain sterling in accordance with its ERM value by using its foreign currency reserves to buy the pound. Soros sparked off a wave of selling of sterling and in a desperate move the British government eventually put interest rates up a total of five percentage points that day in order to attract investors, realizing that it could not realistically defend the pound in the currency markets given the extent of the selling activity.

This did not deter the wave of selling as currency dealers increasingly realized the impact of Soros' actions and joined the bandwagon. Eventually the British government had to give in and announced that it was leaving the ERM. This was a major policy U-turn as the British government had placed ERM membership as a centrepiece of its economic policy and had given strong guarantees that it would strongly defend its membership. In doing so it had not accounted for George Soros. In that one day Soros reputedly earned $1 billion, one of the most profitable pieces of currency dealing ever. Following its departure from the ERM the price of sterling fell considerably. Sterling eventually picked up and settled in a price range well below its lowest permissible ERM value.

Soros has been widely regarded as a master of arbitrage in the financial markets and has been one of the greatest money managers on Wall Street. An investment of $100 000 with Soros in 1969 would have been worth around $300 000 million in 1997. He is President of Soros Fund Management and Chief Investment Advisor to Quantum Fund, a $2.5 billion international investment fund recognized for its high performance during much of its history. Born into a Jewish family in Hungary in 1930, Soros survived the holocaust and experienced first hand the political extremes of both fascism and communism. He emigrated to Britain in the 1940s where he studied at the London School of Economics. It was a combination of his life experiences and his time at the LSE, where he was strongly influenced by the Austrian philosopher Karl Popper, that shaped his strong views about the nature of economic theory.

After studying conventional economic theories of the market at the LSE, he was highly critical of conventional wisdom and developed his own views of how markets operate, which he termed the theory of reflexivity. He put this theory into practice in the financial markets after emigrating to the US in the 1950s and founding his investment fund. By the end of the 1960s he had specialized in financial arbitrage, buying and selling securities in different markets in order to slice profits off the transactions. In particular, he discovered the considerable potential of arbitrage in the currency markets by moving money around the world in order to profit from the rise and fall of currencies. He has written several works outlining his ideas, including his 1987 book *The Alchemy of Finance*.

His theory of reflexivity is based on the notion that people always act on the basis of imperfect knowledge, whether in the financial markets or everyday life, and although they seek the truth about the world they can never attain it because the very act of looking distorts the picture. Peoples' perceptions about reality are therefore incomplete and can never be complete because their very actions change reality. Thus Soros argues that in the economic and social world there is a never ending feedback mechanism between perceptions and reality which is guided by human actions made on the basis of imperfect knowledge. This is the process of reflexivity.

Soros bases this theory on a critique of conventional economic thought, both generally in terms of its impossibly objective view of human behaviour and specifically in terms of its view of the way in which markets operate. He criticizes the conventional economic axioms that market demand and supply are determined independently of each other and that they interact to set an equilibrium price. He further criticizes the concept of perfect knowledge in the economic environment and the view that markets can only work efficiently if they are atomistic with no one individual's actions having a profound impact on the market price. This theoretical framework assumes that reality can be analysed objectively as a set of absolute facts which exist in the world and which are entirely separate from the actions of market participants. In contrast, Soros argues that this view of economic science is inappropriate because of the process of reflexivity.

Furthermore, he argues that actions are not based upon indisputable facts, which he believes cannot possibly exist, but upon people's expectations of what their actions will achieve. Soros therefore views all human action as being essentially speculative and actual outcomes may be different from expected because once actions are implemented they may create a different set of circumstances to those anticipated. Markets are therefore characterized by dynamic disequilibrium, where perceptions of reality may vary considerably from what is actually happening. At best, in circumstances where there is an absence of change and a greater convergence of perceptions and reality, there can be a tendency towards equilibrium. Actual equilibrium, however, can never be attained because the knowledge necessary to facilitate this event can never exist in a complete and generally available form at any point in time. A market equilibrium price must discount the future and this can never happen because the future is dynamically determined by the actions of market participants and therefore cannot be predicted. In this regard, Soros argues that conventional economic theory is particularly inappropriate to the operations of financial markets because the price is primarily the cause of buyers and sellers actions and not merely the end result. He believes that characteristically fast changing circumstances, and widespread imperfect knowledge make dealing in the financial markets particularly speculative, and thus open to arbitrage.

In a speech delivered to the MIT Department of Economics World Economy Laboratory Conference in Washington, D.C. in 1994, Soros cited the ERM episode, his most famous victory, in defence of his theory. For many years the ERM had operated at near equilibrium conditions, which was after all its fundamental purpose, but it was thrown into turmoil by the German reunification in 1989. The period of revolutionary economic and social change which ensued created dynamic disequilibrium in the markets for ERM currencies and presented opportunities to profit from the much greater degree of imperfect knowledge which resulted from this unforeseen event. Soros's shrewdness in recognizing the potential for arbitrage across the markets for ERM currencies and in spotting the opportunity to short-sell the pound were characteristic of his outstanding performance as a money manager. The $1 billion he earned on that fateful day in 1992, to the detriment of the Bank of England, are certainly very powerful arguments in his favour.

Schumpeter – entrepreneurship, innovation and creative destruction

Schumpeter (1934, 1943) also identifies an explicit entrepreneurial function within an economic system in which there is the potential for equilibrium to exist but which is characterized by dynamic forces which cause change and disequilibrium. Schumpeter is concerned with explaining the process by which capitalist societies develop, where capitalism is the social, economic and institutional order associated with market economies. It is important to note that in Schumpeter's theory, by 'development' it is meant the ways in which change occurs and is adapted to.

In explaining the process of capitalist development in this sense, Schumpeter incorporates the Marxist idea that capitalism is a system which is driven by internal conflict which is created within the system (Marx, 1867). Schumpeter assumes that economic development is therefore an organic process, and that change occurs within the system. His concern is to explain the causes of change in consumer preferences and production technologies, in contrast to the neoclassical and Kirznerian theoretical perspectives in which change in these factors is assumed to be exogenous to the economic system. Furthermore, Schumpeter is concerned with the creation of new possibilities and not merely the discovery of existing possibilities, which were hitherto unnoticed.

Within this theoretical framework Schumpeter identifies entrepreneurs as the key agents of change and entrepreneurship as the cause of capitalist development. In relating entrepreneurship to economic evolution, Schumpeter disagrees with Marshall's cautious treatment of evolution as a slow incremental process which is contributed to in a small way by all business managers. In contrast, Schumpeter perceives entrepreneurs as exceptionally gifted individuals that are few and far between and views economic development as a dramatic, turbulent process in which entrepreneurs are revolutionaries. The mechanism through which entrepreneurs' actions are implemented is that of innovation and 'creative destruction'. By innovation it is meant the commercial exploitation of a novel product or production mechanism in the pursuit of profit. There are two aspects to this conceptualization of innovation which must be understood clearly.

First, innovation is not the same thing as invention, entrepreneurs are not advancing knowledge for science's sake; they may develop inventions into usable products and are motivated by profit. Second, by 'novel' it is meant an entirely new idea or the new use of an existing idea. The point is that entrepreneurs both create and commercially exploit new knowledge which hitherto did not exist in the economic system. Schumpeter has very clear ideas of the type of innovations that entrepreneurs create and he is referring to grand innovations which have far-reaching effects throughout the whole economy and which challenge the existing order. As in Marshall's evolutionary framework, change begins in the supply side of the economy.

Entrepreneurs are producers who must convince consumers to buy their products, and therefore they undertake activities such as advertising and marketing in order to sway consumer preferences. Thus both new consumer preferences, and products to meet them, and new production technologies are created by producers in Schumpeterian theory. All of the activities which entrepreneurs must undertake in order to exploit their ideas require a range of intellectual and practical abilities, and personal attributes such as creativity, imagination, intuition, and sheer ambition and drive. Entrepreneurs 'make things happen' and they see their ideas through to the end no matter what obstacles are put in their way.

Thus, only a small proportion of the population of an economy is capable of undertaking entrepreneurial activity. Above all, entrepreneurs have to be leaders, capable of convincing others of the worth of their ideas and capable of overcoming the existing order which, in general, is reluctant to change. Most 'ordinary' individuals like to follow known routines and this resistance to change has to be overcome if entrepreneurs are to profit from their innovations. Profit is thus created by entrepreneurial innovation. In equilibrium there can be no profit therefore entrepreneurship is a disruptive force which causes disequilibrium and which creates profit opportunities. Once disequilibrium is created by entrepreneurial activity, the question may be raised as to how the system adjusts to change. The answer lies in the process of creative destruction.

Schumpeter argues that equilibrium must be the starting point for entrepreneurial activity. Only in equilibrium are all routines known and therefore entrepreneurs can calculate the profit potential of their innovations in the knowledge of all the products, technologies, prices and costs which currently prevail. This information is available to all producers but only entrepreneurs have knowledge of the novel idea which they are about to implement.

It is important to note that while a general equilibrium in its strictest mathematical sense is not a practical possibility, there may be periods of relative stability in market economies and it is this more realistic conceptualization of equilibrium which is important to Schumpeter's theory. Only if entrepreneurs are certain that their innovation will be profitable will they act. This must entail a belief that their ideas will have a competitive advantage over what is currently available. On this basis they can convince a capitalist to finance their new venture and it is the capitalist who bears the risk of the venture failing and not the entrepreneur. Thus entrepreneurs and capitalists enjoy a symbiotic relationship in a mutually beneficial quest for profitable projects which will provide a return on investment.

While these new ventures create new opportunities they also threaten the viability of existing products and production processes. The novelty value of the new ideas leads to a surge in demand for them and thus away from existing producers, who may become obsolete unless they adapt to the changing circumstances. Those that do adapt will merely imitate the new ideas pioneered by entrepreneurs and more new investment projects will ensue. Alternatively, existing producers can develop products or processes which are complementary to entrepreneurs' innovations. However, once the competition to profit from the new opportunities becomes so great as to make further investment unviable, this boom period will come to an end. At the same time consumers will no longer be impressed by the novelty value of the new idea and eventually it becomes routine. The ensuing downturn in the economy towards recession is fuelled further by those producers who were so entrenched in their routines that they could not adapt to the new ideas and whose businesses subsequently fail.

This is the process of creative destruction; the new destroys the old. Only once change has been fully accommodated throughout the economy in a 'new order' of institutions and routines, can some form of stability be restored. There is, however, no explicit equilibriating force in Schumpeter's theory, the whole economy must react and adapt to change in order to restore widespread stability and equilibrium. Once the new equilibrium has been achieved a new wave of innovative activity will follow and the process of creative destruction will again be invoked. Schumpeter argues that this is the turbulent way in which the capitalist system develops, although the time scales he envisages for each wave of innovation and creative destruction is several decades. This is not a theory of short-term business cycles, indeed Schumpeter perceived creative destruction as an unpredictable spiral of change rather than a predictable cycle or a trend.

An important element of Schumpeter's earlier work was the role of new, small firms in the process of innovation. Entrepreneurs create and develop new ventures in order to challenge the monolithic corporations that pursue obsolete routines and which are forced to adapt in order to survive. In his later work Schumpeter took a more pessimistic view in arguing that eventually these monolithic corporations would use their market power to buy out entrepreneurs and thus take over the entrepreneurial function which they would then proceed to stifle. The eventual demise of capitalism through increasing industrial concentration and the stagnation caused by the lack of entrepreneurial change, would seem inevitable in these circumstances. However, Schumpeter was being unduly pessimistic about the potential of small entrepreneurial firms to survive and prosper in markets dominated by large corporations, a fact which Schumpeter himself later recognized. While not all small firms are driven by innovative activity, many have made an outstanding contribution to the creation and commercialization of new ideas in dynamic technology driven industries such as microelectronics and biotechnology.

In summary, Schumpeter's theory is a hybrid of neoclassical, Austrian and Marxist perspectives which aims to explain the process of economic development in the capitalist system. Fundamental to his theory is the recognition that entrepreneurial activity is initiated in periods of equilibrium. In creating disequilibrium through the innovation of new ideas, which in turn leads to the process of creative destruction, entrepreneurs destroy the conditions they need to flourish. In disequilibrium there is no new entrepreneurship, only existing entrepreneurs exploiting the profit opportunities they created initially. While imitators follow the lead of entrepreneurs, they are not themselves entrepreneurs. Imitators, however, benefit from entrepreneurial innovation, as do the capitalists who finance investment projects. Entrepreneurship is thus the driving force of capitalist development.

Illustration

Innovation and entrepreneurship: Bill Gates

Bill Gates, the Chairman of Microsoft Corporation, the world's largest producer of computer software, has come a long way since he founded the company in the mid-1970s whilst a student at Harvard University. As the world's richest man, he is also the youngest ever multi-billionaire and despite coming from a wealthy family, his personal fortune is entirely self-made through his efforts at Microsoft. He is widely acclaimed to have revolutionized the computer industry, having recognized soon after the invention of the personal computer in the early 1970s that the future lay in desktop rather than mainframe systems. The monolithic IBM, the dominant force in the computer industry for many years, had cornered the market for mainframe systems up to that point.

Gates recognized the commercial potential of personal computers and of PC software in particular. In the late 1970s, along with the team of technically brilliant 'microkids' which he had assembled at Microsoft, he created programming languages which he used to develop the software packages with which Microsoft would dominate the market in the 1980s and 1990s. Gates also realized early on that gaining control of the disk operating systems used by PC hardware manufacturers was the key to success in the PC market. In 1980 Gates negotiated a nonexclusive licensing agreement with IBM for the Microsoft operating system MS-DOS, which Microsoft had originally bought from a small software company in Seattle. MS-DOS rapidly became the industry standard as virtually all other hardware manufacturers were developing IBM compatible machines. IBM had belatedly realized the potential of the PC market and sought outside assistance in developing its own PC. As a result of the shrewd tactic of obtaining a nonexclusive agreement, Gates was also able to license MS-DOS to all hardware manufacturers, other than Apple Macintosh (which had developed its own operating system), and therefore gain control of virtually all of the PC market. Apple had previously rejected the option of licensing its operating system to other hardware manufacturers, leaving the way clear for Microsoft.

In a similarly shrewd manner in 1990 Gates apparently offered hardware manufacturers a 'take it or leave it' licensing arrangement for the use of an updated version of MS-DOS, whereby they were required to pay a fee to Microsoft for all computers they sold regardless of whether they used the MS-DOS operating system or not. This provided a clear incentive to use MS-DOS on all computers. In 1997 Gates made a $150 million investment in Apple to tie the remaining segment of the PC market into an alliance with Microsoft, thus making Microsoft's domination of PC operating systems complete.

Importantly, the IBM contract was to provide Microsoft with the financial strength necessary to develop a new graphics based operating system in the 1980s, Windows, which has also become the industry standard since its large scale commercial introduction in 1990. Windows has subsequently been upgraded in new versions for both personal and corporate users, the latter principally using network servers which require more powerful operating systems. In developing the proprietorial Windows based operating system, NT for network server use, Microsoft attacked IBM's traditional dominance in the corporate computing market. This attack was reinforced by providing extensive corporate training programmes in the applications and support of NT and its related Windows software.

Microsoft's domination of the software market was enhanced by the novel step of developing suites of software where data could be transferred between applications rather than individual, self-contained packages. Furthermore, these software suites were integrated with the Windows operating system rather than developed as add-on applications, which reduced development costs and in turn led to substantial reductions in the price of software. Microsoft's domination of the software industry extended further into the development of Internet software.

While this emerging market had initially been dominated by the Netscape, Gates soon realized the potential of the Internet as a new form of computer network technology which could potentially supersede Microsoft's proprietorial PC based software applications. He therefore set about developing Microsoft's own Internet software, which has become an integral part of the Windows PC software suite. In the space of two years Microsoft began to set the standards in the development of Internet software and in doing so Gates has perhaps become the first major entrepreneur in the computer industry, so far, not to fall by the wayside through failing to adapt to new developments.

In the process Gates has incurred the wrath of his competitors, some of whom have pursued law suits against Microsoft for allegedly using anti-competitive practices in building up its dominant market share, and of the US Department of Justice, who have pursued allegations of a monopolistic abuse of market power by Microsoft principally relating to their 'take it or leave it' licensing practices. Critics of Gates and his commercial tactics perceive Microsoft as having previously unconceived of possibilities for monopolistic domination in a vast range of markets using computer applications. In the 1990s Microsoft has engaged in a vigorous programme of company buyouts and equity partnerships in a diverse range of businesses from car sales to satellite communications.

Defenders of Gates, however, perceive this domination to have arisen fairly from the superior abilities of Microsoft to take a long-range view and to innovate new ideas which have increased consumer choice and revolutionized the highly interconnected markets for computing products. In this sense they argue that Microsoft is not a coercive monopoly and that it does not abuse its market power to the detriment of consumers. On the contrary, they argue that consumers have benefited from Microsoft's innovations, as have its competitors in being shown new and better ways of doing things. Even Microsoft cannot rest on its laurels in a fast changing industry, as the Internet episode shows. Microsoft spends hundreds of millions of dollars a year on research and development, and the shrewd business acumen of Gates and his staff has ensured that many innovations have been implemented commercially.

Bill Gates has been the driving force of Microsoft's success. He is not only recognized as a technically brilliant visionary but also as a determined, hard edged businessman who is driven by a desire to be the best. At Harvard he was as well known for his shrewdness and tenacity as a poker player, and for diligently reading widely on business strategy and management, as he was for his skills as a mathematician and a computer scientist. He dropped out of Harvard not long after founding Microsoft and few of his closest friends and confidantes perceived this to be a bad move given his extraordinary range of talents and hard driving ambition. He is renowned for his ability to recruit and motivate brilliant and talented individuals, in both technical and commercial fields, and for his maverick approach to corporate management. While corporate giants such as IBM insist on codes of practice relating to, for example appearance and behaviour, Gates has thrown conventional corporate culture out of the window and fostered a culture of individualism with no restrictions on the ability of individuals to dress as they see fit and to work as many hours as it takes, at whatever time, to complete a job. The binding force in Microsoft is the pursuit of technical excellence and a shared desire to set new standards and to be the best. Whether they agree with his business practices or not, few people would disagree that Bill Gates is one of the leading entrepreneurs of modern times.

Kirzner and Schumpeter – a comparative critique

Both Kirzner and Schumpeter are concerned with explaining some aspect of the dynamic operations of market economies. While their theories incorporate the notion of economic equilibrium in some respect, they are both fundamentally different from the largely static approach of neoclassical economics. In aligning his theory with the Austrian subjectivist approach, Kirzner identifies a key role for entrepreneurship as an equilibriating force within market economies, in which preferences and technologies are always changing somewhere in the system. Entrepreneurs help to restore markets to equilibrium through the process of price adjustment. Schumpeter, on the other hand, bases his theory primarily on the notion of economic development, in which equilibrium is necessary as a starting point. In doing so Schumpeter identifies entrepreneurs as the creators of new preferences and technologies and, therefore, views entrepreneurship as a disequilibriating force which causes economic development.

The issue may be raised of how the theories can be combined in explaining the process of change and adjustment. That is, once Schumpeterian entrepreneurs have acted upon their innovations and caused disequilibrium, why then cannot Kirznerian entrepreneurs act upon the opportunities which are created by their Schumpeterian counterparts? The answer to this is that they cannot imitate innovative ideas and be regarded as entrepreneurs. Schumpeter is quite clear that imitators are not entrepreneurs, even though they benefit from the profit opportunities thrown up by innovation. The point is that only entrepreneurs, by virtue of their unique qualities as individuals, create innovative profit opportunities. All other economic agents, however, benefit from the actions of entrepreneurs. The perspectives adopted by the Kirzner and Schumpeter in identifying an entrepreneurial function are too different to be accommodated within one theory.

Kirzner is not concerned with explaining the process of change and can therefore offer little account of why preferences and technologies change. Of the two theories, only Schumpeter's can offer an explanation of how entrepreneurs add value to the economy and advance production possibilities. In both theories there is the notion that entrepreneurial profit is associated with an element of monopoly. In Kirzner's theory, entrepreneurs have a short lived monopoly over their superior knowledge until this is signalled through their actions and competed away by other entrepreneurs. In Schumpeter's theory, entrepreneurs also have a short lived monopoly over the new knowledge they are seeking to exploit commercially. In both cases though, entrepreneurship is, in a way, self destructive. Entrepreneurs' actions as prime movers cannot fail to signal opportunities to others. On this basis it may be argued that some form of protection of their monopoly, such as trademarks and patents, may motivate Schumpeterian entrepreneurs to innovate new ideas.

In both theories, it is the capitalist who bears uncertainty in financing entrepreneurial ventures, although the possibility of entrepreneurial failure is not really dwelt upon in either theory. Both Kirzner and Schumpeter are primarily concerned with explaining entrepreneurial success, which is largely assured by the unique attributes and abilities which entrepreneurs possess. There is a difference, however, between the theories with regard to their views of what it takes to be an entrepreneur. Entrepreneurship is largely depersonalized in Kirzner's theory in that any individual can potentially be alert or creative at some time, while Schumpeter envisages entrepreneurs in a more personalized way as unique and gifted individuals who have extraordinary talents.

Both Kirzner's and Schumpeter's entrepreneurs rely upon most market participants unquestioningly following well established routines. It is through their greater knowledge and insight that entrepreneurs can profit from the ignorance, and the surprise, of others. Both theories also stress that entrepreneurs show the way for others to follow, although in Kirzner's theory this is in a very localized way with no more than partial reallocation of resources arising from a single entrepreneur's actions. Schumpeter, on the other hand, is concerned with a more general reallocation of resources arising from entrepreneurial innovation. A single entrepreneur can therefore have a profound impact on the whole economy in the Schumpeterian scheme of things.

Conclusion

In this chapter the notion of entrepreneurship as an essential function in the process of market change and adjustment was introduced. This is in contrast to the static neoclassical models of Chapter 3. Identifying a role for entrepreneurs in market dynamics has entailed further analysis of the qualities required to act entrepreneurially, and of the role of entrepreneurship in evolution as well as equilibrium. These themes are developed in Chapter 5 in which a further element will be added to the examination of entrepreneurship in economic theory, the social influences on entrepreneurship, which are largely ignored by the neoclassical, Kirznerian and Schumpeterian theories.

References and further reading

Cusamano, M.A. and R.W. Selby, (1997) *Microsoft Secrets: How the World's Most Powerful Software Company Creates Technology, Shapes Markets, and Manages People*, New York, Free Press.

Kirzner, I.M. (1973) *Competition and Entrepreneurship*, Chicago, University of Chicago Press.

Kirzner, I.M. (1985) *Discovery and the Capitalist Process*, Chicago, University of Chicago Press.

Kirzner, I.M. (1997) 'Entrepreneurial discovery and the competitive market process: an Austrian approach', *Journal of Economic Literature*, Vol. 35, pp. 60–85.

Lachmann, L.M. (1991) 'Austrian economics as an hermeneutic approach', in D. Lavoie, (ed.), *Economics and Hermeneutics*, pp. 134–46, London, Routledge.

Marx, K. (1946, 1867) *Capital: A Critical Analysis of Capitalist Production*, translated by S. Moore, E. Aveling and D. Torr, London, Allen and Unwin.

Schumpeter, J.A. (1934) *The Theory of Economic Development*, Cambridge, Mass., Harvard University Press.

Schumpeter, J.A. (1943) *Capitalism, Socialism and Democracy*, London, Allen and Unwin.

Shackle, G.L.S. (1972) *Epistemics and Economics*, Cambridge, University of Cambridge Press.

Shawcross, W. (1997) 'Turning dollars into change', *Time* magazine, September.

Soros, G. (1987) *The Alchemy of Finance*, New York, Simon & Schuster.

Soros, G. (1997) 'The capitalist threat', *The Atlantic Monthly*, February.

Wallace, J. (1997) *Overdrive: Bill Gates and the Race to Control Cyberspace*, Chichester, John Wiley and Sons.

Wallace, J. and J. Erickson, (1993) *Hard Drive: Bill Gates and the Making of the Microsoft Empire*, Chichester, John Wiley and Sons.

5
Socio-Economic Influences on Entrepreneurship

Introduction

In this chapter we analyse theorists: Casson and Etzioni. They both identify the importance of entrepreneurship as a key function within market economies but do so by relating the concept to a wider societal framework. In this respect they incorporate a socio-economic aspect to their analyses rather than adopting a purely economic perspective. The respective approaches they adopt are somewhat different although it is possible to regard their theories as representing complementary perspectives. Both theorists essentially focus on the socio-economic factors which determine the demand for and supply of entrepreneurs.

Casson, however, is primarily concerned with aligning his theory within the economic equilibrium approach, while Etzioni has a greater concern with the process of economic evolution. Casson and Etzioni also bring together key elements from the theories considered in Chapters 3 and 4. These are, the concepts of judgmental decision-making, imperfect knowledge and market dynamics (in terms of the causes of change and the processes through which economies adapt to change). In this respect both theories represent more comprehensive attempts at identifying the economic importance of entrepreneurship than the theories considered in Chapters 3 and 4. Chapter 5 is something of a pivotal chapter in Part II in that it links economic and socio-economic influences. The notion that entrepreneurs are agents of change who operate within the evolution of a wider socio-economic environment is developed further in Chapter 6. Chapter 7 focuses more specifically on the personal attributes and behaviour of entrepreneurs.

This chapter proceeds by reviewing Casson's theory of entrepreneurship, the central concern of which is the 'market for entrepreneurs'. This is followed by considering Etzioni's theory, which is concerned with the societal legitimization of entrepreneurship as the force which promotes adaptation to a changing environment. Following this the different views of economic evolution elaborated by Marshall and Schumpeter in Chapters 3 and 4 and Etzioni in the present chapter are pulled together. These ideas are examined further in the analysis of the contemporary body of evolutionary economic theory developed by Nelson and Winter (1982). This provides an important basis for the ideas developed in Chapter 6. An illustration is then given to help illuminate the general issues raised, that of Richard Branson, one of the most successful and well known contemporary entrepreneurs in the UK. Finally, the chapter concludes by drawing out the main themes from the discussion thus far in Part II.

Casson – the market for entrepreneurs

Casson (1982, 1990) attempts to combine insights from both the neoclassical and Austrian approaches in a comprehensive economic theory of entrepreneurial decisionmaking. He suggests that, in general, while neoclassical theory cannot explain many observable activities in the real world its strength is in providing a theoretical yardstick against which reality can be compared and any discrepancies identified. Casson also recognizes the value of the Austrian approach in accounting for purposeful human action but recognizes that this approach is limited by its subjectivism, which prevents it from developing a predictive theory of entrepreneurship.

Casson therefore attempts to integrate the positive features of both approaches by incorporating an Austrian view of entrepreneurship into a neoclassical static equilibrium model. In doing so Casson is primarily concerned with explaining the processes of efficient resource allocation in an economy. He identifies a key role for entrepreneurs as the coordinators of this process, following the Austrian view. Casson assumes that all individuals act rationally and make what they believe to be optimal choices according to their perceptions. These perceptions may be incorrect, however, in two ways. First, in the Kirznerian sense that some decisions may be made in ignorance of better information. Second, in the Schumpeterian sense that some individuals continue to follow established routines which are made obsolete in a changing environment but they are unaware of the changes which have occurred.

They are essentially 'behind the times'. Either way, mistakes will be made and these mistakes will throw up profit opportunities for entrepreneurs. The role of entrepreneurs is to assist in the process of allocating resources to their optimal effect by correcting these mistakes. At one level, incorrect choices such as paying too high a price for a good or buying a good when there exists a better alternative, provide opportunities for profitable arbitrage.

At another level Casson argues that entrepreneurs can perceive opportunities through speculation, for example about what products consumers would prefer if they were to be made available. Anyone who perceives and acts on such opportunities, either through arbitrage or speculation, is an entrepreneur. Casson defines an entrepreneur specifically as a specialist in making judgmental decisions in return for profit. His conception of a judgmental decision is very specific and entails the ability to make a correct choice in given circumstances in which a non-entrepreneurial individual would make an incorrect choice. In this situation, although both individuals may be motivated by similar goals, only the entrepreneur would have the knowledge required to make a correct choice and would be able to interpret that knowledge and apply it to achieve the desired goal. Furthermore, entrepreneurs are able to do this repeatedly and therefore they are a unique set of individuals, with unique skills and abilities which allow them to make judgmental decisions.

Casson argues that the ability to make judgmental decisions is determined by a combination of the qualities evident in other economic theories, namely perception, foresight, creativity and imagination. Non-entrepreneurial individuals do not possess these abilities and furthermore do not learn from their mistakes. This proposition is in contrast to Kirzner who argues that all individuals learn from their mistakes and therefore have the potential to act entrepreneurially. Casson appears to disagree with this view and asserts that entrepreneurs are a subset of the population. On this basis, it is important that entrepreneurs, as the key decisionmakers in an economy, are able to gain control of resources in order to co-ordinate the process of resource allocation. In this respect Casson suggests that differences in economic performance between nations are attributable to the quantity, and the quality, of entrepreneurs evident in their populations. Thus it is resource use that is the important issue in economic performance and not the ownership of resources *per se*.

Casson argues that something similar to neoclassical supply and demand analysis can be applied to a perfectly competitive market for entrepreneurs, with an equilibrium price equating demand with supply. Casson's theory therefore represents an aggregate theory of the market for entrepreneurs rather than a theory of entrepreneurship at the individual level. In common with Kirzner's analysis, Casson assumes that individual entrepreneurs can only effect partial and not general resource allocation. However, Casson's application of supply and demand analysis is not conventional. The demand curve is drawn assuming a given pace of change in the economy so that new opportunities are occurring at a certain pace and entrepreneurs will spot and take advantage of them. The demand curve will shift position if the pace of change in the economy increases or decreases. As the number of active entrepreneurs increases, the expected return to each entrepreneur decreases given the higher probability that any given opportunity will have already been spotted and acted upon by other entrepreneurs. The position of the supply curve depends on the stock of entrepreneurial talent existing in the population, which is determined by a random distribution of judgmental decisionmaking ability (thus people are born entrepreneurs or not) and the proportion of those who are actually capable of having command over resources.

In elaborating on this second requirement Casson recognizes the importance of socio-economic factors which can influence entrepreneurial activity. Entrepreneurs can gain access to resources through the capital markets, although unless they have a proven track record or 'establishment' connections they may find it difficult to convince capitalists to back their ideas. On the other hand, they may have been born into wealth or they may know wealthy individuals who are willing to finance their ventures privately. On this point Casson argues that 'family firms' are abundant in most economies because of the problems of accessing finance to gain control of resources. The family firm can provide a reputation for new entrepreneurs even though they may have no personal track record and can provide finance for family members to branch out on their own. The supply curve will therefore change position if there are changes in the socio-economic factors which influence the ability of entrepreneurs to access resources.

As in the production function approaches discussed in Chapter 3, Casson assumes that entrepreneurs reject the opportunity of earning a market determined wage by working for an employer. This wage represents the opportunity cost of entrepreneurship. Thus adjustments occur in the market for entrepreneurs if the opportunity cost of undertaking entrepreneurial activity is greater or less than the expected reward. If it is greater, then potential entrepreneurs choose to become waged employees. If it is less, then potential entrepreneurs choose to undertake entrepreneurial activity. The decision to become active in the market entails that entrepreneurs have to form estimates of their own abilities. New entrants into the market eventually compete away any element of monopoly profit received by existing market participants by virtue of their superior alertness in the first instance. Entrepreneurial profits entail an element of monopoly and entrepreneurs will therefore seek to maintain their monopoly as long as possible before it is competed away by other entrepreneurs.

Casson argues that one of the key ways in which active entrepreneurs can maintain a monopoly over their knowledge is by forming a firm. Casson rejects Kirzner's notion that entrepreneurs require no resources to exploit profit opportunities. In order to capitalize on their superior knowledge, entrepreneurs must overcome the problems associated with the successful development and marketing of their products. Casson describes the process of doing so as 'market making'. By forming a firm entrepreneurs can internalize and monitor those activities which have recurring costs such as hiring labour or leasing machinery. Once those costs have been borne, firms already active in a particular market are in an advantageous position. They do not have to consider sunk costs as relevant to future decisions. A new entrant, on the other hand, does have to consider set up costs and the need to recover them over time. In production activities where fixed costs are high, these can only be recovered through building up the volume of business and expanding the firm's operations.

Casson argues that entrepreneurs will attempt to protect their superior knowledge and profits for as long as possible by erecting barriers to entry into their markets, through undertaking activities such as advertising and quality control. In this respect, an existing firm's reputation is a powerful marketing tool which allows a competitive edge over new firms attempting to break into the market.

However, the management of a firm requires the entrepreneur to possess a wider set of abilities than those of perception, foresight and imagination, which are necessary to identify profit opportunities in the first place. Entrepreneurs must also have managerial abilities such as knowing when to delegate control of the firm to subordinates. In contrast to Knight and Schumpeter, Casson does not distinguish clearly between the skills required to undertake the routine activities involved in the day-to-day management of a firm's activities and the creative abilities which are necessary to make judgmental decisions. For example, successful delegation depends upon subordinates making correct decisions for achieving specific goals. However, even though monitoring of subordinates' decisionmaking is feasible, as are routinized decisionmaking systems, these require the entrepreneur to spend time on low level managerial tasks which could be better spent on making judgmental decisions aimed at identifying and exploiting profit maximizing opportunities.

In summary, Casson's comprehensive theory of entrepreneurship provides a more detailed insight into the nature of entrepreneurial activity than either neoclassical analysis or Austrian analysis on its own. An important additional aspect of Casson's theory is the emphasis on the socio-economic influences on entrepreneurship. While the attempt to incorporate these influences within a supply curve for entrepreneurs is limited, Casson is one of the few economists to have attempted to model these factors as determinants of entrepreneurial activity. The problem with his approach, however, is how can variables such as 'the pace of change', and 'knowing wealthy people' be specified and measured accurately in order to predict the number of active entrepreneurs? Another deficiency of his theory is that he does not attempt to explain what causes change in exogenous factors. Taking a Schumpeterian viewpoint, it may be argued that, rather than the number of active entrepreneurs being determined by the pace of change, the causality in this relationship may be reversed. However, Casson is not concerned with developing a theory of economic evolution so that the market for entrepreneurs is perhaps best conceived of as a benchmark for analysing the concept within an equilibrium framework.

Etzioni – entrepreneurship, adaptation and legitimization

The importance of recognizing the social influences on entrepreneurial activity was raised in Casson's equilibrium-related theory of entrepreneurship. Attention is now directed to the socio-economic school of economic thought, of which Etzioni (1987, 1988) is a key contemporary writer. It is fundamental to this school of thought that the interplay between social and economic behaviour, and the factors which influence this behaviour, cannot be disentangled as in neoclassical economic analysis. In Chapter 3 it was demonstrated that neoclassical economics assume that human decisionmaking is rational, in the face of given preferences and constraints that are known by all individuals. The acquisition of perfect knowledge may entail some search activity but all knowledge can ultimately be accessed.

Etzioni refutes this view of human behaviour and argues that it is impossible for individuals to make rational decisions because of several reasons. First, he argues that search activity can only pay-off if the benefits are known to exceed the costs in advance of undertaking it. In reality it is impossible to know this because of the uncertainty associated with dynamic and ever changing environments. Etzioni therefore agrees with another economist, Simon (1959, 1979), that human behaviour is systematically sub-rational, in that people are content to make satisfactory choices rather than optimal choices. Simon termed this type of decisionmaking 'bounded rationality'. Etzioni also agrees with the subjectivist view that much decisionmaking is intuitive, spontaneous and based upon future expectations rather than past experience. This is not the case if a decision is to be fully rational, where the options have to be weighed up and some decisionmaking routine has to be employed in order to select what is believed to be the optimal choice.

Furthermore, Etzioni acknowledges the importance of human decisionmaking with a wider communitarian and societal framework. That is, individuals do not make choices purely in self interest (even if they do serve the public good), rather they think of the consequences of their actions. For example, it may be rational not to want to pay tax but the choice to actually pay tax is made in the knowledge of the consequences of being caught or the personal benefits gained from things funded by taxes. Etzioni argues that individuals might make choices also because of moral reasons. For example, they may want to pay tax because it funds public services which will benefit their community and the wider society. In this respect, Etzioni argues that collectivism is the basic form of human organization, social and economic, and that collective beliefs and values determine the preferences for, and constraints upon, decisionmaking and therefore upon activities such as entrepreneurship. Collective values can be manifested in both public and private institutional forms, for example governments, markets and firms. The demand for, and supply of, entrepreneurs is therefore a function of the wider socio-economic environment in which cultural values are endemic.

Etzioni also argues that collective, rather than individual decisionmaking, can lead to a greater number of rational choices being made. This proposition may be related to the views of Knight (discussed in Chapter 3), who envisaged firms as 'pools' of entrepreneurs where the law of averages ensures that overall, more 'correct' speculative choices are made than 'incorrect' choices. Etzioni extends this analysis further by suggesting that institutions such as firms can develop decision-making routines which, on aggregate, lead to 'good', rather than 'bad' choices being made. What is regarded as a 'good' or a 'bad' choice entails that some value judgement must be made in the light of the cultural values which prevail in a society. This is not the same issue as determining what is a 'correct' choice at the individual level which may entail that the public good is not served, as in tax evasion.

It is interesting to note here that Hayek, one of the pioneers of modern Austrian economics which stresses the importance of individualistic self-interest, also recognized that collectivism was a basic human instinct. Hayek took the view that small numbers of individuals would naturally combine in some community in order to pursue some common goal such as survival. However, Hayek argued that human organization at a societal level based upon this principle (that is, socialism) was impossible. This is because no common goal could possibly satisfy all individual preferences and there is no mechanism through which individual preferences could be revealed. In his last work, Hayek (1988) argues that socialism is 'The Fatal Conceit' and proposes that there is no such thing as a society. He argues that the only efficient way of organizing production is through individual choice being expressed in the market place. The pursuit of self interest in these circumstances is enough to ensure that the common good is served, a point which is also fundamental to contemporary neoclassical economics in works such as *Capitalism and Freedom* (Friedman, 1982).

Returning to Etzioni, within the scope of his socio-economic analytical framework he develops a theory of entrepreneurship (Etzioni, 1987). It is important to realize, however, that this is not a theory of individual entrepreneurs or a theory which places much emphasis on the possibility of entrepreneurship at an individual level. While Etzioni suggests that some individualistic entrepreneurial activity may occur on an *ad hoc* basis, the most endemic form of entrepreneurship occurs in a collective institutional form in which decisionmaking is made routine and thus entrepreneurship is made routine. Within institutions, entrepreneurs challenge the decisions of other entrepreneurs so that the best routines evolve through a process of natural selection. In common with Casson, Etzioni argues that entrepreneurs are a subset of the population although their individual characteristics and abilities may vary within the same society and between different societies. The key defining feature of entrepreneurs is their willingness to adapt to change and a desire to try out new innovations. In this sense they are the evolutionary force within societies which advance economic and social development.

In common with Schumpeter, Etzioni envisages societal institutions as unwilling to adapt to change, partly because of the fear of the unknown and partly because of the costs associated with devising and implementing new routines, including the time and effort necessary to establish a new consensus. Thus institutions lag behind in a constantly changing environment and it is the job of entrepreneurs to test out new ideas in order to select the best and discard the rest. Etzioni terms this process 'adaptive reality testing'. An important feature of this process is that most new ideas will not be successful in reality and therefore most entrepreneurial activity results in failure. Only the best ideas survive and entrepreneurs speculate that the returns from the few ideas that work will more than compensate for the greater number of failures. Furthermore, entrepreneurs do not cause change to occur, they are purely reactive to change; and they are only required to initiate the process of societal adaptation to change, not to fully implement it.

Etzioni agrees with Marshall that adaptation to environmental change is primarily an incremental evolutionary process, although he acknowledges that there is scope for exceptional revolutionary changes such as those envisaged by Schumpeter. However, unlike Schumpeter, Etzioni refutes equilibrium as the starting point for entrepreneurial activity. His position is similar to Kirzner's in believing that entrepreneurial activity is most needed during periods of disequilibrium. The more rapidly the environment changes the larger the potential gain from adaptation, and the greater the potential reward. A dynamic environment therefore promotes entrepreneurship although Etzioni argues that this is not the only factor to do so. He takes a more sociological stance in arguing that the key factor promoting entrepreneurial activity is societal legitimization of the function. The legitimization of entrepreneurship can vary between societies and is determined by cultural influences such as religious and political beliefs. Thus as Weber (1930) argued, entrepreneurial activity may be promoted more in Protestant societies because they are more predisposed towards a work ethic. Some political ideologies such as communism are not favourably disposed towards legitimising entrepreneurial activity, while others are, such as capitalism. Legitimisation can affect both the societal preferences for, and institutional constraints placed on, activities such as entrepreneurship.

In summary, Etzioni's analysis of the entrepreneurial function is more overtly socio-economic in nature than those considered previously in that it stresses the importance of society wide factors in determining adaptation to change, and thus entrepreneurial activity. Etzioni argues that his theory is not incompatible with conventional notions of a market for entrepreneurs such as that of Casson, when more demand for, or supply of, entrepreneurs will lead to their 'production' in greater numbers. However, Etzioni's theory is not based on the assumption that there is a market for entrepreneurial services and is based on the notion of economic evolution rather than equilibrium. Entrepreneurs promote adaptation to change and entrepreneurship is thus the catalyst of economic evolution.

At this point it is interesting to compare the socio-economic approach adopted by Etzioni in elaborating an entrepreneurial function, with a neoclassical theory of human capital developed by Schultz (1975), in which the wider societal implications of entrepreneurship are also recognized from a conventional economic standpoint. Schultz defends the importance of the equilibrium approach in economic theory and in particular in the analysis of the entrepreneurial function. In a neoclassical context Schultz also defines the concept of entrepreneurship as the ability to deal with disequilibria, although he stresses the ability of all individuals and groups in society in this respect and not just producers. Furthermore, Schultz suggests that disequilibria are not only created by producers but by all individuals and groups. He argues for the importance of education and training, as forms of human capital, in increasing the supply of entrepreneurial services at any point in time in response to the rewards to be gained from these services. In common with the production function approaches reviewed in Chapter 3, entrepreneurial reward represents a return to ability in Schultz's analysis rather than a return to uncertainty as in Knight's analysis. In this respect, Schultz argues that the aggregate rewards from entrepreneurship in a dynamic economy account for a substantial part of the growth of national income.

Although Schultz does not use the term, it is not too difficult to conceptualize of the widespread supply of entrepreneurial services as being synonymous with the notion of an 'enterprise culture'. Following in the path of socio-economists such as Weber, Etzioni would perhaps find this an acceptable interpretation of Schultz's work. In an enterprise culture, societal preferences and institutional constraints would be favourable to and help to legitimise entrepreneurial activity. Schultz, however, is more concerned with demonstrating the effectiveness of the equilibrium approach in explaining economic performance and is not concerned with explaining the impact of cultural influences on entrepreneurship. He predicts that increasing the general level of human capital in an economy through education and training will lead to economic progress. It may be suggested though that in neglecting to take account of cultural influences on entrepreneurship, Schultz's analysis does not deal as rigorously with the impact of socio-economic influences as Etzioni's analysis. While Schultz predicts that increasing the human capital base of an economy will increase the supply of entrepreneurs, this says nothing about the demand for entrepreneurs by a society or the propensity of a society to assimilate new ideas which may conflict with long held cultural values.

Evolutionary economics

At this point it is useful to pull together the various elements of evolutionary thought which have been considered thus far and to relate these to the contemporary body of evolutionary economics developed by writers such as Nelson and Winter (1982). The theories of Marshall, Schumpeter and Etzioni all identify a key role for entrepreneurship in the process of economic evolution, albeit in different ways.

Marshall regards economic evolution as a slow and gradual process which is contributed to in a small way by all business managers, although he did claim that 'the Mecca of the economist lies in economic biology rather than economic dynamics'. Schumpeter (1976, p. 82), on the other hand, argued that while 'in dealing with capitalism we are dealing with an evolutionary process' he defines a specific role for entrepreneurship as a endogenous force which disrupts equilibrium and overturns the status quo, thus causing economic evolution. Only a subset of the population who are exceptionally talented individuals are capable of performing this function according to Schumpeter. Etzioni also identifies entrepreneurs as a subset of the population but regards economic evolution primarily as an incremental process in which entrepreneurship is an endogenous force that promotes the adaptation to change through testing out new ideas.

All of these approaches stress that firms are mechanisms through which change is implemented. Entrepreneurs exist within a wider institutional framework, and firms as organizations in which production takes place play a key role in either assisting or hindering entrepreneurs in exploiting the profit opportunities they have identified. Furthermore, firms are perceived as being organizations in which decisions are made and implemented through an established set of routines. These routines evolve within an environment which is characterized by change and uncertainty; and in which decisionmaking is made with bounded rationality. It is therefore important that the best decisionmaking routines are devised and implemented in order to ensure that resources are not misallocated as economies evolve.

Nelson and Winter (1982) address this issue from an explicitly organizational perspective and in doing so they also identify a key role for entrepreneurs in the process of economic evolution. Their evolutionary theory of economic development is based on the work of Simon (1959) and Cyert and March (1963), who apply the idea of human bounded rationality to the study of organizations and in particular how organizations develop behavioural rules in order to operate efficiently. From this body of work Nelson and Winter develop the concept of an organization as a set of interactive routines. In an organization many decisions are trivial and made by many individuals who each have specialized knowledge. Thus in terms of efficiency, an organization can achieve overall what no single individual in that organization could achieve individually. The capabilities of an organization may also be greater than the sum total of its individual parts because of the synergy which is created by linkages between these parts. Furthermore, an organization can wield power in economic, social and political terms, that no individual can, and therefore has greater scope to influence the environment in which it operates.

Nelson and Winter also incorporate the idea of an organization as a coalition of different interest groups, each with their own agenda. If a firm is divided along functional lines into production, finance, marketing and research and development departments, each department will have its own vested interest, the pursuit of which may raise conflict with other departments. For example, if new products are developed this has consequences for other departments in that new production processes may have to be implemented and a new marketing campaign may have to be organized, both of which have implications for costs and resource allocation within the firm in terms of staffing levels and budget allocations. The efficient operation of an organization depends on the members of that coalition following established routines otherwise the conflict of interests within the coalition becomes so great as to impede efficiency. These routines may be formally stated in a policy document, or accepted informally as acceptable practices, the boundaries of which are commonly known and not contravened.

Nelson and Winter develop this idea further by identifying three main types of routines: (1) operating routines, which are related to all the production and marketing processes; (2) investment routines, which are usually centralized to the key decisionmakers and not delegated as are other routines; (3) search routines, which are intended to gather information which may help to make the other two sets of routines more effective. Within this analytical framework, in common with Marshall and Etzioni they assume that the process of economic evolution is one of natural selection and that not all change is successful. In this context the 'fittest' routines are generated within an organization by a process of trial and error. The complexity of the organization and the diversity of interest groups within the organization make the organization slow to adapt and thus resistant to change.

This analysis follows Schumpeter in arguing that in the face of change, existing organizations are only capable of pursuing existing routines. However, Nelson and Winter do not go as far as Schumpeter in assuming that innovative ideas are so radically different that they require the development of an entirely new set of routines. They argue that most new routines are likely to be largely dependent on adaptations of existing ones. In some cases though, perhaps where obsolete routines are too deeply entrenched and the environment is very fast changing, entirely new routines may have to be developed and implemented. This action may have profound consequences for the organization in that new routines will have to be learned very quickly if the organization is to survive. Once the new pattern of routines has been identified, whether they are adaptations or entirely new, the problem for the organization is then how to create a new coalition in order to implement them.

Within this analytical framework the function of entrepreneurship is again to make judgmental decisions, this time with regard to whether the new pattern of routines is to be a new creation or an adaptation from an existing pattern. Only entrepreneurs, as a subset of the population, are capable of making such judgmental decisions. In doing so, entrepreneurs are able to stand outside current practice, judge whether or not it can be improved, and then determine in what organizational form improvements can be implemented. Entrepreneurial activity is therefore the engine of economic progress; but more than that, it ensures that resources are not misallocated along the way. A key element in this theory of economic evolution is that decisionmaking is 'path dependent' in that present decisions are made in the context of previous decisions, as well as in the face of uncertainty. Evolution is therefore truly historical and products and technologies are the result of interdependent choices. It is therefore a vitally important decision faced by entrepreneurs in choosing whether to adapt existing routines, which entails continuing on the same pathway, or to develop new routines, which may entail taking a new and unexplored pathway.

Conclusion and review of Chapters 3 to 5

This chapter now concludes with a review of the economic perspectives on entrepreneurship discussed in Chapters 3–5. This is helpful at this point in order to identify clearly the line of argument which has developed from considering entrepreneurship in economic equilibrium and evolution. The examination of entrepreneurship in economic theory began in Chapter 3 by considering why conventional neoclassical economic thought tended to neglect the concept. It was concluded that the methodology of static general equilibrium analysis is unable to incorporate aspects of reality such as dynamic and purposeful human behaviour, and the causes of change in the economic environment.

In early general equilibrium models there was no explicit entrepreneurial role identified. Later neoclassical theorists have attempted to incorporate a specific entrepreneurial function although their attempts to do so are rather limited and generally do not differentiate between entrepreneurs and business managers. Marshall, who was concerned with explaining economic evolution within a static equilibrium framework, also does not make this distinction. Knight, does, however, relate entrepreneurial activity to dealing with uncertainty in the economic system and makes a clear distinction between entrepreneurs and managers based on the ability to make judgmental decisions.

Chapter 4 considered the work of economic theorists who identify a clear entrepreneurial role in relation to market dynamics. Kirzner views entrepreneurs as individuals who exploit price differentials created by ignorance on the part of others, in return for profit. In the process entrepreneurs signal information to other market participants and help to restore markets to equilibrium. This view of entrepreneurship as a stabilizing force in market economies is in contrast to Schumpeter's view of the entrepreneur as a creator of disequilibrium through the innovation of new ideas, in return for profit. In both of these theories the ability to undertake the entrepreneurial function required that individuals possess particular attributes.

Chapter 5 has revealed that Casson attempts to synthesize elements from different theoretical approaches into a comprehensive theory of entrepreneurs and their activities. Fundamental to Casson's theory, however, is the notion that entrepreneurs must also be good business managers in order to manage the expansion of their firms in order to exploit profit opportunities. It may be questioned whether entrepreneurs are also necessarily good business managers given the contrast in the skills and abilities it takes to perform each function. Also fundamental to Casson's theory is the recognition of socio-economic influences on entrepreneurial activity, in particular in determining the entrepreneur's ability to gain access to resources. The socio-economic theme was continued by considering the work of Etzioni, who also recognizes the importance of societal influences in promoting entrepreneurial activity.

In all of the economic approaches which are in some way 'alternative' to neoclassical economics, the most important aspect of entrepreneurship relates to the ability to create or adapt to change, and to exploit new ideas and opportunities in the pursuit of profit. Only Schumpeter, however, actually identifies entrepreneurs as creators of new ideas. While Etzioni does not perceive entrepreneurship as the cause of change, he identifies entrepreneurship as the cause of economic evolution in that only entrepreneurs test out new ideas and ensure that the best survive. The organizational theory of economic evolution developed by Nelson and Winter also finds a role for entrepreneurs as the promoters of new and better ideas, and as the decisionmakers who can determine the best organizational forms through which change can be implemented efficiently.

A common feature of all the theories reviewed here is that they concentrate primarily on the 'function' of entrepreneurship, whether the emphasis is purely economic as in Knight and Kirzner, or within a wider social and institutional environment as in Schumpeter, Casson, Etzioni and Nelson and Winter. There is some conflict, however, with regard to whether entrepreneurial activity is best undertaken at an individual or a collective level. Underlying this conflict are differing views of human decisionmaking in the face of imperfect knowledge. The Austrian view of individuals making 'incorrect' rational choices because they lack some information, conflicts with that of the socio-economic and organizational view that imperfect knowledge leads to bounded rationality decisions, which entails that collectives are able to make consistently better choices than individuals. This debate illustrates the importance of the problem of 'knowledge' in economic theory, in terms of how it is created, accessed and used in decisions concerning resource allocation. This issue, along with that of entrepreneurship in a socio-economic and evolutionary context, is developed further in Chapter 6.

Illustration

Richard Branson

Few people would disagree that Richard Branson is an entrepreneur. He is a self-made multi-millionaire. His company, the Virgin Group, has one of the strongest brand images in the world and Branson himself has, for many, entered popular culture as a modern day 'hero'. He is perceived by many as a genuine 'man of the people' despite having personal wealth of around £1.5 billion and as an adventurer who constantly pushed himself beyond conventional limits. In a poll to find out who the British public would want as President, if Britain were to be made a republic, Branson was the clear winner. His record breaking speedboat and hot-air ballooning exploits have given him celebrity status world-wide and also earned the company valuable publicity.

Branson Banks on a Smile

The text in this section is an edited version of an article entitled 'Branson Banks on a Smile', based on an interview with Richard Branson, which was first published in the newspaper *Scotland on Sunday* on 19 October 1997. The authors gratefully acknowledge the Editor of Scotland on Sunday in consenting to allow the article to be adapted for use here as a case study.

There are times when Richard Branson himself cannot believe how far he has come since as a public school dropout in the 1970s he launched into business, first as a magazine publisher and then as backer of some of Britain's best known rock bands. Over the past 18 months Virgin's brand has been stretched into rail, cosmetics, pensions and banking.

Branson is nothing if not ambitious. When he decided to take on the might of British Airways and launch a long-haul scheduled airline from scratch, no one gave him a chance. But he has succeeded where others have failed. To this day competitors cannot understand how he got away with it. The answer lies in Branson's unique mix of irreverence, youthfulness and hard-nosed business sense. Branson is no rocket scientist; no Bill Gates. Most of his innovations are obvious touches that anybody could have come up with: more leg room between seats, video screens on seatbacks and ice-cream during 'inflight' movies. The point is that no one did.

> Most of the companies we start from scratch so we start with a clean sheet of paper. We go out and get the best people. Craft the company to exactly the picture we want, and we don't take on the problems of the past.

Branson is impatient with the past and with convention. Perhaps it took a product of a prestigious English public school, whose father merits his own entry in 'Who's Who', to stand up to the crusty business establishment. Whereas most captains of industry seem to get off on making others feel small, Branson has perfected the art of making people who come into contact with him, as employees or through the media, feel that he is one of them: an outsider battling against the people who think they know best, who tell you that it cannot be done. Branson has his detractors, but somehow the mud never seems to stick. He can pay himself as much as he likes, own speedboats, his own island – Necker, in the British Virgin Islands – and indulge hobbies like balloon racing that only a rich man can afford.

> I think the stereotype you see in films of businessmen who tread all over people to get to the top is not actually a correct stereotype. The world is a very small place. If you have a good, trusted relationship, a good reputation, people will come back for more. Sometimes it is worth not squeezing the last penny out of a deal, leaving a bit behind for the other side, striking a fair balance.

Branson insists that his business style has evolved, rather than having been consciously created.

> At Virgin records we attracted some of the best artists because they liked the way we ran it. We never lost a major artist in 20 years which is quite rare in the record industry. We dressed as we felt comfortable. We worked in pleasant buildings rather than office blocks and people working there had fun, enjoyed the job, enjoyed challenging, taking on the major record companies.

Branson has the advantage of not being answerable to shareholders only interested in the bottom line. Where ventures have turned sour he has been able to dip into his own pocket to ensure that, where divorce has become necessary, it has been on friendly terms. His brief dalliance with the City when he sold 35 per cent of Virgin on the London stockmarket in 1986 was not a success. When the shares failed to perform he bought them all back. Even now there is little love lost on either side. 'Richard's principal gripe with the City is it is too driven by the short term things you can measure rather than the real long term gain', says one close aide. Branson's staff are incredibly loyal and even more touchy about slights than he is. One feels that a man who has got this far must have enemies but they are difficult to find outside BA.

Perhaps that is why he is so loved by the public and so feared by the business establishment. Branson has turned business logic on its head. At a time when the preachers of shareholder value insist that focus is everything, Branson is finding new areas into which to stretch the Virgin brand. Up to now those at the commanding heights of British industry have been able to dismiss Branson as a maverick, a canny operator with an eye for the headline grabbing PR stunt. But they have reason to fear. Branson has an ability to attract talented people and to make the most of his public appeal.

We love tackling big companies, trying to turn them upside down, seeing their vulnerabilities, piercing their soft underbellies and turning them upside down. That is slightly unusual for British companies. With the traditional way the City looks at things, you find what you know and stick at it without straying. That in my opinion is dangerous because the way the world moves so fast you can suddenly find yourself in a business when there is no more need for that business. We wanted Virgin to move into the Internet with V-net, and the net might put out of business something we are in now one day. At least we are putting ourselves out of business, rather than letting someone else do it.

Much of the new activity has prompted suggestions that Branson has taken on more than he can handle. The two biggest successes – Virgin Records which he sold to EMI in 1992 for £560 million, and Virgin Atlantic – were entirely new ventures. But in more recent ventures, such as taking over a dilapidated British railway company, he is having to re-energize a flagging business; a challenge which requires different skills. Fellow directors admit that, looking back, Branson might have done better to keep Virgin's name off the trains until new state-of-the-art rolling stock under order was ready. Branson admits that he is 'gambling with the brand'. But he adds, 'Sometimes you have to take risks. I am determined that three years from now it will be the best in Europe.' However, his eyes are on America. He wants to set up his own airline in the US and believes that the British bank concept will work even better over there. While others fret at how far Virgin can stretch, Branson sounds like a man just getting into his stride.

All the time we have teams looking into new areas which are enormously fat and wealthy which seem to have a monopoly which we can shake up. We don't sit still and we love to learn.

It is the supreme accolade that in his recent venture into financial services, the public is prepared to put its money and blind faith for future financial security into a company that does not publish its accounts, yet turns against long established mutual businesses who rank among the most democratic institutions in the country. For Branson, the City ill serves British industry and the consumer. In his view it is a vastly inefficient machine whose rules have been organized in favour of the self-serving elite of bankers and fund managers who grow fat on ordinary people's savings. Virgin has stood industry wisdom on its head. It has no investment managers to manage its products, no salesforce and does not deal through independent financial advisors driven by commission. Branson says, 'Financial services is a commodity business. If you get rid of the salesmen, you get rid of 50% of the cost and 95% of the compliance problem.' The new Virgin account is a 24 hour telephone banking operation and Branson claims that it could save people £100 000 over 20 years. Publicly, Britain's big financial institutions insist that banking is far too complex a business for a man like Branson to understand. Privately, they are deeply worried. Since moving into financial services in the areas of pensions and personal equity plans, Virgin has captured a significant slice of the market. Tellingly, most of its customers are precisely the well paid 'forty-somethings' that the established financial companies regard as their own, almost by right.

So what does Branson think Virgin is all about?

> We are beginning to cover people's needs from birth to death. If Virgin goes into something it is because it can shake up the industry – do something that has not been done before.

References and further reading

Casson, M. (1982) *The Entrepreneur: An Economic Theory*, Oxford, Martin Robertson.

Casson, M. (1990) *Entrepreneurship*, Aldershot, Edward Elgar.

Cyert, R.M. and J.G. March (1963) *A Behavioural Theory of the Firm*, Englewoods-Cliffs, NJ, Prentice-Hall.

Etzioni, A. (1987) 'Entrepreneurship, Adaptation and Legitimation: A macro-behavioural perspective', *Journal of Economic Behaviour and Organization*, Vol. 8, pp. 175–89.

Etzioni, A. (1988) *A Moral Dimension: Towards a New Economics*, New York, Harvester Free Press.

Friedman, M. (1982) *Capitalism and Freedom*, 2nd edn, Chicago, University of Chicago Press.

Hayek, F. (1988) *The Fatal Conceit: The Errors of Socialism*, London, Routledge.

Jackson, T. (1995) *Virgin King: Inside Richard Branson's Business Empire*, London, Harper Collins.

Nelson, R.R. and S.G. Winter (1982) *An Evolutionary Theory of Economic Change*, Cambridge, Mass., Harvard University Press.

Schultz, T.W. (1975) 'The value of the ability to deal with disequilibria', *Journal of Economic Literature*, Vol. 13, pp. 827–46.

Schumpeter, J.A. (1976) *Capitalism, Socialism and Democracy*, 5th edn, London, George Allen and Unwin.

Scotland on Sunday (1997) 'Branson Banks on a Smile', 19 October.

Simon, H.A. (1959) *Administrative Behaviour*, New York, Macmillan.

Simon, H.A. (1979) 'Rational decision-making in business organizations', *American Economic Review*, Vol. 69, pp. 493–513.

Weber, M. (1930) *The Protestant Ethic and the Spirit of Capitalism*, London, Allen and Unwin.

6
Entrepreneurship, Contracts and Networks

Introduction

The aim of this chapter is to build upon the major issues raised in Chapters 3 to 5, those of entrepreneurship in an individual and collective form and within a socio-economic and institutional environment. In developing these issues this chapter brings together key elements of the neoclassical, Austrian, socio-economic and evolutionary schools of economic thought. More specifically, the points which are addressed relate to the role of entrepreneurship in determining: (1) the nature of relationships between firms; (2) the evolution of production modes; (3) the economic and social mechanisms which govern relationships between firms, within production modes, and which lead to efficient resource usage.

In previous chapters it has been recognized that firms exist as economic organizations and social institutions, in which resources are deployed in production. Entrepreneurs are perceived as the key judgmental decisionmakers who determine which products are produced and what is the most efficient way of organizing the production process. In this chapter these ideas are developed further, by first of all considering two other bodies of thought which are of relevance to the issues raised, those of contractarian economics and social networks theory. While both of these bodies of thought address the issues of why there are firms in the first place and what form the firms take, they do so in different but complementary ways.

Contractarian economics focuses on the choice faced by entrepreneurs between using the market or the firm as alternative means of organizing production. In addressing this issue it regards cost minimization as the most important determinant of the choice between firm and market. Social networks theory, on the other hand, recognizes that many business relationships are informal in the sense that they are not based on formal contractually binding economic obligations, but on socially binding obligations such as trust and reputation. Both of these bodies of thought raise the question 'where are the boundaries of the firm?'.

After considering contractarian economics and social networks theory, attention is directed to relating the issues raised by these bodies of thought to the function of evolution of production modes and the role of entrepreneurship in this process. This is not an exhaustive treatment of this topic, rather the focus is on the evolution and operations of two of the most widely studied forms of production, the multinational enterprise (MNE) and the 'industrial district'. The MNE is characterized by an international division of production and considerable economic, social and political power concentrated within one large integrated firm. The industrial district, on the other hand, is characterized by geographically clustered groups of small independent producers who exist in socio-economic networks of collaborative competition. In terms of the evolutionary economics developed by Nelson and Winter (1982), these represent alternative 'pathways' of production. Illustrations of entrepreneurship in MNEs and industrial districts follow the discussion of the theory. The chapter then concludes by drawing out the main themes from the discussion.

Contractarian economics

Contractarian economics focuses on the contractual nature of business transactions, and addresses the question 'when is it better to contract production activities out to the market or to undertake them in-house?'. This notion is introduced in the discussion of 'outsourcing' by large firms in Chapter 2 and in Casson's theory of entrepreneurship in Chapter 5, where the entrepreneur is required to create a firm in order to exploit a profit opportunity. This is in contrast to the Kirznerian approach in which production could be organized purely through contractual relationships in the product and factor markets.

The problem of how resources are allocated to optimal effect is fundamental to contractarian economics, as in neoclassical analysis, but the contractarian approach seeks to address how this is possible given that decisionmaking is made in the face of imperfect knowledge and uncertainty. In addressing this issue the contractarian approach incorporates greater institutional detail into analytical models than the neoclassical approach, and focuses on the way in which organizational structures affect incentives and behaviour. In common with the neo-classical and Austrian schools of thought, contractarian economics assumes that individuals will pursue their own self-interest. In common with the evolutionary approach, it assumes that competition ensures that the most efficient institutions survive. It is important to realize, however, that the contractarian approach employs a static analytical framework and is not concerned with explaining economic evolution. Its concern is with predicting what will be the optimal organization of production in a static equilibrium. It assumes that the economic environment is uncertain and is determined by exogenous factors and that knowledge is imperfectly distributed between market participants. If exogenous factors change, a reorganization of production may be necessary to ensure that resources are allocated to optimal effect.

Contractarian economics developed from the work of Coase (1937), who pointed out that using markets involves costs. For example, search costs must be incurred in discovering the relevant prices of factors of production and every market transaction involves an implicit or explicit contract. These contracts entail costs, for example, of negotiation. All activities undertaken by firms can be explained only if 'transaction costs' are recognized. In this regard Coase argues that transaction costs can be avoided to some extent by bringing production activities within the boundaries of a firm rather than contracting out through the market. Firms are essentially 'internal markets', with firms and markets representing alternative means of co-ordinating resource allocation.

Williamson (1975, 1985) extends Coase's work to identify more precisely those factors which favour undertaking activities within the firm as opposed to using the market. Williamson's analysis is based on three main factors: bounded rationality, uncertainty and opportunism. Opportunism entails that individuals will exploit imperfect knowledge in the pursuit of self-interest at the expense of others. Opportunistic behaviour arises as a result of an imperfect distribution of knowledge between individuals, and it is rational and predictable behaviour in that it serves the self-interest of individuals.

The problem, therefore, is one of how production can be organized so as to curb opportunistic behaviour and ensure that resources are allocated to optimal effect. In terms of the decision to contract out to the market or to undertake production in-house, the particular problems created by imperfect knowledge are: (1) adverse selection, which entails that potential contractors will overstate their potential to secure a contract; (2) moral hazard, which entails that a contractor's performance will diminish once the contract is secured; (3) rent-seeking behaviour, which entails that contractors will attempt to get more income without improving their productivity.

Williamson argues that the greater the degree of imperfect knowledge and uncertainty, and therefore the greater the scope for contractors to engage in opportunistic behaviour, the more likely it is that contracting will be prohibitively expensive. In these circumstances it may be better to monitor behaviour within a firm by implementing a system of sanctions and rewards which direct behaviour towards fulfilling contractual obligations. Furthermore, the greater the degree of asset specificity, which refers to the degree of specialization of an asset's use, the more likely it is that co-ordination within the firm will be preferred in order to derive learning advantages from the intensive use of the asset.

Setting up and developing a firm, however, entails that costs have to be incurred. These are most obviously perceived of in financial terms, but also exist in terms of the time and effort required to draw up employment contracts and to monitor employee performance. Thus in-house production is only the most efficient means if the likely benefits exceed the set-up costs plus the transaction costs of contracting out to the market. On the other hand, if markets are information-efficient and very competitive the more likely it is that contracting will be an efficient way of undertaking production. In these circumstances a good deal of knowledge will exist about the ability of contractors to perform well and there is an incentive for them to do so in order to secure future contracts. Moreover, the lower the degree of asset specificity the more likely it is that contracting will be undertaken rather than in-house production.

Central to the choice of production mode is the availability and use of knowledge within the economic system. If imperfect knowledge and uncertainty persist in the long term, Williamson argues that firms are the only efficient means of minimizing transaction costs and of organizing production efficiently. Firms are therefore institutional mechanisms through which imperfect knowledge and uncertainty are dealt with. This notion is extended to explain: (1) the development of large firms, which operate predominantly within the uncertain environment of oligopolistic markets; (2) the organizational structures which are developed within large firms, for example managerial hierarchies. In this analysis hierarchies are mechanisms through which sanctions and rewards are implemented and through which employees' performance is monitored to ensure that it is in accordance with contractual obligations. Conversely, if the economic environment changes and markets become more information-efficient and competitive as a result, there may be greater efficiencies to be gained through contracting out production activities and thus there may be a disintegration of production into smaller units.

If production is organized within firms rather than through the market, the question arises of how resource allocation is co-ordinated within firms in the absence of a price mechanism. In the contractarian approach this function is served by a central decisionmaking authority within the firm who acts in the same way as entrepreneurs in the theories of Kirzner, in arranging contracts through the market, and Casson, in arranging contracts within a firm. This element of Casson's theory is derived from contractarian economics. Entrepreneurship is central to the formation of new firms, whether these are entirely new firms or larger entities which are formed through the integration of firms which had previously existed independently. In either case resources should be reallocated more efficiently within the boundaries of a new production unit through the actions of entrepreneurs.

In creating a new firm an entrepreneur will have spotted a more efficient and therefore more profitable form of production. This would only be the case if the firm is a more efficient way of monitoring and controlling these activities. In this regard, the entrepreneurial role also encompasses the ability to devise and implement monitoring and control mechanisms to achieve optimum efficiency in production. It is therefore a judgmental decision which entrepreneurs face concerning the optimal organization of production in a given economic environment, which requires the ability to acquire and use knowledge effectively. If the economic environment changes and the availability and distribution of knowledge changes as a result, entrepreneurs must react by reorganizing production in its most efficient new form in accordance with the new set of economic circumstances. There is no assumption, however, that the organization of production at one point of static equilibrium has any bearing on the organization of production in another state of equilibrium. The determination of production is not path dependent. In common with Casson's theory it is also recognized that knowledge can be monopolized to some extent within the internal environment of a firm, and that this is an important way in which entrepreneurs can gain a competitive advantage over their rivals.

In summary, the contractarian economic approach recognizes the importance of institutional factors in analysing the cost minimizing behaviour of atomistic competitors. The integration of production activity within firms is a response to changes in the economic environment. The greater the degree of uncertainty, the more integrated production will be. Contracts are arranged by entrepreneurs through the market or within a firm, with the choice being determined by efficiency considerations. Contracts are a way of ensuring that opportunistic behaviour is avoided. In this analytical framework there is no consideration given to social relationships. It is concerned solely with economic mechanisms through which human behaviour can be governed in order to achieve efficient resource allocation. Furthermore, even though it places emphasis on institutions as forms of economic organization, it is essentially based upon an individualistic rather than a collectivist view of the world.

Embeddedness and social networks

In the neoclassical, Austrian and contractarian economic approaches, the emphasis is on individualistic human behaviour motivated by self interest. Institutional collectives such as firms arise because entrepreneurs, acting in their own self-interest choose firms rather than markets as the most efficient form of production in the pursuit of profit. The firm is a response to uncertainty and imperfect knowledge in the economic environment. In all of these approaches human economic behaviour is not related to the social sphere and the importance of social relations as determinants of economic behaviour are given no consideration. While Casson and Etzioni recognize the importance of social factors, they both view these largely as parameters on economic activity.

Another body of thought which has been termed the 'new economic sociology', a term which reflects its greater emphasis on the sociological underpinnings of economic life, has addressed the importance of social and cultural determinants of economic relations. A key writer in this school of thought is Granovetter (1973, 1985, 1991) who has developed the notion that economic relations between individuals and organizations are 'embedded' in social and cultural relations. Granovetter argues that firms are essentially 'networks' of economic and social relations which are socially constructed and culturally defined. In contrast to contractarian economics, Granovetter argues that regardless of the formal economic relationships which exist between individuals and firms, social relationships can extend beyond these economic relationships and can 'tie' individuals and firms together in wider social and cultural networks. For example, these social ties may take the form of personal relationships with family, friends and acquaintances, who in turn may have different friends and acquaintances and so on.

Social ties can also arise from more formal business relationships such as interlocking directorships and memberships of commercial and trade associations. These social networks are important in economic terms in that knowledge can be dispersed and accessed far beyond the boundaries of contractual economic relationships between individuals and firms. Social networks can therefore provide entrepreneurs with greater access to knowledge, which can reduce uncertainty in their environment and allow them to generate more profit opportunities. Furthermore, the nature of these non-contractual relationships may be such that they can create synergistic linkages, the advantages of which are not confined to any one firm but can be derived from all members of the network.

In more explicitly economic terms, networks have also been regarded as 'loose coalitions' of firms within production chains, which are bound together economically and socially through the pursuit of a common goal, and which exist in a framework of collaborative competition. As such it has been suggested that networks represent an intermediate organization of production between that of the vertically integrated firm and the atomistic market. Networks in this sense may arise because there is so much uncertainty in the economic environment that opportunistic behaviour cannot be governed through formal economic contractual relations, either within firms or through markets.

Storper (1995) identifies the importance of 'untraded interdependencies' within networks, which exist beyond the boundaries of formally stated and binding contractual relationships within production chains. Untraded interdependencies relate to the social and cultural customs, conventions and routines which bind firms together but which are not specified in any formal contractual terms. In a sense they represent acceptable 'ways of doing business'. All firms within a network accept these routines and do not contravene them as this would serve to act against their best interests. It is interesting to note that Storper (1995) compares the contractarian view of the vertically integrated firm as a 'nexus of contracts' with the view of the network as a 'nexus of untraded interdependencies'. In defence of the contractarian viewpoint, Williamson has argued that networks are merely transient arrangements characterized by incomplete contracting. Once formal contracts are implemented which govern all economic relations, Williamson argues that social relations are irrelevant. The evidence suggests though, that networks have historically been a pervasive feature in many economies, which the notion of incomplete contracting cannot explain.

The routines which govern networks are assumed to develop through time so that informal business transactions rather than formal contractual obligations can take place. Informal transactions are based on: (1) the solidarity which is developed within a common culture; (2) the trust which is built up through shared experience. Imperfect knowledge, uncertainty and opportunistic behaviour are reduced by the existence of trustworthy relationships within networks. These relationships develop through repeated transactions between network members and they propagate the widespread availability of knowledge within the network. The fear of being alienated and losing the economic and social advantages gained from membership of the network, ensures that knowledge will not be exploited opportunistically in win–lose transactions between network members. The desire to maintain a reputation for being trustworthy in serving the common good is the key monitoring mechanism. This is a product, however, of the social relations between network members and not formal contractual economic relations. It also suggests long-term advantages for organizations or individuals who act and have a reputation for strong ethical standards.

In many cases informal transactions will take place with no formal contract existing at all and the basis of the transaction will be an amicable 'gentlemen's' agreement'. Aside from the advantages gained from the information-efficient environment which is fostered within the network, there are other advantages to be gained in terms of having a greater degree of flexibility in production arrangements. This flexibility ensures that the network overall is highly adaptive to rapid changes in demand and can respond quickly to accommodate new production arrangements in order to meet new market conditions. Game theory, such as the Prisoner's dilemma, suggests that a strong 'shadow of the future' (for instance the need to act as agreed to maintain one's reputation and future transactions) is important in keeping people to their agreements.

However, just as the success of the network depends upon the routines which bind it together, the same routines can also serve to hinder its overall productive efficiency if there are changes in the economic and social environment which make them obsolete. For example, networks based upon socially binding economic relations such as 'family firms' or 'community enterprises' will be affected by social changes which cause the disintegration of family units and the breakdown of communities. In terms of evolutionary theory a new social and economic order is required to ensure that the network survives and prospers in the face of such change. The new routines which evolve must provide a cohesive framework in which social and economic relations are such that trust and solidarity are maintained.

Trust and solidarity are the essential factors which create the synergistic linkages between members, which in turn generate a collective productive efficiency over and above the sum total of the capabilities of individual members. New routines must evolve through consensus, or the solidarity of the network's membership will break down. Here a function for entrepreneurship may be identified which is similar to that in evolutionary economic theories. It is important to note, that social network theorists do not themselves identify an entrepreneurial function. The following suggestions for an entrepreneurial function within the social networks framework are made in the light of the entrepreneurship theories considered in other chapters.

In terms of Marshall's evolutionary theory, entrepreneurship in a collective form will develop new routines which evolve as a result of the shared knowledge which is contributed to by all firms in the network. In terms of Nelson and Winter's evolutionary theory, a judgmental choice will be faced as to whether the new order should be an adaptation of the old or an entirely new creation. Networks are therefore a path-dependent mode of production. Some members of the network may be more reluctant to change than others, so that there may be a role for entrepreneurship in creating and testing out new routines and convincing others of their worth.

In this case, perhaps only the most respected and trustworthy members of the network, who wield a relatively higher degree of social influence, can undertake the entrepreneurial role. In doing so they risk damaging their reputations if the new routines do not prove to be successful. The question arises again of whether entrepreneurship is a collective or an individual activity. It may be that the success of a network depends upon a few individuals who have greater abilities to process information and to make judgmental decisions regarding how resources can be deployed to optimal effect. At the same time, however, the social environment is important to allow entrepreneurs to act effectively, and entrepreneurs must preserve and foster the social order and the non-contractual relations which facilitate the efficient use of knowledge within the network, and which allow it to function more effectively as a collective form of production.

In summary, the social networks approach provides an alternative viewpoint to more traditional economic approaches, in that it emphasizes the importance of social relations as determinants of economic behaviour and of the efficient organization of production in an uncertain environment. It also addresses the question of where the boundaries of a firm are, but does so in an entirely different way from that of contractarian economics. The networks approach recognizes the evolutionary process through which the social routines which govern the economic operations of networks develop. It also recognizes that there is an historical context to the decisions faced by entrepreneurs in adapting to change. This is in sharp contrast to the static equilibrium approach of contractarian economics, which does not recognize the temporal interdependence of production decisions.

Entrepreneurship and the evolution of production modes

The developments of two alternative production modes which have attracted a great deal of interest in the last two decades are now examined, those of the Multinational Enterprise (MNE) and the Industrial District. These production modes are analysed in the context of the previous considerations of the function of entrepreneurship, and the role of individuals, firms and networks in determining the temporal and spatial pattern of production. One starting point for this discussion is that of the 'industrial divide' which has developed in the last quarter of the twentieth century and was formally addressed by writers such as Piore and Sabel (1984).

The divide in question refers to widespread changes in both demand and supply side factors which have meant that production modes have had to become more flexible and responsive to a rapidly changing market environment. Flexible production modes are regarded as being 'post-Fordist' in that they are not directed at achieving economies of scale through the mass production of standardized products, but rather are geared to more 'individualized' or niche products produced in more flexible production processes. For much of this century the Fordist model of mass production has been predominant. This has been associated with the development of large vertically integrated firms which operate in mature oligopolistic markets for generic products. In these market conditions cost efficiency, in terms of both monetary and transaction costs, is the predominant competitive strategy. In mass production systems technology is a large scale capital investment and is only cost effective if used at, or near, full capacity over a prolonged period of time. There is therefore little incentive to implement innovations in products or processes in these circumstances. Mass production systems can therefore be relatively inflexible.

Major changes have occurred, however, which have challenged the predominance of mass production. In terms of market demand, this has become increasingly globalized and has become typified by changing patterns of consumer behaviour away from standardized mass produced products to customized products. However, by expanding the market from relatively small national or regional markets to the global level, demand may be great enough to achieve economies of scale. In terms of market supply, there has been a rapid development of flexible technology which can be implemented cost effectively on a smaller scale. At the same time, transport improvements have also allowed large-scale plants to serve the entire global market.

Both of these demand and supply changes have served to create the more diverse array of production modes which now exist and which involve alternative possibilities in production arrangements between individuals, firms and networks. Another element to the debate about the nature of post-Fordist production modes is the spatial dimension, which is expressed in terms of the geographical placement of production activity. This dimension has been analysed at international, national and regional levels in an attempt to determine the reasons which underpin the spatial evolution of alternative post-Fordist production modes and the competitive advantages which they enjoy relative to others.

Fundamental to the debate centred on the development of post-Fordist production, is the nature of knowledge in production modes, and the ways in which knowledge is created and used to best effect in determining the most efficient organization of production. Here a key role can be identified for entrepreneurship and the following discussion of MNEs and industrial districts is intended to illustrate this point. MNEs are typically large, highly integrated and geographically dispersed firms, while industrial districts are typically geographical clusters of many small independent firms. It must be appreciated though, that many other post-Fordist production modes exist other than MNEs and industrial districts; that the pattern of relationships between firms may take many other forms. No attempt is made to summarize the full range of theoretical developments in this area. It is, however, worth noting that a key aspect of much literature on such industrial clusters has been the 'Schumpeterian' processes involving the creation and interaction of knowledge and resources, rather than analysing comparative statics in an equilibrium setting.

Large firms may develop dependent chains of small subcontractors in which the large firm is the ultimate driver. This model is typical in Japan, for example 'Toyota City', where advantages can be gained from subcontracting to local small firms in operating efficient 'just-in-time' production systems. The inventory costs are minimized for the large firm, each small firm within the subcontracting chain has to be efficient to keep its place, and the chain overall has to be responsive to the large firm's needs. A substantial degree of co-operation is required between subcontractors along the supply chain and this is facilitated by their mutual interest in serving the large firm. In other cases a diverse range of large firm–small firm linkages can exist in a mutually beneficial production mode. The success of 'Silicon Valley' in California, where some of the world's largest computer manufacturers exist alongside small design houses and components manufacturers, has been attributed to extensive interfirm linkages and a highly developed technical and social infrastructure. Silicon Valley is claimed to represent an oligopolistic industrial structure in which there is considerable industrial decentralization, localized interdependencies and flexibility.

Other relationships between firms may exist in mutually beneficial partnerships such as strategic alliances and joint ventures, in which there is no formal degree of integration but potentially synergistic linkages can be exploited so that each partner can achieve individually an enhanced degree of competitive advantage. Such arrangements may occur for purposes of short-term expediency and as such they may not be so path-dependent in an evolutionary sense. In contrast, MNEs and industrial districts have a much stronger evolutionary context and this feature, allied to the fact that they represent very different forms of production, means that they are of particular interest in elaborating an entrepreneurial role in their functioning and development.

Multinational enterprises

MNEs are firms that own and control productive assets outside the country in which their headquarters is based. These are the largest players in both international and national oligopolistic markets and as such they wield a substantial degree of economic, social and political power. Indeed their power to influence markets and institutions, and therefore to control their environment and develop monopoly power on a global scale, has been suggested to be one of the major reasons for their evolution. Other explanations have suggested the need for domestic mass producers to diversify production into overseas economies in order to gain cost advantages offered by international wage differentials. The interdependence of behaviour in oligopolistic markets is such that all producers may have to follow a prime mover in order to remain competitive and retain their market share.

This explanation cannot hold, however, in the more economically sophisticated post-Fordist world where flexibility is required to remain competitive. The evidence, in high technology sectors in particular, suggests that multinational production is a deliberate strategy from the outset. A key feature of technology driven industries is that they are highly dynamic and their evolution can be somewhat turbulent. This creates a great deal of uncertainty in the market environment, and knowledge which is created by research and development is a highly important firm-specific asset which provides a competitive advantage over both national and international rivals. The desire to retain a degree of monopoly over this knowledge is therefore a natural consequence of dynamic industries, although this must be traded off against the benefits which can be derived from potentially synergistic linkages with other firms.

The choice to locate production overseas and compete in international markets in this way is different to that of locating all production operations domestically in the home economy and exporting into international markets. Exporting can occur either through internally controlled distribution networks which are located in overseas markets or through external production arrangements with overseas firms, which may take forms such as licensing and franchising. The decision to actually undertake production in overseas markets must therefore entail advantages to the firm in doing so which are not realized simply through exporting.

Furthermore, the benefits from undertaking multinational production must be greater than the considerable costs which must be involved in setting up and developing production facilities in a foreign culture, in which social, economic and institutional routines may be entirely different from the home economy. These factors essentially create transaction costs which only multinational producers must incur because they do not possess the same knowledge as domestic producers when they make the decision to locate a new production facility overseas. This knowledge can be acquired through time, although it will be seen later that there are ways in which MNEs can avoid this problem through inculcating their own organizational culture. At face value, the costs of multinational production would seem prohibitive, and strategies such as licensing arrangements and joint ventures with overseas producers, who have greater access to country-specific knowledge, would seem to be more appropriate.

The problem with these arrangements is that the producer risks disseminating knowledge about their products or production processes to rivals, both actual and potential. These arrangements may only be effective if opportunistic behaviour on the part of the partner firm can be curbed. If the knowledge which will be released is very product-specific then this can be well protected by a formal monopolistic arrangement such as a trademark or a patent. In these cases, licensing and franchising may be the most efficient forms of production. If knowledge is very process-specific and can be applied to produce a range of different products, there will be no gains at all from releasing this knowledge to potential competitors either at home or overseas. In these cases, there is obviously scope for imitating this knowledge in the development of entirely different products, some of which may prove to be in direct competition. It may therefore be more efficient to retain this knowledge entirely within the firm's headquarters and pursue a strategy of product diversification within the domestic economy and only export overseas if the domestic market becomes saturated.

The intermediate stage of knowledge which is partially product-specific and partly process-specific is a particular problem for an expanding producer. Buckley and Casson (1976) suggest that it is in this situation that multinational production is most likely to be undertaken. They argue that firms locate production overseas in order to retain control of the knowledge which gives them a competitive advantage, within the firm. They term this feature of multinational production 'internalization'. A benefit of internalization is that this knowledge is freely available to other overseas subsidiaries within the MNE, while it remains protected from rival firms. MNEs can therefore gain a substantial competitive advantage from the transfer of knowledge within the firm.

While this may form the competitive strategy of MNEs, it has also been suggested that MNEs derive further competitive advantages from their organizational structures. These structures are typically multidivisional, organized along geographical and functional lines, which are all ultimately accountable to the headquarters based in the home economy. The key research and development function is also typically located in the home economy. Monitoring and control systems are also typically devised and implemented by the headquarters. It is also typical that all of the key managerial functions within overseas divisions and subsidiaries are filled by managers recruited in the home economy by the headquarters, so that the line of control is readily apparent to the hierarchical structures beneath them. Each subsidiary is regarded as a separate profit centre whose performance is transparent, so that there is a spur to efficiency at all levels of the organization. Recruitment policies in the host economy are designed to prevent the possibility of vital knowledge being released to potential rivals, to the extent that it may only be highly standardized and low level production tasks which are undertaken by staff recruited from local labour markets.

Control is further maintained by the implementation of routines, both formal and informal, which are common to all subsidiaries in the organization. Essentially, an internal organizational culture is fostered. Local labour from the host economy is governed by the routines specified by the firm's headquarters and their work behaviour has to conform to the organizational culture of the MNE rather than their indigenous culture. MNEs can also develop a generic 'product culture' which gives them a competitive advantage over international and national rivals; and products can be customized for particular national markets from a standard form in order to gain a further edge over rivals. Only MNEs can accrue these benefits on a global scale and the whole organization benefits from the core activities undertaken by the firm's headquarters.

In terms of identifying an entrepreneurship function in the evolution of MNEs, it can be argued that it must be a judgmental choice as to whether multinational production is the most efficient production mode in globalized, dynamic and uncertain markets, where knowledge is the critical resource from which all competitive advantages are derived. Furthermore, this knowledge is very costly to acquire so that the benefits which can be derived from its use must be fully realized to recoup the substantial development costs and gain a return on investment over and above these costs.

The decision to undertake multinational production therefore requires considerable foresight, perception and resolution on the part of the firm's entrepreneurs in creating and exploiting profitable opportunities in a diverse range of national markets. In the process of doing so, entrepreneurs must determine the efficient creation, dissemination and protection of knowledge through devising and implementing organizational structures and routines which can be tightly controlled and adapted if circumstances change. The evolution of MNEs is therefore determined by the abilities of entrepreneurs who make the key judgmental decisions that determine the firm's strategy and structure.

Industrial districts

The notion that similar economic activities will benefit through spatial clustering was first observed last century by Marshall. He observed that many small firms could exist together harmoniously in spatial clusters and derive benefits similar to those of large firms, with whom each individual small firm could not possibly compete. Marshall (1919) referred to these benefits as economics of agglomeration, which are generated by the close proximity of firms within the cluster. These economies arise from shared access to common factors of production and the efficient dissemination of knowledge within the cluster. Furthermore, firms within the cluster tend to specialize in certain functions and synergistic linkages that form between firms so that the cluster overall evolves into an efficient productive unit. It does so without developing the inflexibilities of highly integrated production modes, which require to be closely monitored through formal structures and routines controlled by some ultimate authority.

In recent years there has been a resurgence of interest in industrial districts as viable production modes in a post-Fordist world. Contemporary theorists such as Porter (1990), Pyke and Sengenberger (1992) and Storper (1995) have proposed a number of reasons why spatial clustering is a necessary requirement of flexible production modes. More specifically they have also addressed the issue of why small firm-led industrial districts, in particular, can generate competitive advantages which cannot be realized in other production modes.

It has been suggested that the key elements which determine the success of industrial districts are the propagation of a collective identity, a shared business culture and the development of co-operative relationships based on trust. These represent untraded interdependencies, rather than formal contractual economic relationships. These elements arise from the spatial proximity of firms, although shared benefits may also be derived from the wider network of social and economic relations of each firm within the cluster. The success of each firm depends upon the success of the community of firms, so that important information is shared within the cluster rather than monopolized to the advantage of a single firm.

The desire for each firm to remain within the cluster through proving how trustworthy it is and how dedicated it is to serving the common good, ensures that opportunistic behaviour is curbed. The collective identity which is formed in social and cultural terms may involve a moral or ideological commitment to maintaining the well being of the community, so that rational decisionmaking, bounded or otherwise, is directed at serving the community's best interest rather than self-interest.

The mesh of informal economic relations in a close-knit social structure is a powerful means of achieving productive efficiency, and the degree of co-operation is such that adaptations in response to changes in market conditions can be implemented rapidly and efficiently. At the same time as the high degree of co-operation that exists vertically up and down the supply chain, there may be a strong element of competition between firms at the same stage of the supply chain. This competition, however, may not be manifested in detrimental price-cutting behaviour which could lead to a breakdown of social cohesion, but rather in terms of reputation for quality and good service. (Individuals take a pride in their work and firms are willing to increase the skills base through undertaking training, which is in the community's interest and allows them to demonstrate their skills to their peers.)

Furthermore, firms typically are willing to promote a satisfying work environment as a point of principle and wage bargaining processes do not involve a high degree of conflict. Compromises are informally agreed on the basis of trust and not in formalized contracts. The sales and marketing functions at the top end of the supply chain can be undertaken by specialist firms or through collaborative institutions such as marketing agencies and commercial associations. Collaborative institutions can also exist to provide collective services such as access to finance and the promotion of new ventures. In the event of a firm failing, its employees are readily absorbed into the district's collective workforce. Overall then, the industrial district as a socio-economic collective can achieve substantial competitive advantages as a production mode through its cohesion. Its nature is such that it can meet competitive challenges through the speed of development of differentiated quality products, the rapid innovation of new production methods and the flexibility of adjustment to new circumstances. This combination of flexibility and specialization has been termed 'flexible specialization'.

It is important to note that industrial districts are not dependent on large firms for their well being. They represent a separate production mode which can compete with large firms effectively in dynamic markets. In contrast to the extremely globalized nature of MNE production, industrial districts represent an extremely localized production mode. For MNEs, globalized production is the source of their competitive advantage, whereas in industrial districts it is localization which provides the source of competitive advantage.

What then is the form and function of entrepreneurship in industrial districts? The collective identity and interfirm linkages which naturally develop within a territorially defined socio-economic culture, eliminate the major problems that are faced in globally dispersed multinational production, that is those of protecting knowledge and controlling opportunistic behaviour. There is no need for a central decisionmaking authority to identify new profit opportunities and to devise and enforce new structures and routines. Nor is there a need to create an artificial common culture in order to develop loyalty within the organization. The industrial district as a 'collective entrepreneur', displays the dynamism which allows it to adapt to change and to evolve. It is not dependent on the success of any one individual or firm in generating and exploiting profit opportunities. All members of the collective may be entrepreneurial at some point in time, for example in acquiring an important piece of knowledge which they will release to the collective in order for its potential to be realized.

It may be that within industrial districts there are some key individuals or firms, for example at the marketing end of the supply chain, who are more alert to changes in consumer preferences and developments in technology, and who make relatively more of the judgmental decisions which determine the flow of resources within the district. While these key decisionmakers may have a relatively greater say in determining the success of the district, this success ultimately depends upon the district's collective ability. This important element of the entrepreneurial function may be institutionalized in a public agency which is contributed to by all firms in the district.

In summary, the consideration of two very different production modes, MNEs and industrial districts, has served to demonstrate that regardless of the organization of productive resources within path-dependent production modes, the role of entrepreneurship is vital in providing the driving force behind their efficient functioning and adaptation to change. Regardless of the form which entrepreneurship takes within different production modes, it is the ability to create or acquire, and ultimately to deploy knowledge to its best effect, which underpins the entrepreneurial function.

Illustration

Entrepreneurship in path-dependent production modes

Presented in this section are illustrations of the multinational enterprise, NEC, which has become one of the largest and most successful

Japanese companies, and the Italian province of Modena, which has come to exemplify a successful industrial district of small firms. The aim of these illustrations is to illuminate the role of entrepreneurship in the evolution and functioning of different production modes, in a post-Fordist market environment in which flexibility is vital to business success.

NEC – entrepreneurship in an MNE

NEC Corporation, founded in 1899 as Nippon Electric Company Ltd, a partnership between US and Japanese investors, has grown into one of the world's largest industrial corporations with particular strengths in the electronics, computer and communications (C&C) sectors. NEC is one of the world's leading producer of semiconductors and its major competitive advantages are accrued in what is termed the 'computer and communications' field, known within NEC as C&C operations. Under the stewardship of its president Koji Kobayashi, NEC became the predominant C&C producer. Since the 1960s, Kobayashi – widely regarded as a visionary in the electronics industry – was one of the first industrialists to identify the vital importance of the interface between computers and communications. In the US and Europe the computer industry chiefly grew out of the office equipment sector.

Kobayashi, an engineer by training, was the first president of NEC to have risen through the ranks of the corporation's organizational structure. Prior to his appointment in 1964, presidents of the corporation were appointed from one of the major companies in the massive Japanese industrial conglomeration, the Sumitomo Group, which NEC investors had entrusted with the running of the company in the 1940s. During this decade, management difficulties were experienced in the face of a world-wide recession and the rise of Japanese nationalism. In the 1990s the Sumitomo Group still owned 25 per cent of NEC stock and supplied 33 per cent of its loan finance. This strong connection has ensured that NEC is firmly embedded in the Japanese corporate system, which provides a stable environment. In many ways, NEC was the archetypal Japanese corporation, in terms of its organizational structure and management philosophy, which are geared towards maintaining a 'cradle-to-the-grave' ethos of company loyalty by all employees.

The globalization of the world's electronic industry began in the 1960s when US producers began setting up subsidiaries overseas to secure supplies of cheap raw materials and labour in order to reduce production costs. By the 1980s, the nature of the industry had changed substantially, with Japanese corporations beginning to dominate some sectors of the industry. NEC was foremost among the new order of world leaders in electronics. In the 1980s many Japanese corporations shifted their activities away from domestic exports to multinational production, partly to overcome problems caused by the strength of the Yen, and partly to overcome the protectionist trade policies pursued by governments in their overseas markets. A more important factor, however, was the increasingly competitive nature of the electronics sector, when producers realized the importance of global markets in which income levels were rising, production cycles were becoming shorter, and consumer tastes were becoming more sophisticated and diverse.

Only by locating in overseas markets, principally the US, Europe and South East Asia, could corporations such as NEC gain access to the market information that they needed to compete effectively against domestic producers in these countries. Also locating some production overseas helped overcome looming labour shortages due to a sharply ageing population in Japan, and also might have reduced the risk of possible trade sanctions. Like many of the major Japanese corporations, NEC also apparently felt that it could exploit competitive advantages gained from the accumulated managerial and technical expertise which it had developed since the 1940s. An important manifestation of this expertise was an organizational restructuring from a predominantly 'functional' form into product based divisional forms. All of the key functional activities such as sales, marketing and personnel management were undertaken at the head office under the divisional structure, and instead of having general functional managers in charge of plants, the aim was to have divisional managers in charge of research and production in each product line. NEC introduced this divisional structure in the 1950s and refined it in the 1960s by devolving a greater degree of responsibility for sales and marketing to a larger number of product divisions.

Kobayashi developed this multi-divisional structure more fully in the 1970s in response to the burgeoning diverse markets for electronic goods, by implementing a complex matrix structure where divisional heads were jointly responsible for production and marketing over a wide range of products and markets, both domestic and overseas. A further reorganization in 1991 aimed at making NEC even more market-oriented, in response to the need to meet an ever increasing demand for customized products and to exploit the advantages arising from a convergence of technologies in computers and communications. This reorganization included the creation of a 'customer satisfaction management' department based at head office, which has retained control over key functions such as personnel, treasury, corporate planning and shareholder relations throughout the various restructuring of the corporation.

In NEC emphasis was always placed on developing a corporate culture within the complex multi-divisional structure, which is based on the 'pillars' of Japanese management philosophy. These include, for example, collective decisionmaking, job rotation, multi-skilling and small group activities, all of which were aimed at creating a strong sense of teamwork and a collective identity in the pursuit of a common goal. Kobayashi believed that all workers should be flexible in adapting their skills to meet new requirements and that all employees should have the opportunity to develop their latent talents. Essentially, an 'internal labour market' has been created within NEC, in which long-term employment is sustained through incentives such as the opportunity to gain accelerated internal promotion based on merit, and hierarchical wage structures based on seniority. Strictly applied quality management systems and codes of practice are evident in all NEC plants, and all employees – domestic and overseas managerial and otherwise – are encouraged to participate voluntarily in maintaining the highest standards and contributing towards the attainment of a 'common destiny'.

The critically important research and development function has also undergone substantial restructuring under Kobayashi's stewardship of NEC. Central research laboratories set up in 1965 and based at head office had become inflexible over the years and unable to keep up with the rapid pace of change in the market environment. In 1980, the need for a more flexible R&D structure led to the dissolving of the central laboratories and the setting up of five new research groups covering all of the major areas of NEC production activities. This reorganization brought R&D closer to the individual production divisions and ultimately to the market for final products. A policy was adopted of undertaking most of the high value-added R&D at home and contracting-out work to overseas divisions depending on the relative distribution of knowledge and skills. Any perceived gaps in the research and development work activated the setting up of an overseas facility. NEC also created a research institute at Princeton University in 1988, in order to tap into the skills of US academics and engineers. This move was prompted by smaller volume of academic scientific literature emanating from Japan in the 1980s and 1990s compared with the US.

While most of NEC's high quality R&D was focused on Japan, an important part of the R&D process occurred in host economies. This R&D work was mostly of a different nature to that undertaken in the home economy, in that it was directed at developing process adaptation technologies to customize products in order to meet the requirements of local markets. Some product development occurs in NEC's overseas facilities, although the mix between process-adaptation R&D and product development in overseas facilities depends upon the skills levels in the host economy. High standards of product quality must be maintained as part of the overall corporate strategy and this is easier to attain with highly skilled workers.

To this end NEC placed importance on undertaking the early stage of new product development in the home based R&D facilities and transferring this responsibility to overseas R&D facilities, in response to skills levels and market demand. The corporation's R&D strategy was market driven, in line with Kobayashi's other organizational reforms, and is aimed at meeting his objective of maintaining NEC's dominant position in an industrial sector which was characterized by dynamic change and extreme competitive pressures.

Modena – entrepreneurship in an industrial district

The province of Modena is the manufacturing heartland of the region of Emilia-Romagna in North Central Italy, which has come to be known as the 'Third Italy'. The economic geography of the region is distinct from other regions of Italy, in that it is based on groups of small entrepreneurial firms which pursue a strategy of continuous innovation and flexibility in production. The region is widely regarded as an ideal example of what a close-knit community of small firms can achieve. In recent years, Emilia-Romagna has been the fastest growing of Italy's 20 regions, with the highest per capita income in the country. The province of Modena is famous for the production of prestige cars (Ferrari, Maserati), ceramics, textiles and clothing, and it has the highest level of exports per capita in Italy.

The province has a population of around 600 000, with a workforce of around 140 000. In a population of around 22 000 registered industrial firms, the average firm size is only six to seven workers. Fewer than 300 firms employ more than 50 workers so that large firms are rare in Modena. The success of Modena is proof that small firms can compete effectively in international markets. This success is based on the nature of firms in the province, the relationships between firms and the municipal institutions which perform important roles on behalf of all firms. In this respect, three types of small firms can be distinguished:

(1) traditional firms that produce non-tradables for the local market;
(2) design-dependent firms that subcontract to leading firms which shape product design and control a critical phase of the production chain such as assembly or retailing. Lead firms interact with regional,

national and international markets while subcontractors compete with each other on the basis of price and lack independent design and marketing capabilities;

(3) design-independent suppliers that have the capacity to refine designs and thereby shape products and markets. They may not produce own-brands, but they are not tied to the designs of assembly or retailing firms.

There are interfirm trade associations at all stages along the production chain, which can collectively and simultaneously redesign products and allow the chain to restructure without a managerial hierarchy. Municipal agencies, in conjunction with interfirm associations, oversee areas such as land management and provide sector-specific collective service centres for information dissemination in areas such as market developments and technology. Changes in market conditions are continually tracked and lead times between design and delivery are reduced substantially through the implementation of 'semi-planned' production channels in which firms rely upon fewer suppliers with whom they develop strong, lasting relations. Access to expensive cutting edge technology is available to all firms, who can pay a membership fee to use the collective service centre, rather than bear the costs of acquiring the technology themselves.

Legally governed financial and marketing consortia exist as non-profit associations to the equal benefit of all members, who also pay a membership fee to use these services. New firms, and spin-off firms in particular, are encouraged and in each case the spin-off is created in response to an existing need by an individual with experience in the same or a related phase of production. In most cases the new firms are headed by family members or trusted previous employees who wish to establish independent firms. Together such firms form a socially integrated system. Wage agreements are negotiated at a collective level and the standard wage for small firms is public information. The wage settlements in Modena have become a standard for wage bargaining by trade unions at a national level in Italy.

The high skill levels in Modena support high productivity and wages so that the collective bargaining process is relatively straightforward with little conflict. The final wage settlements are adjusted up and down by individual firms from the provincial standard. Firms are encouraged by trade associations and unions to compete on the basis of innovation and quality rather than wages. Firms paying lower than standard wages must explain their actions and higher than standard wages must be justified in terms of productivity. All workers have the option of creating their own small firm, so that employers are under pressure to maintain attractive conditions or they risk losing a valued employee and gaining a competitor at the same time. Wages are roughly the same in small and large firms so the small firms have to constantly seek ways of increasing productivity to match productivity gains in large firms.

Modena has a history of economic co-operation. The province has been governed by the Communist Party since the end of the Second World War. Two guiding principles have been followed in developing the Modena local economy as a communist municipality: (1) to distinguish between monopoly capital, or big business, and artisan capital run by crafts-based in small firms, which is the favoured form of economic activity in communist doctrine; (2) to govern by consensus through invoking democratic processes at all levels of economic activity. All productive associations, consortia and municipal agencies are governed by committee, with all members being duly elected by democratic processes.

The notion of free enterprise therefore takes on a new meaning in the communist municipality of Modena. A strong heritage of public and private sector economic partnership has developed out of the highly integrated social infrastructure and an ideological commitment to placing the common good ahead of private interest. Local government in Modena has been able to pursue a dynamic economic programme by creating a range of interfirm associations and municipal institutions.

Modena operates effectively as a collective entrepreneur. The local economy is led by internationally competitive independent small firms, productive associations, municipal government and a strong civic culture which encourages good citizenship. Private enterprise in the form of small businesses activity is fostered within a democratically accountable political environment. Owners of small firms are both entrepreneurs and skilled workers. By co-operating in the collective provision of services, small firms can maintain their independence in production without being reduced to fulfilling a subservient role as subcontractors for products designed by large firms.

Conclusion

This concludes the examination of entrepreneurship in an evolutionary and socio-economic context. In Chapters 3 to 6, a diverse range of economic perspectives on entrepreneurship were considered, most of which are in some way 'alternative' to conventional neoclassical economics. While individual theories may adopt different perspectives and identify different functions for entrepreneurship, it is clear that all of these approaches consider entrepreneurship to be a specific and vital economic function. Regardless of the individual viewpoints which have been expressed by economic theorists, entrepreneurship is perceived overall as the key force within economies which allows them to function efficiently and to develop.

The remaining chapter in Part II considers 'non-economic' perspectives on entrepreneurship which, in general, have placed greater emphasis on the sociological and psychological determinants of entrepreneurial activity. Non-economic perspectives pay greater attention to entrepreneurs as people, with personal attributes, needs and ambitions, and to entrepreneurship as a form of managerial behaviour which is associated with successful businesses.

References and further reading

Amin, A. (1993) 'The globalization of the economy: an erosion of regional networks?', in G. Grabher, *The embedded firm: On the socioeconomics of industrial networks*, London, Routledge.

Brusco, S. (1982) 'The Emilian model: productive decentralisation and social integration', *Cambridge Journal of Economics*, Vol. 6, pp. 167–84.

Buckley, P. and M. Casson (1976) *The Future of the Multinational Enterprise*, London, Macmillan.

Coase, R.H. (1937) 'The nature of the firm', *Economica*, Vol. 4, pp. 386–405.

Emmott, W. (1992) *Japan's Global Growth*, London, Century Business.

Granovetter, M. (1973) 'The strength of weak ties', *American Journal of Sociology*, Vol. 78, pp. 1360–80.

Granovetter, M. (1985) 'Economic action and the social structure: the problem of embeddedness', *American Journal of Sociology*, Vol. 91, pp. 481–510.

Granovetter, M. (1991) 'The social construction of economic institutions', in A. Etzioni and R. Lawrence (eds), *Socioeconomics: Towards a New Synthesis*, pp. 75–81, New York, Armonk.

Griffiths, A. and T. Nakakita (1993) 'Structure and strategy in a global environment: the case of NEC Corporation', in J. Preston (ed.), *International Business: Text and Cases*, pp. 241–56, London, Pitman.

Kobayashi, K. (1991) *The Rise of NEC: How the World's Greatest C&C Company is Managed*, Oxford, Blackwell Business.

Marshall, A. (1919) *Principles of Economics*, London, Macmillan.

Nelson, R.R. and S.G. Winter (1982) *An Evolutionary Theory of Economic Change*, Cambridge, Mass., Harvard University Press.

OECD (Organization for Economic Co-operation and Development) (1997) *The World in 2020: A New Global Age*, Paris, OECD.

Piore, M. and C. Sabel (1984) *The Second Industrial Divide*, New York, Basic Books.

Porter, M. (1990) *The Competitive Advantage of Nations*, London, Macmillan.

Pyke, F. and G. Becattini (eds) (1989) *Industrial Districts and Inter-Firm Cooperation in Italy*, International Institute for Labour Studies, Geneva.

Pyke, F. and W. Sengenberger (eds) (1992) *Industrial Districts and Local Economic Regeneration*, International Institute for Labour Studies, Geneva.

Ricketts, M. (1994) *The Economics of Business Enterprise* 2nd edn, London, Harvester Wheatsheaf.

Storper, M. (1995) 'The resurgence of regional economies, ten years later', *European Urban and Regional Studies*, Vol. 2, pp. 191–221.

Williamson, O.E. (1975) *Markets and Hierarchies: Analysis and Antitrust Implications: A Study in the Economics of Internal Organization*, New York, Free Press.

Williamson, O.E. (1985) *The Economic Institutions of Capitalism: Firms, Markets, Relational Contracting*, London, Macmillan.

7
Non-Economic Perspectives on Entrepreneurship

Introduction

This chapter concludes the examination of theoretical perspectives on entrepreneurship undertaken in Part II. Chapters 3 to 6 demonstrated that economic approaches have generally focused on the function of entrepreneurship in the economic system, rather than on the personal characteristics of those individuals who are entrepreneurial. However, economic theorists have recognized the importance of sociological factors such as social background and cultural attitudes, and psychological attributes such as creativity and imagination. In economic approaches the prime motivation to undertake entrepreneurial activities is utility maximization generally based upon profit and the intrinsic gains to the individual of undertaking entrepreneurial activity are relegated to relatively minor importance. Some would argue that without profit there is no entrepreneurship (although this view ignores the view of entrepreneurship as a form of behaviour).

In this chapter the discussion turns to non-economic approaches to entrepreneurship and their economic implications. One of the key implications involves the relationship between entrepreneurship and small firm performance. In conventional economic theory it is assumed that pursuit of profits and growth is rational business behaviour. The statistical evidence presented in Table 2.1, however, shows that the vast majority of small firms remain small and that in many places there has been an upsurge in small firm numbers in the advanced Western economies. There has been a growing realization by economists that in advanced capitalist economies small and new firms have much to contribute to economic prosperity.

The key players in the small firm sector are generally assumed to be entrepreneurs although more is said about this later in this chapter. In the previous discussion of economic theories of entrepreneurship, roles were identified for entrepreneurs not only in new, small firms, but also in growing firms and in large corporate firms. Common to all these approaches is the notion that it is only entrepreneurs who are capable of strategically deploying resources in production to create profit, regardless of firm size. In larger businesses there is generally a distinction between entrepreneurs and administrative managers who do not possess entrepreneurial abilities. Other approaches which are rooted in sociological, psychological and management science, have also developed theories of entrepreneurship and have made a contribution to the small business debate. These non-economic perspectives are considered here. The chapter begins with an overview of the major sociological and psychological perspectives on entrepreneurship. This review is not intended to be exhaustive, rather it is aimed at identifying the main strands of thought on entrepreneurship in each of these disciplines, which represent the other major social sciences in addition to economics. Accordingly, the methodologies of sociological and psychological perspectives on entrepreneurship are then compared with each other and with that of economics.

Following the review of sociological and psychological theories, perspectives on entrepreneurship developed within the particular discipline of management science are considered. This discussion focuses on the key analytical models which management theorists have developed in seeking to explain the nature of entrepreneurial activity, and in particular its impact on business performance. Approaches which can be considered 'generalist', in the sense that they synthesize elements from a range of different subject perspectives, are then considered, along with illustrations of small firm entrepreneurship to help illuminate the major issues raised in this discussion. The strengths and limitations of adopting a multi-disciplinary approach to analysing entrepreneurship are then examined in terms of their ability to analyse the economic impact of both economic and non-economic influences on entrepreneurial activity. The proposition that the study of entrepreneurship is an emerging science in its own right is then considered.

Sociological theories of entrepreneurship

The nature of sociology may be defined in broad terms as representing an attempt to analyse the ways in which groups of individuals interact in societies and the ways in which the social environment determines the behaviour of these groups. Sociological approaches to entrepreneurship stress the societal influences on entrepreneurial activity and are largely concerned with the social group which constitute the *petite bourgeoisie*. This group is defined by the small-scale ownership of capital and represents a contemporary interpretation of Marxist analysis. While Marx predicted that large-scale capital accumulation would occur in the hands of an elite group of bourgeois capitalists, this does not explain the increasing trend towards small-scale economic activity which has become prevalent in capitalist economies. Accordingly, sociologists have turned their attention to examine the characteristics of the *petite bourgeoisie*, and there are essentially two main pillars of sociological analysis in the field of entrepreneurship.

The first key pillar in the sociological analysis of entrepreneurship revolves around the concept of social marginality, or of social groups which are outside mainstream society. This work originated with Weber (1930) who argued that activities such as entrepreneurship can differ between societies or groups within a society. Some groups hold values outside the cultural norm and are thus marginalized. This pushes them into pursuing certain forms of activity in order to achieve self-actualization within their own sphere of reference. Weber stressed the importance of holding certain religious beliefs, such as the Calvinist doctrine of predestination, which stresses the importance of austerity and hard work, and is commonly referred to as the 'protestant work ethic'.

Other writers have widened the scope of the 'outsider' and have linked outsider groups to small-scale economic activity. The social marginality thesis proposes that when an individual's perception of their own worth differs from their social role, this may serve to stimulate entrepreneurial behaviour, which in this sense is a way of proving their own self worth and showing others what they are capable of achieving. Entrepreneurship may therefore represent a means of social mobility to some people when other doors are closed to them. This need not only apply to ethnic groups but also to individuals frustrated by a lack of promotion opportunities in large organizations. The social marginality thesis does not suggest that all individuals in this situation will undertake entrepreneurial activity, rather it is one form of self-actualization and social mobility which is open to them, and some will follow this route.

Furthermore, outsider groups are not necessarily forced into entrepreneurship by discrimination, it may be that their cultural beliefs are more in favour of entrepreneurial activity than those of mainstream society. Correspondingly, individuals may be socialized into an entrepreneurial culture even if mainstream culture does not favour entrepreneurial activity and their role models will be drawn from their own social group. In this regard, it has been suggested that family groupings, in either mainstream or outsider cultures, which have a history of self-employment, can socialize siblings into entrepreneurship and provide role models of entrepreneurial success.

A second key pillar of sociological analysis in the field of entrepreneurship revolves around the notion that there are different 'types' of entrepreneurs that can be grouped according to the possession of common attributes. For example, the social development model proposed by Gibb and Ritchie (1981) suggests a typology of entrepreneurs relating to different stages of the life-cycle. Different attitudes to entrepreneurship may be determined by different societal pressures, circumstances and opportunities throughout the course of a person's life. This suggests that age may be an important factor at the onset of entrepreneurial activity because different attitudes may arise at different stages of the life-cycle. For example, the attitudes of a 35-year-old starting a business may vary considerably from those of a person nearing retirement. Much research has found the middle stage of the life-cycle to be the most common category in terms of first-time entrepreneurial activity. Individuals at this stage of the life-cycle may have accumulated substantial human and financial capital and may feel the need for greater self-actualization. Shapero (1984) also suggests the importance of a 'triggering factor' such as redundancy or divorce, or some other life crisis or event, which provides the final push into entrepreneurship for many people.

Along similar lines, Scase and Goffee (1982) propose a typology of the 'entrepreneurial middle-class' of small-scale capitalists. They suggest that there are four distinct types of small-scale capitalist: (1) the self-employed, which statistics have shown to be the most prevalent form of small business; (2) the small employer, in which a small number of employees are supervised directly by the owner-manager; (3) the owner-controllers, in which the owner-manager takes a more administrative managerial role in the firm, although still has direct control as far as possible; (4) the owner-director, in which control has to be devolved due to the substantial size of the firm.

Each of these entrepreneurial types is therefore related to a different size of small firm, with the largest of these small firms clearly displaying different organizational structures to the smallest firms. Within each type of small entrepreneurial firm, there will be different organizational cultures and different attitudes on the part of entrepreneurs in managing the firm. In larger small firms it is more likely that there will be formal management systems and a more structured organizational form, which will lead to a more 'professional' managerial culture within the firm. This is in contrast to the smallest firms, which are under the direct control of the entrepreneur, who adopts a more autocratic and personalized style of management.

In summary, the thrust of sociological analysis is to examine the impact of the social environment on entrepreneurial activity in terms of the wider societal influences on entrepreneurship and the influence of specific social groupings.

Psychological theories of entrepreneurship

While the concern of sociological approaches is with the environmental influences on entrepreneurial activity, the concern of psychological theory is with the intrinsic influences on individual entrepreneurs. Psychological approaches generally focus on analysing the internal cognitive development in individuals who display entrepreneurial behaviour, although they also recognize that behaviour can be shaped to some extent by the social environment. Two distinctive approaches have been developed by psychologists in the study of entrepreneurship, these are: the psychodynamic model proposed by Kets de Vries (1977) and personality trait models – the seminal work in this field being McClelland (1961).

The psychodynamic model suggests that entrepreneurial behaviour arises from deviant personalities which are developed through abnormal childhood experiences such as deprivation. Current actions and behaviour are the result of early life experiences. It is argued that the experience of deprivation in childhood results in psychological problems in adulthood, such as low self-esteem and an inability to accept authority or work with others. Entrepreneurial activity for such individuals represents a chance to create their own empire, where there are no authority figures presiding over them and thus their self-esteem and self-confidence is bolstered.

In common with the social marginality thesis the psychodynamic model does not explain why entrepreneurship is the likely choice for all such individuals. Not all small business owner-managers have had a deprived childhood, although the 'rags-to-riches' story is commonly told as a model for successful entrepreneurship. Furthermore, this approach does not incorporate current life experiences or situations as possible determinants of the decision to undertake entrepreneurial activity. The question then arises of why some individuals who have had similar childhood experiences to others choose to undertake entrepreneurship at different times in their lives to others, or even at all.

The main approach adopted by psychologists, however, is that of correlating certain personality traits with entrepreneurial activity. McClelland (1961) sought to prove that much economic history could be explained in terms of psychological variables. He defined three personality traits which he believed explained social, political and economic change in societies. These are: (1) need for power – the means for influencing other people; (2) need for affiliation – the means for developing friendships with other people; (3) need for achievement (nAch). The last of these traits McClelland predicted to be associated specifically with entrepreneurial activity.

McClelland found all societies showing substantial economic development to be associated with the presence of entrepreneurship and high scores for nAch. This study triggered a substantial body of research on the relationship between certain personality traits and entrepreneurial behaviour. For example, Rotter (1975) suggests that an 'internal locus of control' is associated with entrepreneurial activity, where a person believes their destiny is of their own making and is not predetermined by fate. Such people are driven by a need for autonomy over strategic decisions affecting the course of their lives and desire independence from external influences. Brockhaus (1980) suggests that entrepreneurs have a higher risk-taking propensity than other individuals, in that they may choose to undertake ventures even when the probability of succeeding is low.

The methodology adopted in studies of entrepreneurial personality traits entails the precise specification and measurement of traits using standardized personality inventories. This approach to analysing entrepreneurship has been strongly criticized on the basis that the attributes being specified and measured are complex processes which cannot be reduced into simple categories. The trait approach assumes that they can and furthermore, once specified, traits are stable enough to provide universally reliable and valid indicators of human qualities such as creativity and imagination. Research carried out in this field of study has, in general, failed to identify any traits which are associated specifically with successful entrepreneurs. More sophisticated versions of this approach have attempted to develop constellations of personality traits which are specifically associated with entrepreneurs, but these have not proven to be any more successful at predicting who will become entrepreneurs.

A key feature of the personality trait approach is that traits must also be independent of social context so that an enterprise culture cannot create more entrepreneurs, only more people possessing such traits can. The debate between 'nature or nurture' is therefore raised in this context, although it may be argued that economic development cannot depend solely upon more entrepreneurs being born.

Even in economic perspectives such as Casson's, which argues that judgmental decisionmaking ability is randomly distributed among the population, the supply of entrepreneurs is still partly determined by social factors. On this point, Robinson *et al.* (1991) have emphasized the importance of attitude as a psychological predictor of entrepreneurial behaviour rather than personality. They assume, however, that while attitude can be determined to an extent by social influences, it can be specified as a psychological variable and measured accurately in the same way that personality traits can, by using standardized psychological testing procedures. Their rationale for pursuing this line of enquiry is that attitudes can be changed by propaganda and education programmes, while personality traits cannot. Thus entrepreneurs can, to an extent, be made if their attitudes can be influenced.

However, Oswald and Blanchflower (1998) used psychological and other tests on 1300 entrepreneurs among the 11 400 people born in Britain in a given week in 1958, and found that those who became entrepreneurs were not any more persistent, self-motivated or risk taking than the others. One of the few things those setting up business had in common was that they had received money as an inheritance or a gift. It is worth noting that those starting up a business may have a different profile from 'high flyers'.

In summary, psychological perspectives place emphasis on the internal cognitive development of entrepreneurial personalities and attitudes, and in doing so place less emphasis on the social, environmental and situational influences on the decision to undertake entrepreneurial activity. However, there has been some criticism that most psychological studies have concentrated upon male entrepreneurs and do not fully reflect the traits, objectives, growth mechanisms and obstacles faced by female entrepreneurs.

The methodologies of sociology and psychology

It is useful at this point to compare sociological and psychological approaches with each other, and with economic approaches. It has been seen that the main strand of thought in economic approaches to entrepreneurship has been to identify the function of entrepreneurship in the economic system. In doing so, simplifying assumptions are made about the personal characteristics, motivations, objectives and behaviour of individuals who are able to undertake the entrepreneurial function. The nature of sociology has been defined broadly as representing an attempt to analyse the ways in which groups of individuals interact in societies, and the ways in which the social environment determines the behaviour of social groups. Sociologists are not concerned with the economic function of entrepreneurs but with identifying the defining features of the social groups which undertake entrepreneurial activity, and the ways in which these groups interact with society at large in terms of their cultural beliefs and attitudes. The 'typology' approach is used to differentiate between different types of entrepreneurial groups within a general grouping of the small-scale capitalists that comprise the *petite bourgeoisie*. Social environmental and situational influences on entrepreneurship are the key concern of sociology, and not the innate determinants of individual behaviour.

In broad terms, psychologists, on the other hand, are primarily concerned with the internal influences on the behaviour of individuals. They also equate entrepreneurial behaviour with choosing to own and control a firm in preference to paid employment. As such, they are seeking to predict which individuals will become entrepreneurs in terms of personal experiences and psychological attributes. Some of these experiences and attributes are very specific, such as having a deprived childhood, or a having a need to make the key decisions which influence the course of one's life. Psychologists generally adopt a more quantitative empirical methodology in that they attempt to specify these attributes in terms of variables which can be then measured with precision using psychological testing procedures. In common with sociologists, psychologists are also not generally concerned with the economic function of entrepreneurship or with its economic impact.

In general, psychologists place greater concern on the predictive accuracy of their methodologies than sociologists, who are primarily interested in explaining who entrepreneurs are rather than predicting who will become entrepreneurs. Thus sociology and psychology are both concerned with determinants of human behaviour, albeit from different perspectives. Both regard entrepreneurial behaviour as being manifested in terms of owning and controlling a small firm. The approaches of sociology and psychology differ broadly from that of economics in the degree of detail which they go into in explaining the personal attributes and experiences of entrepreneurs, and ultimately in terms of the purpose for which the theories are intended.

Management theories of entrepreneurship

While the broad concerns of sociological and psychological work in the entrepreneurship and small firm field are with the questions 'which individuals will start their own small firms, and why?', another body of thought has been developed in the management science literature. This focuses on the types of managerial behaviour associated with entrepreneurial organizations, defined as those which create and exploit new opportunities for profits and growth, in the process redeploying resources in the pursuit of these opportunities (Stevenson and Sahlman, 1989; Sandberg, 1992). Fundamental to this body of thought is the view that there is a difference between entrepreneurial management and administrative management, the latter being associated with merely overseeing the pattern of existing resource allocation within organizations in response to known and existing opportunities. Entrepreneurial management is the driving force for change and is associated with innovation and the implementation of strategic policies and flexible organizational structures, in order to maximize the potential of new opportunities.

In this respect there are strong similarities between this perspective on entrepreneurship and many of the economic perspectives reviewed earlier. As in these economic approaches, the concern of the entrepreneurial management school is not predominantly with new and small firms but with large corporate firms. However, the entrepreneurial management school go into greater detail concerning the types of managerial behaviour and strategic policies which are thought to be associated with successful entrepreneurial organizations. These relate not only to the development of efficient organizational structures in response to the exploitation of opportunities, but also to strategic management activities which are aimed at securing competitive advantages over rivals. Particular strategic management activities in the specific context of small firms are discussed in the section which follows.

It is also recognized in this approach that entrepreneurial management is a process, which begins with the identification of an opportunity and ends with the rewards being derived from its exploitation. In between the start and end points of this process, strategies are formed to ensure that resources are deployed and managed efficiently in order to maximize the potential of the opportunity. It is suggested that firms which are governed by opportunity-oriented entrepreneurial management styles, rather than bureaucratic administrative management styles, are better able to develop and implement effective business strategies and policies and will, therefore, be more successful. In this respect there are similarities between this approach and the views of evolutionary economic thought which also emphasizes the importance of entrepreneurial management in creating and adapting to change.

A variant on this theme examines the nature of the evolution of management styles in small firms. In this respect some management theorists have developed 'stage' models of small business development. These models take a longitudinal view of the forms of managerial behaviour which are likely to evolve in businesses during the course of their life-cycle, and identify clear stages in the evolution of managerial styles in new and developing businesses. It may be noted, however, that there is no one model of the stages of business development and that the principle focus for attention in models of this nature is upon the types of problems encountered and the consequent behaviour of the business owner. The key variables in stage models are the size and age of the business. It is proposed that particular management styles and strategic policies are only appropriate to certain stages of a business' development in terms of its organizational structures and the problems it faces.

For example, Churchill and Lewis (1983) identify five stages in the process of business development, these being existence, survival, success, take-off and resource maturation. Thus at the start of the business venture the owner has to be concerned with ensuring the viability of the business, particularly in terms of its customer base and financial security. As the business becomes established and more profitable, the owner is faced with a choice of whether to pursue growth or stabilization. If growth is pursued, a more strategic managerial style is required in which the owner is disengaged from the day-to-day affairs of the business. Once the business has reached a certain size, the owner begins delegating managerial tasks and decentralizing control of the business, at which point growth 'takes off' and eventually the business matures into its optimal organizational structure. However, the owner is now faced with the problem of maintaining the business' 'entrepreneurial spirit' in a more bureaucratic organization.

Flamholtz (1986), on the other hand, identifies a four-stage model of business growth beginning with two 'entrepreneurial phases'. These stages entail, first of all, the identification of a market opportunity and the initial assembling of resources to produce the product or service in response to that opportunity. A flexible organizational structure must then be developed which can respond efficiently to the day-to-day needs of the business as it expands rapidly in order to exploit its opportunity. Following these entrepreneurial stages Flamholtz suggests that the owner must make a transition to a professionally managed business, so that stage three is the beginning of the process of professionalization. The final stage entails the consolidation of the business as a professionally managed corporate entity in which a corporate culture must be developed to remedy the problems associated with a loss of control over its overall direction because of its greater size.

The key problem with the stages modelling approach in general, is that it is by no means certain that all businesses will develop from one stage to the next in a rational and predictable manner. Many researchers have strongly criticized the stages approach in failing to account for the fact that the vast majority of small firms do not grow in a predictable linear fashion, or do not grow at all.

In summary, managerial theories of entrepreneurship focus on the forms of managerial behaviour which are associated with entrepreneurial, opportunity-seeking organizations. The focus is on the policies and actions of entrepreneurial managers rather than their personal attributes and influences. Entrepreneurial management is regarded as a process in two senses. First, in terms of the actions which managers take in order to create and exploit profit and growth opportunities. Second, in terms of the managerial styles which must evolve in the process of pursuing these opportunities, in response to problems which managers face at certain points of a business' development.

Key themes in non-economic perspectives

The consideration of entrepreneurship in the disciplines of sociology, psychology and management science has identified a number of issues relating to the types of people who become entrepreneurs, the reasons why they do it, and the forms of management behaviour they adopt in creating and developing small firms. The following discussion is concerned with the nature of the personal characteristics, motivations, objectives, strategic choices and management practices of entrepreneurs that are suggested to be associated with successful small firms. Insights are provided from recent empirical studies which have examined sociological, psychological and managerial aspects of small firm performance.

Personal characteristics

Beginning with the personal characteristics of entrepreneurs, the key variables in this regard which have been suggested to have some bearing on small business success are: the entrepreneur's age, level of educational attainment, employment history (in terms of previous managerial and small firm experience), if they have a family history of entrepreneurship, and if they are the founders of the firm. Regarding age, in line with Gibb and Ritchie's (1981) model of life-cycle effects, there is thought to be a non-linear relationship between age and firm performance. The middle stage of the life-cycle (35–45 years) is thought to be associated with the highest levels of small firm performance. This is broadly because of two effects, the first of which relates to levels of motivation to succeed, and the second of which relates to the possession of 'human capital', that is the relevant skills and abilities required to manage a small firm. Entrepreneurs younger than this optimal age group may have the enthusiasm to succeed but not the experience and they will find it more difficult to raise capital because of their inexperience. Older entrepreneurs, on the other hand, are likely to have the experience and perhaps the financial capital, but not the motivation as they near retirement.

Also with regard to human capital, it is thought that higher levels of education and the possession of previous managerial experience, previous experience of working for a small employer and a family history of entrepreneurship, may be associated with higher levels of performance. These variables represent elements of human capital which should be positively associated with the skills and abilities which are necessary to achieve business success. However, Storey (1994: p. 137) takes an overview of these variables and cautions against placing too much emphasis on the impact of the personal characteristics of entrepreneurs on the performance of their businesses. He indicates that 'the identikit picture of the entrepreneur whose business is likely to grow is extremely fuzzy', and that 'what the entrepreneur has done prior to establishing the business exerts only a modest influence upon the success of the business'.

With regard to the impact of having the firm's founder in control, it has been suggested that founder managers are more likely to have a vested interest in the firm's success. It has also been suggested that founder managers are more likely to accept lower remuneration in order to plough back profits into the firm. Higher levels of profitability and growth may therefore be expected in small firms managed by the founder. On the other hand, it has also been suggested that the managerial styles of founders are likely to be different from non-founder managers, in that the latter may have more professional managerial styles. Non-founder managers, may also have little vested interest in the firm, other than to gain peer recognition of their managerial abilities, thus they may be more willing to pursue riskier opportunities.

Motivations and goals

Regarding motivations for undertaking entrepreneurial activity, a key point to emerge from the previous discussion of economic, sociological and psychological perspectives on entrepreneurship is that motivations for undertaking entrepreneurial activity can be divided into two sets of factors, those that 'push' and 'pull' people into undertaking entrepreneurial activity. Individuals can be pushed into entrepreneurship by factors such as a desire for greater job security or redundancy. In such cases entrepreneurship may be preferable to insecure employment or unemployment. Economic factors that may pull individuals into entrepreneurship relate to the identification of market opportunities in the pursuit of profit. There may also be sociological and psychological pull factors, such as a feeling of frustration with working in a large organization, a desire for independence and a desire for greater self-esteem and social mobility.

Other researchers have emphasized the importance of motivations for choosing to sustain entrepreneurial activity. In this respect Kuratko *et al.* (1997) identify four sets of motivations: (1) extrinsic rewards, which relate to the accumulation of personal wealth and income; (2) independence/autonomy, which relate to a need for personal freedom and control; (3) intrinsic rewards, which relate to peer recognition and personal growth through meeting new challenges; (4) family security, which relate to the desire to build up a family business in order to pass it on to family members and to provide security for the family. In particular the importance of the non-pecuniary 'independence' motive as a factor contributing to the choice to undertake entrepreneurial activity is widely reported. It has also been suggested that there may be different facets to intrinsic motivations which are broadly termed 'independence'. On the one hand, creating a potentially profitable firm using sound business practices may be one way of achieving independence. On the other hand, independence in terms of 'leave me alone', and allowing the firm to be at the mercy of its environment implies something completely different. A small business cannot be completely self-contained, it is dependent upon suppliers, bankers, customers and so on.

Strategic choices and management practices

Turning now to consider the forms of managerial behaviour which are thought to be associated with successful small firms, it has been suggested that successful entrepreneurial strategies in small firms are likely to display a greater strategic awareness of the market environment and customers' requirements. In particular, it is suggested that an entrepreneurial strategy of focusing on market niches and developing a reputation within these niches, is a successful way for small firms to develop profit opportunities (Porter, 1980, 1985). An additional advantage of the niche market strategy is that small firms can remain protected from the typically more hostile competitive environments of wider markets for generic products. It may also be, however, that in niche markets for specialized products the level of demand is less than in wider markets for generic products, so that growth opportunities are constrained. In this regard, another strategy entrepreneurs in small firms may employ is diversification, although this may be difficult for small firms given the resources required. This may entail either supplying new products to the same geographical market or supplying the same products to new geographical markets, including export markets. Both of these approaches are potentially resource intensive and if a small firm's resource base is small, the risks of diversification are greater in that resources may be overstretched.

It has also been suggested that in developing an appropriate competitive strategy, entrepreneurs in successful small firms will: (1) undertake information gathering activities (also referred to as 'environmental scanning') in order to identify their market position; (2) develop formal strategic planning cycles; (3) make necessary adjustments to their product and customer base in order to keep ahead of the competition and set the pace in their markets; (4) develop their social network (see Chapter 6), which can increase both their reputation and knowledge base, thus reducing uncertainty in their economic environment and enabling them to identify new opportunities for profits and growth.

However, it has been suggested that the extent to which strategic management activities are adopted in small firms may be limited by the reluctance of some entrepreneurs to disengage from day-to-day management of the business, in favour of assuming a more strategic role. If entrepreneurs become too embroiled in addressing day-to-day management issues, they have less time to concentrate on strategic decisionmaking and planning the business's future direction. The inability of some entrepreneurs to take a more strategic managerial role in their business is a widely reported constraint on the performance of small firms.

Generalist theories of entrepreneurship

Attention now turns to consider approaches which have synthesized elements from economics, sociology, psychology and management science into what may be regarded as multi-disciplinary 'generalist' approaches. These approaches are more 'applied' in their orientation in that they seek to explain why some small businesses perform better than others, and in doing so they relate particular aspects of entrepreneurial attributes and behaviour to small firm performance. It is from these generalist approaches that a more rounded view of entrepreneurship and its relationship with the performance of individual firms can be derived. There are some problems with adopting such a micro-level analytical perspective, however, and these are commented on at the end of this section.

In broad terms, generalist approaches address the questions, 'what is the impact of personal attributes on small business performance?', and 'what are the features of entrepreneurship as a process and as a form of behaviour in developing a business?'. The second of these questions is not concerned with the personal attributes of individuals *per se*, but with the types of behaviour that are displayed by individuals (who may possess a variety of personal attributes) in the process of undertaking entrepreneurial activity. This broad categorization of the two main issues addressed in the generalist theories of entrepreneurship represents what has been a vigorous debate in the multi-disciplinary literature in this field of study.

The first of the generalist theories to be considered is that of Smith (1967), who differentiates between different types of entrepreneur who possess different personal characteristics, and who have different motivations and objectives. Smith differentiates between two types of entrepreneurs, which he labels 'craft' and 'opportunistic'. The craft entrepreneur is characterized by a working-class, blue-collar background, limited education but successful work experiences, a paternalistic management style and a reluctance to use outside sources of advice and finance. Craft entrepreneurs are not motivated by rational economic objectives such as profit and growth, but by intrinsic satisfactions such as independence and autonomy, although pursuit of these goals are subject to earning a sufficient minimum level of income to make a living from the business. For these individuals entrepreneurship represents a livelihood rather than a vehicle to accumulate personal wealth.

On the other hand, the opportunistic entrepreneur is characterized by a middle-class, white-collar background, a well rounded education, previous managerial experience, an aloof professional management style and a willingness to use external sources of advice and finance. These entrepreneurs are primarily motivated by profit and growth, although the pursuit of these objectives may be subject to an autonomy constraint when the firm grows to some size which is beyond their 'comfort level' of control. At this point opportunistic entrepreneurs may choose to sell their business. Furthermore, Smith suggests that only opportunistic entrepreneurs run flexible, adaptive firms which employ long-term planning horizons and use strategic marketing practices to achieve their goals.

Filley and Aldag (1978) also propose a typology of entrepreneurs similar to that of Smith's, but they distinguish further between two types of opportunistic entrepreneur. They propose a 'promotion' type of entrepreneur, who will pursue profit and high growth rates in the short term, employing a flexible organizational structure in which they are the nexus of control; in comparison to a 'administrative' type of entrepreneur, who is more managerial orientated and will grow the firm at a steady rate by developing a hierarchical organizational structure. Thus the performance of a firm will be determined by the type of entrepreneur who is in control of it.

The problem with these approaches is that while they recognize the importance of multi-disciplinary determinants of entrepreneurial activity, they implicitly assume that there can be no dynamic change in entrepreneurial type. At the time of forming their firm, an entrepreneur is either 'craft' or 'opportunistic' and the performance of the firm is determined from that moment on. There is, however, a body of thought which realizes that entrepreneurial activity is a dynamic process. Over time a particular individual may also learn and develop different forms of behaviour, skills and motivations. This body of thought also appreciates that the process of choosing to undertake entrepreneurship and the subsequent development of the business is dependent upon a range of economic, sociological and psychological factors.

For example, Chell (1985) has proposed a model which incorporates a range of these factors, which are termed 'appropriate person variables'. These include skills, perception of new experiences, behaviour towards options, and individual values and standards. Every individual is assumed to be on a learning curve and does not have a fixed entrepreneurial personality, but reacts and defines matters in relation to continuous experiences. Chell argues that at the start of the process of development an entrepreneur has limited skills and finds it hard to cope with the vast amount of new information with which he or she is faced. After a period in which the entrepreneur adapts to their new role and has acquired some of the skills needed to run a business, the firm becomes established. Growth beyond this point depends upon the motivation and objectives of the entrepreneur, which in turn, are influenced by their own expectations of what they are capable of achieving, the recognition of their efforts by outside parties, and their ability to deal with the even greater amount of information which must be processed if expansion is pursued. One way in which this information processing constraint may be overcome is by delegating specialist functions to a management team, although this may be limited by the desire of entrepreneurs to retain control over their firm.

Chell's model reflects a theme evident in other dynamic generalist models such as the 'social action' model proposed by Stanworth and Curran (1976). This approach is different to the 'stage' models evident in the management literature, in which all firms go through clearly defined and hierarchical stages of development. Stanworth and Curran argue that stage theory does not explain why most firms opt to remain at a certain size and why some people leave employment with large firms to start their own small firm. Their model stresses that firm growth depends upon the willingness of the entrepreneur to assume certain roles at different phases of the firm's development. They identify three such roles, which they term 'latent social identities'. The first of these is the 'artisan' identity, which is broadly comparable to Smith's craft entrepreneurial type, where income generation is secondary to intrinsic satisfactions such as life-style and job satisfaction. After a period in which the entrepreneur has gained confidence in running the business, he or she may assume a 'classical entrepreneur' identity, similar to Smith's 'opportunistic' type, where earnings are a core component of the entrepreneur's motivation.

The business may expand rapidly during this phase, although as it does so, forces emerge which push it towards a more bureaucratic structure. This necessitates the delegation of managerial functions and the entrepreneur has to assume a 'manager' identity, adopting a more administrative function, where goals are oriented towards peer recognition of managerial excellence. The desire to build up a substantial enough capital base to pass on to offspring may also be an important motivating factor in the manager identity. Firms which have grown to this size and organizational structure are the relatively more 'successful' small firms and thus offspring will be socialized into successful entrepreneurship.

Not all entrepreneurs, however, will be willing to adopt the latter two identities, as they may conflict with their original motivations for choosing to undertake entrepreneurship. Some entrepreneurs may simply not want to expand their firms, whether or not they are capable of doing so, in terms of both internal competencies and external market conditions. Other entrepreneurs may be willing to assume these latter identities regardless of whether or not they conflict with, or reinforce, their original motivations for undertaking entrepreneurship.

While non-economic approaches to analysing small firm performance have stressed entrepreneur-specific and firm-specific attributes, some researchers have argued that it is difficult to disentangle these variables from exogenous factors. Many of these variables, such as social class, education and possession of managerial experience may be highly interrelated, so that it is difficult to separate out causal variables determining the process of why individuals choose entrepreneurial activity and the subsequent performance of their business. For example, if an entrepreneur does not want to grow because he or she has reached some 'comfort level' of firm size, is this because of intrinsic motivations and objectives, or because the firm has already reached its optimum level of output given the market it trades in and further expansion would require a degree of business acumen which the entrepreneur does not possess? Incorporating too much of reality into theories has its weaknesses – in terms of confusing matters – as well as its strengths.

The advantages of adopting a generalist approach are evident, in that it can help to explain in greater detail the practical nature of entrepreneurship, and as such it can provide a better all-round focus of thought than any of the social sciences on their own. This is not a criticism of the individual social sciences, they all provide a valid insight into entrepreneurship in their own right, but combining elements from all approaches undoubtedly provides a better overview of the concept at an applied analytical level. The main disadvantages, however, arise from the greater level of detail. Sometimes incorporating too much detail into theory can make it difficult to develop a clear perspective on a concept. The purpose of a theory is to provide a clear focus of thought on a concept and not to account for all aspects of the concept in reality.

Theories offering alternative viewpoints on a concept such as entrepreneurship can be compared against each other and their relative value in helping to understand the concept can be judged. By considering too much reality at one time it is sometimes difficult to disentangle the important factors which influence a concept, and thus isolate the key variables which can be applied across a range of contexts. The illustrations which follow are intended to help illuminate some of the advantages and disadvantages of adopting a generalist perspective on entrepreneurship and its relationships with the performance of small firms.

Illustration

Small firm entrepreneurs

Presented below are three profiles of small firm entrepreneurs prepared from fieldwork research undertaken by the authors. All three firms are single establishment manufacturing companies located in Britain. All three firms have less than 25 employees, are owned and managed by one distinctive entrepreneur and have been established for at least 10 years. The three profiles provided have been selected to illustrate a broad range of the multi-disciplinary themes considered in this chapter. It is by no means suggested that the three profiles are typical of small firms in general, rather they are intended to allow the reader to help illuminate the theoretical perspectives on small firm entrepreneurship.

Profile 1: Mr A – 'Engines Inc.'

The firm's main activity is subcontracted light engineering although larger scale heavy engineering projects are also undertaken periodically. Mr A is 51 years old and is the sole owner of the firm, which he founded at the age of 40. He previously had other business interests in the form of a minority stockholding in another engineering company. This company failed and he 'would not consider it again', having made a large loss on his investment.

Mr A has no formal educational qualifications and served an apprenticeship in a shipyard after leaving school. He remained in the shipyards for the duration of his working life before forming his own firm. In the three years previous to this event he was employed as a foreman in a large engineering plant specializing in ship repair. However, this plant closed when the owners relocated its operations, thus making Mr A redundant. At the time, he did not believe that there were any other job opportunities available and that he was 'forced' to start his own business 'in order to earn a living'. He did not perceive the venture as risky, believing that there were good opportunities for small engineering firms to specialize in ship repair. His considerable knowledge of the industry, and the network of contacts he had made over the years, 'gave the business a running start', the finance being provided from his redundancy package. He had no ambitions for the firm initially in terms of growth and profitability, his goal for the business was merely survival.

Initially, he obtained work through his network of contacts, but the firm's customer base grew quickly. This increase in demand led Mr A to expand the firm's operations rapidly and to seek out larger premises to accommodate the growing workforce and stock of capital equipment. The firm's workforce had quadrupled during the course of his stewardship. He attributes the firm's success largely to growing demand for its work; he has been reactive to the needs of his growing customer base. The only problem he encountered in the early days of the venture was his own ability to manage not just the production side of the firm but also to make 'business decisions'. 'There's no manual telling you how to be a managing director. You just have to learn by doing, and by making mistakes.'

He made no active attempt to seek out customers and had 'turned down nothing' that was offered to him. His customer base is diverse, ranging from very small scale precision engineering work for small, local companies, to larger scale projects for multinational companies. The nature of the work undertaken has changed over the years away from heavy engineering work such as ship repair, to light engineering work such as components manufacture. This has been largely determined, however, by the nature of the contracts offered. There was no conscious strategy to target an expanding market for light engineering work instead of a declining market for heavy engineering work. He is satisfied with the firm's performance in terms of growth and profitability. 'It just happened. The jobs got bigger and we just branched out. We have always been profitable.'

Mr A's wife undertakes all of the administration and he relies heavily on his accountant for advice as he has 'no commercial acumen'. Mr A concentrates on supervising production activities and he still derives the greatest satisfaction from being in the workshop 'with the men'. However, he is unable to do as much hands-on work as he would like to due to ill-health, and his role in the workshop is largely as a foreman. Ill-health has 'forced' him to delegate more, but he still prefers to oversee the workshop. His reputation has been built on the quality of his work and he does not trust the workforce to come up to his own high standards unless he is there 'to push them on'.

The financial rewards from his firm have always been much greater than those from his previous employment. He has never been primarily motivated by financial gain, however, believing that his motivations are more personal, in terms of 'surviving when many go down', and 'a sense of achievement'. Another satisfying aspect of the entrepreneurial position for him, is being able to 'help men in employment'. He has always encouraged his workers to undergo training, and he has always been reluctant to lay workers off. Throughout his stewardship of the firm there has been little staff turnover. He has no plans, however, to expand the business beyond its current size in any respect. He is satisfied with the size of the workforce, which he regards as 'still manageable', and taking on a larger volume of work would require larger premises and more capital equipment. This in turn would require some borrowing which he is opposed to, preferring to be entirely self-financed through retained profits. He does not like 'too many overheads', and if the firm grew larger, 'there would be more hassle with admin'. Further expansion would require him to assume a more active role in the commercial administration of the business, which he has no intention of doing.

He believes that constraints on the firm's activities are largely self-imposed. Mr A's sole objective is to maintain the firm's profitability and to ensure its survival at the present level of production, although he would have no qualms about selling the firm if offered the right price. While he does not mind working the long hours required, he admits that his motivation has 'waned through time'.

Profile 2: Mr B – 'Wood Inc.'

The firm's main activities are wooden furniture manufacture and specialized wooden goods manufactured to order. Mr B is 56 years old and is the majority owner of the firm, with his son being a minority owner. He bought the firm from receivers when he was 38 years old.

Mr B emigrated to Britain from Eastern Europe after the Second World War, having received only 'basic schooling' in his home country. Soon after arriving in Britain, he attended evening classes in order to gain university entrance qualifications. He then won a scholarship at a prestigious British university and graduated in mathematics. Mr B's son is also a graduate and Mr B has strong views about the importance of education, believing that 'an education gives you a better chance.'

After graduating, Mr B worked for a large company as a mathematician. He held several senior posts and his last post before leaving the company entailed heading a team responsible for mathematical simulations of the company's operations. While in this post he had a failed attempt at a part-time data processing business. Mr B attributes the failure of this venture to a lack of demand for the service at that time.

Mr B formed his own firm after working for 15 years in secure and highly paid employment. He had accumulated substantial personal capital and his wife also had a highly paid job. Having planned to become self-employed over a period of five years, he had easy access to company information at the time and had looked for a 'good buy'. This turned out to be a failed business in a remote rural area, and no problems had been encountered in buying over the firm from receivers. The capital was provided mostly from personal savings, although a small grant was obtained from a development agency. Mr B's motivation for instigating the buy-over was a dissatisfaction with his previous employment. 'I had gone as high as I could, and I saw a lot of my colleagues being moved sideways, but not up the way. I wanted some control over where I was going, more stability'.

Financial rewards were not a consideration at the time and the financial rewards from entrepreneurship have never been near the same level as those from his previous employment. He had no experience of manufacturing furniture prior to the event, but the firm came with a sizeable house in a scenic location and his wife was also able to transfer employment to the area, thus providing some financial stability to the venture. A steady income along with no external borrowing reduced the risk of the venture, although Mr B was not sure if he would be 'any good at the job'. However, he was sure that this was going to be a long-term venture. Mr B's primary goal, which has not changed since the beginning is 'to make enough money to keep ticking over'.

Expansion had never been an objective, although currently he has plans for 'steady expansion on the mass production side'. A second workshop on the premises had just been equipped with second-hand machinery to this end. The expansion of the firm was being financed out of a 'small' profit and working capital. While Mr B formed the firm to gain more control over his life, and the firm had provided a livelihood, his main concern now is to develop the firm in order to hand it onto his son. What his son did with the firm (sell, expand, maintain at present level of activity) was entirely up to him.

Mr B is winding down his involvement in the firm, concentrating primarily on the financial and commercial side of the business. His son is responsible for high volume production and Mr B indicates that 'things really took off when my son joined the firm after graduating'. On the production side Mr B still undertakes 'craftsman jobs' for custom-made products, which gives him a great deal of satisfaction given that he is self-taught. While he undertakes the 'office jobs', he still feels the need for hands-on work. This need, however, is not directed at the financially important, but routine, mass production activities, but the specialist one-off jobs. Employee numbers had remained unchanged during his stewardship of the firm, with all his workers being long-term. He places great emphasis on fostering good working relations with employees.

The firm has one major customer for the mass produced products which 'helps to keep the place going'. In addition to this customer, the firm has supplied specialist products to customers nation-wide. Mr B makes no effort to seek out new customers and relies entirely on the firm's reputation. With respect to external finance, while he has no objection to leasing assets or taking them on hire purchase, he does not want to borrow from banks. He had made an approach to a development agency for financial assistance with his current expansion plans, but found them 'too bureaucratic'. He refused a proposed loan because he did not want 'to feel indebted to them'. He prefers to be self-financed in order to 'retain control of the firm', and he has never sought advice or information from external parties. While trading conditions in general had been 'slow and competitive', the contract with the major customer and the good relations with smaller customers throughout the country had helped to stabilize trading. Mr B believes that 'it could have been a lot tougher'.

Profile 3: Mr C – 'Cloth Inc.'

The firm's main activity is cloth manufacture. Mr C is 46 years old and the sole owner of the firm. He founded the firm at the age of 36 through a management buyout of a plant owned by his previous employers. His family has a history of self-employment with the previous three generations of his family having owned a firm, which was also in the textiles business.

Mr C is a graduate in business administration. He regards this qualification as a valuable aid to his business career, although it had been supplemented heavily by knowledge acquired through 'hands-on' experience. After graduating from university, Mr C joined the family firm, gaining experience in all aspects of the business and eventually settling into the role of sales director. He remained with the firm for several years until his father sold the firm to a multinational company. The company retained the services of Mr C, although they relocated him to another of their subsidiaries, where he remained in the position of sales manager. After two years in the post, the holding company indicated that they intended to run down the subsidiary and Mr C was asked to preside over the streamlining. At the same time he was allowed to act as an overseas agent for other textile companies. This experience was invaluable for Mr C in building up a network of trade contacts.

After the streamlining, the holding company indicated that they intended to sell off the subsidiary and offered it to Mr C as a management buyout. However, they gave only one month's notice before the firm's impending closure. At the time, Mr C felt that he had no option other than to accept the offer although he perceived it as being risky given 'family considerations'. His motivation was 'necessity', having perceived that alternative employment opportunities in the area were not good. He had not previously considered starting his own firm and had no other motivations at the start of the venture other than 'to make it work'. This entailed ensuring the firm's survival in the short term and providing a livelihood. His accountant assisted him in putting together a financial package to buy out the subsidiary, which consisted largely of long-term bank loans. He has no objections against borrowing and has subsequently obtained an additional term loan from a development agency. He believes that 'the borrowing requirement will never decrease' in an expansion-minded firm.

His primary strategy at the start of the venture was 'to make the company more efficient', which was aimed at increasing the volume of production gradually and expanding the turnover of the firm in the longer term. 'The potential was there for a high quality element in the market, but the market has tight margins, therefore the price has to be right'. Consequently, by improving the efficiency of production and operating with minimal overheads and as small a workforce as possible, Mr C hoped to maintain the profitability of the firm while gradually expanding turnover. The workforce inherited from the subsidiary had been cut to a third of its original level during his stewardship. His experience in the industry had taught him that, 'There's no such thing as an overnight success. The secret is stability and gradual expansion'.

The family firm owned by his father had expanded too rapidly and had subsequently experienced difficulties through overtrading. This experience meant that Mr C had 'learned the hard way'. His strategy had not changed during his stewardship of the firm and it had taken several years to 'get the gross margin right', and to 'establish volume consistent with turnover'. He had increased profitability by clearing out the least profitable lines and concentrating on the most viable in terms of production and sales. He has restored the firm's turnover to the same level it was when it was most successful as a subsidiary, although the product base was narrower and the customer base was wider. The firm also has a strong export base, a factor which had prompted Mr C to computerize the firm's administration systems, an action which he believes has facilitated the expansion of turnover.

Mr C's motivations have always been largely personal, rather than financial, although he is satisfied with the level of financial reward. They have provided 'a comfortable rather than extravagant living'. 'The way of life is more important for me. Its been a very interesting experience'. He regards the downside to the entrepreneurial position as being the level of commitment required which impacts on family life, although he has tried to minimize this as far as possible. The years, however, have taken their toll. 'I have the experience and knowledge, but not the same drive or energy'.

He has thought about selling the firm, but this is dependent on whether his family wishes to perpetuate the firm as a family business. If the decision was entirely his own he 'would not hesitate to sell it'. In these circumstances he is sure that he would never work for another employer and would only consider entrepreneurship as an alternative. He believes that the firm is in a good position as only the 'strongest firms in the industry have survived'. The 'next big jump in turnover' was dependent on more marketing, and to reach the demand for the product he plans to undertake more advertising and publicity. His marketing strategy in the past has been to personally visit customers, although he had not been able to do this recently, having had to devote all of his time to the day-to-day management of the firm. Mr C is responsible for all the managerial functions in the firm, only delegating shopfloor production activities. 'Delegation only works if you have the right people. Its very difficult to delegate, having done it all yourself to begin with'.

He perceives this to be the biggest constraint on the firm's activities and that 'we really need another body'. The greatest need is to take over the financial management of the firm in particular, which takes up most of his time. He feels that he will 'be forced' to delegate managerial duties in the future. Despite his reluctance to delegate managerial duties, he has no qualms about using the services of external business advisers and has done so on several occasions.

Multi-disciplinary themes

The aim of this section is twofold: first, to derive general themes from the previous considerations of economic, sociological, psychological, management and generalist theories of entrepreneurship; second to derive the economic implications of non-economic perspectives on entrepreneurship. In doing so, it must be appreciated that there are no 'correct' interpretations of the material and this section is merely intended to be indicative of the major issues which may be identified across a wide range of the academic literature on entrepreneurship.

It was suggested earlier that motivations for undertaking entrepreneurial activity may be divided into two sets of factors, those which push and pull individuals into undertaking entrepreneurial activity. Research work (for example, see Storey, 1994) suggests that there is no evidence to support any claim that firms managed by entrepreneurs who are pushed into entrepreneurial activity are more likely to fail than those pulled into it. They are, however, far less likely to grow. From the perspective of economic regeneration, it has been suggested that entrepreneurs who are pushed into self-employment generally have less impact, because they tend to undertake such activity at the lowest point in the economic cycle, when low aggregate demand offsets any positive contribution they may make to economic regeneration. These entrepreneurs tend to set up in the industries in which they have previous experience. Unfortunately, these industries tend to be the ones in decline, in which lack of demand has led to job insecurity or redundancy in the first place.

On the other hand, entrepreneurs who are pulled into entrepreneurial activity through identifying a new market opportunity, will tend to set up in new industries employing new technologies, in which there is growing product demand. It is these firms, in which entrepreneurs are generally motivated by profit and growth, that form the seedbed of new firms with growth potential. Some researchers have raised the question, 'are all small firm owner-managers necessarily entrepreneurs?'. In this regard, it has been suggested that the term 'entrepreneur' has cultural values attached to it which give approval to certain forms of activity that contribute positively to economic development. However, the vast majority of people who start their own business are not entrepreneurs in this ideal sense. The hallowed term entrepreneur, it is argued, should be reserved for those individuals who are in the mould of the opportunistic, innovative type.

Despite the limited number of small firms which do expand to any significant size, the aggregate importance of the small firm sector is not disputed by most writers. The small firm sector on aggregate is an important source of employment generation and many small firms provide goods for specialist markets which large firms are not interested in, to the benefit of consumers. Furthermore, the dynamic and turbulent nature of the small firm sector, with its high rates of firm births and firm deaths, is in contrast to the relatively stable corporate sector. Some researchers have therefore argued that it is a sterile debate as to whether there is a distinction between an owner-manager and an entrepreneur in the small firm sector. The key point to emerge from the literature is that small business entrepreneurs are a heterogeneous group. Motivations for undertaking entrepreneurial activity are not consistent between individuals, with some motivations orientated towards rational economic objectives, and some not.

Small firm performance is evidently a more complex process than is proposed in conventional economic theory, which mainly emphasizes exogenous determinants. Furthermore, assumptions made by economic models that entrepreneurs are motivated primarily by financial gain are not, on the whole, borne out by the evidence. Research on the motivations and objectives of small business owner-managers has stressed the importance of the 'independence' motive, both as a pull factor contributing to entrepreneurial choice and as a constraint on the ensuing performance of the firm. The desire to retain control of the firm, and a failure to delegate authority, imposes a constraint on further growth after some 'comfort' level of organizational size has been reached.

The relationships between end goals and means goals in small entrepreneurial firms may be important in this regard. Goal-setting and behavioural practices aimed at achieving goals in small entrepreneurial firms are more sophisticated than simple assumptions of profit maximization, constrained profit maximization (for those entrepreneurs primarily motivated by autonomy), growth maximization, or constrained growth maximization. Profits affect other objectives as well as being an end goal in their own right. Growth orientated entrepreneurs will need profits to either provide internal finance for expansion, or to convince lenders or investors to provide external finance. A profitable business also provides greater security for entrepreneurs motivated by life-style goals and who do not wish to pursue growth. On the other hand, addressing the profit performance of their business may only be forced upon some entrepreneurs by periods of crisis, and profit performance may be improved by retrenchment and cost reduction rather than by targeting new market opportunities.

For other entrepreneurs, building up a portfolio of businesses may be one way of achieving security and growth at the same time. It has been suggested that the view of business growth being expressed in terms of a single small business unit becoming larger is too limited. There may be 'portfolio' entrepreneurs who own several small businesses, which on aggregate may represent substantial levels of employment, output and turnover in local economies. The closure of a business unit may not necessarily constitute entrepreneurial failure. Entrepreneurs may choose to close or sell one business to concentrate on others.

It is evident that these features may not be identified by concentrating on the business as the unit of analysis and not the entrepreneur. It was suggested in Chapter 6 that supply chains are becoming more fragmented in many sectors, and interconnections between businesses are such that it is becoming more difficult to judge where the boundaries of any single business lie. The implications of this distinction are important in these circumstances, as judging entrepreneurial performance on the basis of a single business unit does not take account of the jobs created and value added along the supply chain. If an entrepreneur secures a major contract, subcontracts work down the supply chain and helps create £1 million turnover and 100 jobs in other businesses, this is not reflected when measuring the performance of the entrepreneur's own business.

Another dimension to business growth is that there may be societal pressures in favour of it. If it is socially accepted that growth represents the purpose of being in business in an 'enterprise culture', then failure to grow may be culturally perceived as failure outright. This may be a negative influence for many entrepreneurs who try to expand their businesses too rapidly and fail through stretching their resources too far. Some researchers have questioned what is entailed by the term 'small firm performance'. It has been suggested that if a small firm can survive through the economic cycle, then that is the best measure of success. It is the aggregate importance of the whole of the small firm sector which determines its contribution to the economy and not the performance of a few high growth small firms. Survival in itself requires the ability to adapt to change and to make judgmental decisions. Thus small firm entrepreneurs on aggregate are every bit as important as large firm entrepreneurs in deploying scarce resources.

The entrepreneurship paradigm

The discussion of the different theoretical approaches to studying entrepreneurship and small firm performance identifies the fundamentally multi-disciplinary nature of the topic. This argument can be taken further and it has been suggested that the study of entrepreneurship may be an emerging 'science' in its own right. This has important implications for empirical methodologies and the process of theory construction in the study of entrepreneurship. In this regard, the study of entrepreneurship has been suggested as being a unique academic discipline which requires the adoption of a fresh perspective, which Bygrave (1989) has termed the 'entrepreneurship paradigm'.

Here it is argued that the study of entrepreneurial choice and development has evolved by using the theories and methodologies of established social sciences such as economics, sociology and psychology. Such methods need to be developed to be able to take account of the complexity of the variables which determine entrepreneurship. Statistical methods developed for studying predictable linear production functions or processes may often not be applicable to the study of entrepreneurship, which is typically a non-linear and discontinuous process. Bygrave levels this criticism at studies which, he argues, have been dominated by 'physics envy', in the application of sophisticated mathematical procedures to analyse hypotheses derived using deductive reasoning. Rather less precise, but more meaningful, models may generate important insights.

It can be argued that in an emerging scientific paradigm, the emphasis should be placed on developing qualitative conceptual models which help to 'ground' theory in reality. Interpretation of statistics from quantitative analyses is often a subjective, qualitative process, which requires an advanced field of study where the knowledge base has been built up to a sufficient extent across a diverse range of contexts. An inductive approach, in parallel to a deductive approach, to theory development is a precursor to the development of many academic disciplines. Even in physics great theories such as the law of gravity were developed from empirical observation. Description and explanation precede prediction.

Bygrave argues that in the study of entrepreneurship, an understanding of the basic concepts has been overridden by a desire to apply analytical techniques which were developed in more advanced fields of study, to the prediction of entrepreneurial choice and performance. Thus in an emerging entrepreneurship paradigm, in which emphasis is placed upon the dynamic process of entrepreneurship, it is argued that there should be greater analysis of the performance of small entrepreneurial firms using fieldwork methods such as in-depth interviews and observation. This is in order to generate theory which is grounded in reality, and which can provide the building blocks for the development of a body of higher level theory for an entrepreneurship science. It is perhaps worth noting that the argument for the development of an 'entrepreneurship science' is in itself entrepreneurial. This is in the sense that it challenges established routines and ways of thinking, and suggests that change and adaptation to change are required to establish a new order.

Conclusion

The main economic implications which arise from incorporating non-economic factors influencing entrepreneurial activity can be considered in terms of the reasons why individuals decide to undertake entrepreneurial activity and the subsequent performance of their firms. It is suggested that two broad sets of factors which determine entrepreneurial activity can be identified, they are, 'push' factors and 'pull' factors. Only the latter corresponds to the perception of entrepreneurship in economic theory of opportunistic and innovative activity. People who are 'pushed' into entrepreneurial activity will generally not manage small firms with growth potential.

This is not to say that this will always be the case. Dynamic generalist theories of entrepreneurial development suggest that some of these entrepreneurs may develop into more 'businesslike' entrepreneurs pursuing profit and growth and implementing strategic managerial practices to achieve those goals. However, the evidence is that the majority will not, and their firms will remain small and will not individually add much value to the economy, although the firm will still contribute to the employment of the owner and their employees. It is important though, to look at the issue of entrepreneurship in the small firm sector at an aggregate level, taking account of wider relationships between firms and not to disproportionately concentrate on the performance of a few exceptional high growth firms.

References and further reading

Brockhaus, R.H., Snr (1980) 'Risk taking propensity of entrepreneurs', *Academy of Management Journal*, Vol. 23, pp. 509–20.
Bygrave, W.D. (1989) 'The entrepreneurship paradigm (I): A philosophical look at its research methodologies', *Entrepreneurship Theory and Practice*, Vol. 12, pp. 7–26.

Chell, E. (1985) 'The entrepreneurial personality: A few ghosts laid to rest', *International Small Business Journal*, Vol. 3, pp. 43–54.

Churchill, N.C. and V.L. Lewis (1983) 'The five stages of business growth', *Harvard Business Review*, Vol. 61, pp. 30–50.

Filley, A.C. and R.J. Aldag (1978) 'Characteristics and measurement of an organizational typology', *Academy of Management Journal*, Vol. 21, pp. 578–91.

Flamholtz, E.G. (1986) *How to Make the Transition from Entrepreneurship to a Professionally Managed Firm*, San Francisco, Jossey Bass.

Gibb, A.A. and J. Ritchie (1981) 'Understanding the process of starting small businesses', *European Journal of Small Business*, Vol. 1, pp. 26–45.

Kets de Vries, M.F.R. (1977) 'The entrepreneurial personality: A person at the crossroads', *Journal of Management Studies*, Vol. 14, pp. 34–57.

Kuratko, D.F, J.S. Hornsby and D.W. Naffziger (1997) 'An examination of owners' goals in sustaining entrepreneurship', *Journal of Small Business Management*, Vol. 35, pp. 3525–30.

McClelland, D.C. (1961) *The Achieving Society*, Princeton, NJ Van Nostrand.

Oswald, A.J. and D.G. Blanchflower (1998) What makes an entrepreneur? *Journal of Labor Economics*, Vol. 16, pp. 26–60.

Porter, M.E. (1980) *Competitive Strategy*, New York, Free Press.

Porter, M.E. (1985) *Competitive Advantage*, New York, Free Press.

Reynolds, P.D. (1991) 'Sociology and entrepreneurship: Concepts and contributions', *Entrepreneurship Theory and Practice*, Vol. 14, pp. 47–70.

Robinson, P.B., D.V. Stimpson, J.C. Huefner and H.K. Hunt (1991) 'An attitude approach to the prediction of entrepreneurship', *Entrepreneurship Theory and Practice*, Vol. 14, pp. 13–31.

Rotter, J.B. (1975) 'Some problems and misconceptions related to the construct of internal versus external control of reinforcement', *Journal of Consulting and Clinical Psychology*, Vol. 43, pp. 489–93.

Sandberg, W.R. (1992) 'Strategic management's potential contributions to a theory of entrepreneurship', *Entrepreneurship Theory and Practice*, Vol. 15, pp. 73–90.

Scase, R. and R. Goffee (1982) *The Entrepreneurial Middle Class*, London, Croom Helm.

Shapero, A. (1984) 'The entrepreneurial event', in C.A. Kent, (ed.), *The Environment for Entrepreneurship*, pp. 21–40, Lexington, Mass., D.C. Heath.

Shaver, K.G. and L.R. Scott (1991) 'Person, process, choice: The psychology of new venture creation', *Entrepreneurship Theory and Practice*, Vol. 14, pp. 23–45.

Smith, N.R. (1967) *The Entrepreneur and his Firm: The Relationship between Type of Man and Type of Company*, East Lansing, Michigan State University Press.

Stanworth, M.J.K and J. Curran (1976) 'Growth and the smaller firm – An alternative view', *Journal of Management Studies*, Vol. 12, pp. 95–110.

Stevenson, H.H. and W.A. Sahlman, (1989) 'The entrepreneurial process', in P. Burns, and J. Dewhurst (eds), *Small Business and Entrepreneurship*, pp. 94–157, Basingstoke, Macmillan Education.

Storey, D.J. (1994) *Understanding the Small Business Sector*, London, Routledge.

Weber, M. (1930) *The Protestant Ethic and the Spirit of Capitalism*, London, Allen and Unwin.

Part III

Policy and Entrepreneurship in the Wider Society

8
Social Entrepreneurship

Introduction

As with profit orientated entrepreneurs, social entrepreneurs apply new perspectives and innovations and significantly change what things or services are produced, how they are produced and/or how their organizations operate. There have been many such social entrepreneurs and innovators down the ages. We start by looking at some examples of these before considering social entrepreneurship in business related organizations and civic entrepreneurship in government.

Florence Nightingale used her creativity to act innovatively, change how medical care was practised and develop new types of medical organizations. She changed peoples' ideas of healthcare and set up organizations to nurture the new nursing profession. Similarly, Mozart created dramatic new musical forms as well as developing a commercial opera house. Thinkers may also generate ideas which open up vistas for others to act on entrepreneurially. For instance, in the fifteenth century Copernicus showed that the earth is not the centre of the solar system but rather that the sun is. This went against the views of both his professional scientific peers and of the most powerful religious leaders. In the end scientific evidence showed his idea to be more valid and he completely changed the perception or paradigm with which people viewed the earth and its relationship to the universe.

More recently there are many examples of innovative individuals or groups setting-up major organizations with social rather than profit aims. Some examples include organizations such as Greenpeace who have excelled in 'marketing' their environmental message, or Oxfam who developed new ways of raising funds for charity and new policies to promote the long-term development of areas facing famine. Indeed many of the best hospitals and universities in the United States and elsewhere employ social entrepreneurs. These organizations are major employers and 'businesses' with large turnovers, which remain wedded to their wider social goals and their commitments to their core social values.

Peter Drucker (1985, p. 21) suggested that there was no better text for the history of entrepreneurship than the creation and development of the modern university. He used as an example Humboldt University in Berlin which was developed in 1809 to help give Germany and its industry scientific and intellectual leadership. Then by the end of that century US universities developed and expanded giving them leadership in research and scholarship in many areas. A new type of US university developed in the second-half of the twentieth century with part-time and flexible hours for attendance, in order to meet the needs of students in work. The educational entrepreneur has also risen to greater prominence in the last decade. For instance, in the UK and elsewhere High School headteachers have increasingly taken an explicit leadership and entrepreneurial role involving: the identification and taking of opportunities; innovation; and the co-ordination of resources. However, many argue that this is only successful if professional standards, and the primacy of their educational mission and of the students' learning, are fully maintained and improved.

In the US there is a long history of innovation and entrepreneurship in the non-profit sector which, according to 'Giving USA', accounted for 8 per cent of the GDP. Americans donated some $175 billion to non-profit organizations in 1998. In the UK the not-for-profit sector has an estimated turnover of over £12 billion per year, and has a share of GDP comparable to that of agriculture.

There are also many examples of commercial entrepreneurs who acted upon their feelings of strong social and moral responsibilities. From the Victorian era examples include Lord Lever, the founder of the soap manufacturer who built a strong commercial firm (which became the giant Lever Bros. Corporation), but at his initial Sunlight factory at Port Sunlight in north-west England he also built a high quality (for its time) village with housing for the workers. Similarly, the Quaker food and chocolate producers such as Cadbury near Birmingham and Rowntree in York provided housing and educational facilities for their workers and families, that were far ahead of their time and were not motivated by purely commercial factors.

This chapter does not attempt to describe and analyse the history or breadth of social or scientific innovators and social entrepreneurship. It concentrates upon those organizations with predominantly social objectives, but which also operate, at least in part, as businesses. It starts by discussing social entrepreneurs, then it goes on to consider one type of business (community business) specifically set up with social and commercial objectives. Another form of business (co-operatives) which can often exhibit collective entrepreneurship is then considered, and finally civic entrepreneurship in government is briefly discussed.

Social entrepreneurs

Entrepreneurship assumes many forms. It may be manifested through usual business structures such as public corporations or companies, partnerships or sole traders. It may also occur in other forms of business such as co-operatives or community businesses, or in other organizations including third or not-for-profit sector bodies, government or educational institutions.

The changing causes and nature of social problems requires much innovative thinking and entrepreneurial action. Society continually undergoes social, economic and political changes, generating new needs, such as community-based urban regeneration, or refashioning old problems, such as drugs, crime, bad housing, lack of facilities for young or old people and so on. Although in absolute terms a poor person in most developed countries may be much better off today than a skilled working person a century ago, in relative terms they are still poor. So poverty is likely to remain a permanent issue, although its nature may change. So entrepreneurial thinking and behaviour will constantly be required to deal with such social issues.

Innovative solutions, often with limited resources, are regularly called for. This may involve generating and acting on new ideas, or providing new services or 'old' services in a new way. It may also involve creating new organizations or ways of delivering services such as combining the activities of many different agencies to tackle a multi-faceted problem. All of these require entrepreneurship, so social entrepreneurs need to use the entrepreneurial skills discussed in Chapter 1 to meet social needs.

In the last two decades there has also been a move by public sector bodies, such as local government, from directly providing welfare and other services themselves toward them contracting with other organizations for the provision of the service. Often these are not-for-profit bodies particularly in areas such as social services. This is often done to increase competition among producers and choice for consumers and to provide more flexible services. This has partly resulted in such not-for-profit bodies becoming more 'business like' and entrepreneurial, so as to get contracts to deliver the services and to operate more efficiently and effectively when they have the contracts.

In considering the growth in importance of social entrepreneurs in meeting such challenges, Leadbetter (1997) suggests: they concentrate on social outputs, that is, ones that promote health, welfare and well being; their core assets are forms of social capital (relationships, networks, trust and co-operation) which then give them access to other physical and financial resources; the organizations they operate in are not-for-profit, that is, they do not have profit as their main aim and usually do not distribute their profits to their owners; they may have a variety of motivations; and often social entrepreneurs are seeking to regenerate particular communities. Hence their main differences from profit orientated entrepreneurs are their motivation and resulting aims, and they should have a strong moral integrity underlying how they go about achieving their aims.

Social entrepreneurs achieve their aims through realizing innovative solutions to social problems, and utilizing under-used resources (for example, people, premises, equipment) to meet identified community or client needs. Hence they may work in public, private or the third sector organizations. This echoes Say's nineteenth-century view of an entrepreneur as organizer of resources (see Chapter 1). Of course, innovative solutions should not simply be innovative for their own sake but must also be effective and efficient or else they may be wasteful and use resources that would be better allocated elsewhere. As Peter Drucker (1992) argues, effective non-profit organizations, or social entrepreneurs, should be governed by good performance in achieving their objectives rather than by their good intentions.

Young (1983) suggests that social entrepreneurs follow a similar process to other entrepreneurs. In general they follow a sequence which starts with idea generation, which may include an opportunity or new solution to a problem identified, usually through systematic analysis of the situation. In the next phase resources have to be gathered or developed, through reallocation of existing resources or gaining new resources from potential stakeholders. Next the path-clearing phase involves overcoming other institutional barriers, such as licences, changing mandates for the organization and so on. Then the leadership and management of the venture must be organized so that it will be self-sustaining, although the entrepreneur, or entrepreneurial team, may not necessarily take the management role. This latter point contrasts with the view of entrepreneurs as being both the initiator or founder of an organization and its manager, but may be consistent with the view of entrepreneurship as the 'event' of setting-up a new organization. Finally after the plans, resources and leadership are in place and necessary permissions obtained, the project itself must be organized and implemented through obtaining and directing, for instance, staff hire, securing and occupation of premises and equipment.

This process is similar to the general strategic decisionmaking and implementation process (see the Appendix on business plans). It involves networking and collaboration among potential stakeholders who may have a stake in the project, including clients and funders of the project, and the entrepreneur (or team of entrepreneurs). It will normally involve a division of labour with delegation of various activities, but with the entrepreneur assuming responsibility for making things happen and driving the project forward. The success in generating the project will depend on both the entrepreneur and other stakeholders and on other factors such as the surrounding economic, social, political, cultural environments. People and organizations are not static and may go through stages of intense entrepreneurial activity and change followed by equilibrium or even stagnation. So the act of setting-up a project needs to be followed by effective and efficient operation and further development.

In organizational terms, social entrepreneurs often create flexible organizations with flat structures, using paid and voluntary workers. Crucially they have the skills to effectively help combine a complex network of various individuals and organizations to tackle social needs. The entrepreneurs may generate and pilot new solutions or provide services more efficiently and effectively than before. To do this they often help build-up the social capital and capacity of the communities or client groups they work with in order to enable them to take greater control of their own destinies. The social entrepreneurs may share many common characteristics with private high-growth firms, for instance having clear vision and goals, professionalism, dynamism, and the ability and willingness to identify and realize opportunities. There is an important difference however, in that the needs of all the stakeholders are paramount, in particular those receiving the services or goods, rather than concentrating on growth or profits or the needs of shareholders. This means that social and private entrepreneurs may take different opportunities. For instance, some identified opportunities may not be taken by the social entrepreneur if they detract from meeting the needs of clients.

In summary social entrepreneurs exhibit entrepreneurial behaviour in a variety of ways, including developing innovative ways of operating, pulling together and allocating resources from many sources, and sometimes setting up or transforming new organizations. They differ from private commercial entrepreneurs in their focus upon their performance in achieving their social objectives rather than private or financial returns.

Illustration – Robert Owen

One of the most famous social entrepreneurs of the Victorian era was Robert Owen (1771–1858). He spanned both commercial and social entrepreneurship in Britain and America becoming one of the greatest social reformers of his time. Born the son of an ironmonger and saddler in Newtown in Wales, Owen started work as a shop assistant. By the time he was 30 he was managing a cotton-spinning mill in New Lanark, Scotland, eventually employing 2000 workers, including 500 apprenticed children from local pauper workhouses. He introduced radical management practices to his mill based upon 'principles of justice and kindness'. These included moving towards an eight-hour working day and good housing for the mill workers in 'co-operative' villages. He also set up an experimental, utopian community in New Harmony, Indiana, but that community lasted only a few years.

Owen also wrote about and provided education for the workers' children. This was innovative, at the time, being based upon offering a good living and schooling environment with patience and kindness in class rather than education based on punishment. He became the part-owner of the New Lanark cotton mill (which today is a World Heritage museum) and reduced working hours from 14-hours-a-day to 12 and tried to reduce them further to 10 hours or lower. Despite high profits at the mill he was prevented in doing this by his partners, so he found new investors to buy the mill.

Owen combined 'goodwill' towards staff and others with efficient organization. He was extremely innovative in both commercial and social terms, and well ahead of his time. Many of his management and social ideas are now accepted so widely that they are considered 'common sense'. Although some of his approaches to worker discipline would today be described as a 'paternalistic', they helped lead the way to the better conditions of today. In later life he became more radical in his criticism of the 'social system' and stressed even more vigorously the importance of reforming human character (Robert Owen, 1991).

Community businesses

Community businesses (or community enterprises as they are sometimes called) are mainly focused upon the wider benefits to the wider community rather than to individual members. A prime community benefit is often the provision of work, while others include physical improvements to neighbourhoods such as tree planting, or social services to local residents. A community business can be defined as a trading organization which is set-up and controlled by the local community and which aims to create community benefits and ultimately self-supporting jobs for local people. The profits of the business go towards creating further employment or providing local services or assisting other schemes of community benefit. The distinguishing features of community businesses are: that they trade their goods or services and so are businesses; their purpose is to provide economic, social or physical benefits for the community; they should be accountable to and controlled by people in the community; and profit is not the main objective. They normally try to make a profit in terms of income covering costs (otherwise a continuous subsidy would be required) but they do not distribute this profit to the members or owners of the business.

The members or owners of the community business are usually restricted to local people or those with an interest in the area who then contribute a nominal membership fee and have voting rights but have no claim on the assets or profits of the business. Hence this is a part of a social as well as an economic network as discussed in Chapter 6. Commonly in the UK the businesses are set up as companies limited by guarantee (so the owners only risk their membership fee if the business goes bankrupt) and with charitable tax status. The actual trading is then carried out by subsidiary companies (such as shops, factories, services and so on) who pay taxes but who pass their profits back to the charitable main company.

In terms of economic theory, the community business would seek to value the externalities it creates (such as extra jobs, or a more pleasant physical environment in a run-down area) as major components of its benefits. So it may achieve a much lower financial return than, say, a private company, but this would be compensated for by taking account of the non-pecuniary social benefits. Hence, taking an extreme example, a community business which only just breaks-even in financial terms (without any return on its original capital) may still be worthwhile if other net benefits outweigh the opportunity cost of its resources. While the marginal private costs may be equal to, or even lower than, the marginal private benefits for the business, the marginal social benefits are greater than the marginal social costs. In such circumstances no private company would normally set-up a business there in the long-term expectation of only breaking-even in financial terms and without an adequate return on capital. Hence community businesses may often be started in depressed neighbourhoods or sectors where other businesses would not enter. Of course, most community businesses will seek to obtain a higher return than break-even, subject to their other objectives, as the surplus can be distributed for the benefit of the community (see also Chapter 6 on contracts). From a public policy perspective, the externalities resulting from support to any such business would be included in the decision on whether to offer any grants and so on.

During the last two decades community businesses have undergone considerable change in many places, such as Scotland or US inner city areas. In the past many community businesses have focused upon satisfying perceived social needs of the community, such as the desire for jobs in depressed communities or local services like a cafe, where these have often been unable to survive financially without public subsidy. Many such community businesses failed partly due to lack of management expertise and limited markets. After such closures later community businesses often focused upon creating financially viable (at least break-even) businesses so that they would not have to rely upon the uncertainty of public subsidy. Other community businesses moved on to trying to create a 'community of interest'. In this approach, rather than locate a business (such as a childcare facility) in a poor neighbourhood where demand may be low, they would locate it in a more profitable location such as a city centre site. The benefits would go back to the poor neighbourhood in terms of the jobs in the facility going to local people and financial surpluses being spent for the benefit of the neighbourhood. The community business hence seeks to create a coalition of interested groups such as parents, employers with staff needing childcare and so on. There may, of course, be some conflicting interests between the various stakeholders, with parents wanting cheaper care and the staff wanting better paid jobs.

Community businesses have sometimes been successful in industries ranging from wood manufacturing to recycling companies, housing and cafes. However, in practice it is extremely difficult to measure the real benefits of community businesses and many of the businesses have failed once their subsidies from the public sector were removed. Nevertheless, hundreds of such businesses exist in the UK and many other countries providing useful benefits to their local economies. They also help develop new enterprises, and entrepreneurial skills and behaviour, often among the most disadvantaged communities, and provide some help in empowering local people to gain some control over their lives and their communities.

For over a century in the US, community-based non-profit (or 'not-for-profit') organizations have been active in operating businesses, from providing and running hospital and social services to property development and providing loans or even venture capital. Many of the government training schemes, such as the Federal JTPA training programme, have been delivered by these organizations, a common form of which is the Community Development Corporation (CDC). For instance, Watts Labor Community Action was set-up with funding from various foundations, government and other sources in Los Angeles after severe riots in the 1960s. The view was that a community controlled company would be able to invest to help local employment and training, to improve housing for local poor people and to reinvest profits back into socially useful projects. CDCs have received considerable support from government. For instance, in Massachusetts the Community Development Finance Corporation provide finance on flexible terms for working capital and property costs, together with management advice, to CDCs where there is a clear public and community benefit. However, some critics have said that CDCs lack professional expertise and business experience. Also there has sometimes been conflict within the organizations over the relative importance of the social and economic objectives and between the organization's advocacy and developmental roles.

Co-operatives

Another form of 'non traditional' business structure is the co-operative. These primarily seek to benefit their members rather than specifically the wider community, but they often also have wider social objectives. Most common are retail co-operatives where customers gain a share of the profits or 'dividends', marketing co-operatives where a number of private producers come together to market their products, or producer co-operatives where the members of the co-operative are its workers.

Retail co-operatives have been popular for centuries. In England, the Sheerness Economical Society in Kent started a co-operative shop linked to a bakery in 1816. In the next decade the London Co-operative and Economical Society set up the first co-operative newspaper called *The Economist* and started bulk buying goods for the needs of their members with an estimated saving of a third in their living expenses (Birchall, 1994).

The most famous early retail co-operatives were those of the Rochdale Pioneers in the Lancashire cradle of the industrial revolution. In the 1840s the life expectancy in the town was 21 years, 6 years less than the rest of England and starvation was quite common. The co-operative started with 40 members and £28 in capital. They sold butter, sugar, flour, oatmeal, candles, tea and tobacco. The first year's takings were

£710 and their capital had grown to £181 with a surplus of £22. By 1880 membership was 379 times greater at over 10 000 while capital and sales were both around £300 000 (over a million dollars at the time) and the surplus around £50 000. This provides clear evidence of remarkable collective entrepreneurial endeavour which succeeded despite having very poor members and customers and a depressed local economy. It's success was also despite major difficulties in the external environment during the period, such as the cotton famine during the American Civil War and a number of major recessions.

Since then retail co-operatives have spread throughout the world including the Harvard Coop beside Harvard University in Cambridge, Massachusetts. They have also moved into sectors such as banks or savings and loans societies. Indeed, although not strictly co-operatives, in the UK the main funders of loans for house purchase have been the mutual Building Societies, owned by their borrowers and savers. In the 1990s many of them converted into public companies, which immediately became some of the largest UK banks. There still remains a commercial Co-operative Bank operating throughout the UK.

Marketing co-operatives are widespread especially in farming areas and it is still common to see grain stores of farmer co-operatives alongside the rail tracks in North America where the farmers may share storage facilities and jointly transport and sell their grain to far-off markets.

Producer co-operation also have a long history. A co-operative flour mill was established in Woolwich in London as long ago as 1760. In theory the co-operative members trade off their utility curve (which will include the social or non-pecuniary benefits of being a member) against the revenue curve. Hence, they may forgo increased net revenue per member in order to maintain or increase employment and so may employ more people than an equivalent private firm. While there are still small producer co-operatives scattered across many countries there are few successful large-scale ones.

In most of the developed world, co-operatives are generally no longer particularly significant forces in retailing or production. One notable exception is that of the Mondragon Co-operative in the Basque region of Spain (Barker, 1997). This was set up in 1954 by a local priest Don José Maria Arizmendiarreta to help combat high unemployment of over 20 per cent and wide-spread poverty (Whyte and Whyte, 1991). At the start the first five young members of the co-operative raised $361 604 (and worth about $2 million in today's money) – a very large sum in such a poor area. Within two years there were 24 employees and by 1958 the number rose to 149 employees. In 1990 the Mondragon Co-operative Complex had 21 241 member employees in over 100 enterprises, worth over \$2.6 billion. The co-operatives at Mondragon are based upon a number of principles such as democracy, where each worker gets a vote, links with education (with the school providing related business training), financial input by employees (which can normally only be withdrawn on retirement) and equity (with originally the top paid staff getting no more than 6 times the lowest wage, although now this gap is wider in order to improve efficiency and to reflect the relative contributions of different members).

All the co-operatives use the Mondragon Co-operative Bank which, unusually for a bank, has a clear objective of funding new jobs rather than protecting its capital. The bank deliberately supports entrepreneurship through funding, advising and mentoring new co-operative businesses as well as existing ones, with a claimed high success rate of 80 per cent for new enterprises which start up. The bank has therefore both commercial and non-commercial contractual relationships with its clients (the provision of artisan capital and the importance of contracts and social relationships were discussed in Chapter 6). This shows the enormous effect that such collective enterprise, along with other entrepreneurs, can make even in areas of low income or high unemployment. However in recent decades there has been declining membership of co-operatives in some countries (ENSR, 1997), so there has been a need to market their services to non-members to a greater degree, in order to maintain economies of scale and competitiveness, which may entail a reduction in the cohesiveness of the co-operative.

The public sector – civic entrepreneurship

In the field of government there has been a call for public sector employees and organizations to act more entrepreneurially in order to deal more effectively with key issues, as resources are limited. Peter Drucker (1992) has argued that in recent years one of the major growth areas for entrepreneurship has been in public bodies (especially local government such as municipalities). These include new ways of developing and implementing policies, making effective and innovative use of new technologies, and taking greater account of the impacts of government on entrepreneurship in the wider economy and society.

Osborne and Gaebler (1992) argue that the old ways of doing things and of looking at things is the greatest stumbling block to reinventing more entrepreneurial government. By entrepreneurial governments they mean ones that have a number of specific features. These include: the promotion of competition between service providers (which opens opportunities for existing public sector staff and for new private or not-for-profit bodies); empowerment of citizens through giving greater control to the community rather than the bureaucracy; concentrating on outcomes rather than inputs (which is manifest by the rise in output measures published by public bodies); the emphasis on choice for clients of services (who are often redefined as customers); the organizations being 'goal driven' rather than driven by rules or regulations; an emphasis on the prevention of emerging problems rather than seeking to cure or ameliorate the results; and acting as catalysts, pulling together public, private and not-for-profit sectors rather than just providing services themselves. Finally entrepreneurial governments focus on using market mechanisms where appropriate, decentralize the management and authority, and concentrate more on earning money and other resources rather than simply spending their allocated budgets.

Some of the features of entrepreneurial government have resulted in a shift in thinking about many government functions from seeing government as a provider of the services (for example, employing people to collect household refuse) to taking on an enabling role. This enabling role is where government sets performance standards and ensures that the service is adequately and equitably supplied by private or not-for-profit organizations (usually following competitive tendering), and allows more entrepreneurial, opportunistic and demand led approaches to the provision of the service to be taken. However, although it no longer directly employs people to carry out the function, the government still pays all or most of the costs. As mentioned previously, in Chapter 2, a somewhat similar process has also been going on within the private sector with firms sub-contracting out non-core activities.

This enabling process has been underway since at least 1975 in places such as Lincoln, Nebraska. Many local government functions in the UK have been put out to tender, although the existing employees can also bid to continue to run the service. At the national scale the privatization of many government-owned industries, from British Telecom to British Rail and British Airways in the UK and many other firms world-wide, has now become common place although this was virtually unheard of 20 years ago. This has removed some of the constraints upon the way the businesses operate, including the removal of previous limitations on opportunities they could take. Crucially, it has also usually brought in competition, so forcing the businesses to

reconsider what they do and how they do things and to act more entrepreneurially (except those that they retain a high level of monopoly
power).

However, there are limits to how entrepreneurial a government department or employee should be. Bureaucratic systems and organizations
are usually designed to try to withstand pressures from vested interests
and despotism by the powerful and these benefits must be balanced
against any hindering of more entrepreneurial actions. Also people's
perceptions of risk and of equity may vary between public and private
services, with public bodies usually taking lower risks due to the fear of
voter reaction if a risky venture fails. In addition public bodies usually
need to deal with all citizens rather targeting only the most profitable.
These factors may each mitigate against opportunity taking. For example one way to raise tax revenue would be to have different tax rates
depending on how cheap it was to collect from different people, but
this would likely be opposed on grounds of equity. Similarly, imagine
the uproar if people in one neighbourhood of a town were charged for
taking out library books but people in another similar neighbourhood
were not. Of course, despite these legitimate constraints on government
activities, there remains large scope for greater entrepreneurial behaviour in government, especially in terms of changing what they do and
how they do it.

In assisting to develop their local economies, more entrepreneurial
approaches have often been used by governments. For instance, in many
cities and regions innovative attempts have been made by various government, private and 'third-sector' organizations to create partnerships
and to develop opportunities for the area or for specific industries, 'clusters' of industries or industrial districts (see Chapter 6). Many publicly-
funded local economic development agencies have been set up by
government and other bodies to support new firm formation by giving
advice, grants and information (see Chapter 9). In the last decade,
increasing efforts have been made by many such agencies to play an
'enabling' role whereby services are provided by third parties and paid
for by the agency. This means that the agency can keep a more strategic
perspective rather than getting involved in the operational details of providing the service. For example a regional development agency trying to
support new firms may part-fund a separate body such as a local Enterprise Trust to provide advice to anyone wishing to set up in business.

Another approach is for an agency to use temporary or sub-contracted staff or external consultants to provide some of their services.
Given the large range of firms to be dealt with, it is often not possible

to have agency employees with specialist knowledge of a number of industries. Hence they may gain the benefits of economies of scale by using specialist outside consultants or funding specialist organizations who, because of their large number of clients, have specialist knowledge of certain industries.

However, there can be dangers in moving too far along the 'enabling' policy, especially in a small-scale unit or organization, as it is often essential to learn the lessons from providing the service in order to develop an effective and efficient policy. Also there are transactions costs in identifying and choosing those with the necessary expertise, be they in private, public or 'third' sectors. Finally, the theoretical benefits of economies of scale in providing services are often outweighed by the disadvantages of lack of local knowledge and the lack of continuity on the part of the sub-contracted providers.

In summary there is considerable scope for more entrepreneurial behaviour at all levels of government. However, this must be constrained by legitimate pressures from citizens for government to act in a relatively risk averse, accountable and equitable manner which takes account of all the long-term needs of the community. Hence in some ways it may be too simplistic to compare entrepreneurship in government directly with entrepreneurship in private, profit orientated organizations.

Conclusion

This chapter has shown that entrepreneurship can have an important role throughout the economy. It illustrated how attempts have been made to bridge social and commercial objectives through business organizations such as community businesses and co-operatives.

Social entrepreneurship shares many of the characteristics of entrepreneurship within the private sector, although there are differences in their aims. However, many social entrepreneurs still seek to obtain profits, although these profits are used to support social objectives to further the purposes of the organization or to ensure its survival, rather than being distributed to shareholders. Social entrepreneurship is important throughout the economy especially in the development of the growing third or 'not-for-profit' sector of the economy. Hence it influences the dynamism of the economy and its ability to deal with crucial social, environmental and other changing issues. Finally, while there is scope for greater entrepreneurial behaviour in government, it needs to be recognized that there are legitimate constraints on such behaviour.

References and further reading

Barker, J.A. (1997) 'The Mondragon Model: A New Pathway for the Twenty-First Century' in F. Hesselbein, M. Goldsmith, and R. Bechard (eds) *The Organisation of the Future*, San Francisco, Jossey-Bass.

Birchall, J. (1994) *Co-op: the People's Business*, Manchester, Manchester University Press.

Boyett, I. and D. Finlay (1993) 'The Emergence of the Educational Entrepreneur' *Long Range Planning*, Vol. 26, 114–20.

Drucker P.F. (1985) *Innovation and Entrepreneurship*, London, Heinemann.

Drucker P.F. (1992) *Managing for the Future*, Oxford, Butterworth-Heinemann.

ENSR (1997) *The European Observatory for SMEs, 45th Report*, Brussels, European Network for SME Research.

LAURA (1990) *Community Businesses, Good Practice in Urban Regeneration*, London, HMSO.

Leadbeater, C. (1997) *The Rise of the Social Entrepreneur*, London, Demos.

Osborne, D. and T. Gaebler (1992) *Reinventing Government*, Reading, Mass., Addison-Wesley.

Owen, Robert (1991) *A New View of Society and Other Writings (1813–1849)*, London, Penguin.

Whyte, W.F. and K.K. Whyte (1991) *Making Mondragon*, 2nd edn, Ithaca, NY, ILR Press.

Young, D (1983) *If Not for Profit, for What? A Behavioural Theory of the Non-profit Sector and Based on Entrepreneurship*, Lexington, Mass., Lexington.

9
Public Policies to Promote Entrepreneurship

Introduction

The aim of this chapter is to consider government policies to encourage entrepreneurial activity. Generally such policies have focused upon aiding new and small businesses, although as discussed in Chapter 8 various policies have tried to increase entrepreneurial behaviour in the government and 'not-for-profit' sectors. The first question is why should governments intervene in the market to support new or small firms? The importance of entrepreneurship generally, and of new and small firms in terms of employment in particular, was discussed in Chapter 2. As was seen in earlier chapters some theories suggest that a rise in entrepreneurship will help the economy move towards equilibrium. Alternatively other writers argue that entrepreneurship may result in greater disequilibrium forces (Chapters 3–4).

So should the market be left alone to achieve whichever outcome the market dictates? In the following section, the economic rationale for government intervention is briefly discussed. However, as analysed in Chapters 5 and 6 entrepreneurs operate in a wider socio-economic environment which is constantly evolving, and which public policies also need to understand and take account of, if they are to be effective. Similarly the variety of economic, social and political motives should be taken into account when analysing such policies.

The next question is that given that there is a case for government intervention in particular circumstances, what form should this intervention take? Policies will depend to a large degree upon our understanding of entrepreneurs or potential entrepreneurs, their motives, their decisionmaking processes, and the socio-economic environments within which they operate, as was discussed in Chapter 7. So if policies are to influence entrepreneurs then we need to understand now different types of potential policies may influence entrepreneurs.

This chapter considers the economic reasons for government to intervene in the market in order to support new firm creation and more general entrepreneurship. It continues by examining macroeconomic policies, and then moves on to microeconomic policies. Finally it discusses some wider issues that need to be considered when developing such policies.

The rationale for policies

The general economic rationale for supporting entrepreneurship development is to remove or reduce market failure. In particular the market may not correctly or fully value the social benefits and costs of job generation, improved innovation and flexibility resulting from greater entrepreneurship. Hence market failure results in a misallocation of resources. There are a number of specific reasons why market failures occur.

The first main reason for market failure is due to the divergence of private and social costs, that is, externalities. This is where the production or consumption of a good or service directly affects others not involved in buying or selling it and these spill-over effects are not reflected in the market price. So the economic benefits (that is, positive externalities) such as greater competition, flexibility and job benefits of having more entrepreneurs may not be fully incorporated in the market. Another way in which externalities can affect entrepreneurship is where the full social costs of pollution are not included in firms' prices. Hence there are lower returns for other entrepreneurs who, for instance, develop innovative pollution control products, and such products might not be introduced. These negative externalities can be dealt with through government action (for example, taxes or regulations) and through the allocation of property rights (Coase, 1960). Environmental taxes or tradable permits which are designed to reflect the full cost of pollution may potentially help create new opportunities for entrepreneurs.

A second reason for market failure is inadequate information for consumers and producers to make decisions. These include missing, inadequate or incorrect information concerning current or future goals, risk and so on. Third, monopoly or concentrated market power may be present and there may be barriers to entry for new firms or other market imperfections. So large firms may be able to stop new products or businesses entering the market or new ways of doing business, and this would stifle entrepreneurship. Even at a local level there may be a high degree of monopoly power among suppliers of some services or property.

Fourth, income redistribution resulting from the workings of the market may not be considered fair or efficient, and, for instance, poorer people may require support. While this usually involves taxation and expenditure policies, there may be discrimination or other barriers to less well off groups, including many minority groups and women, becoming entrepreneurs or small business owners and improving their income prospects.

Fifth, there may be wider reasons for public policies to support entrepreneurship based upon market failure. These include the provision of merit goods (where insufficient amounts of the good would be provided for optimum public benefit), or public goods (due to non-exclusivity and non-rivalry of the good where, for instance, those benefiting from a good cannot be excluded from consuming it and made to pay for it, and the marginal cost of another consumer is zero at any level of production), or policies to reduce the severity of business cycles.

Besides these general reasons for public intervention, there are other related specific problems faced by new or small firms. These include difficulties with obtaining finance, and knowledge of the accounting and tax systems, having no guaranteed income in the early stages of start-up, getting customers and, especially for innovative products, getting the product to a marketable stage. If there is market failure in any of these areas then the number of business start-ups or expansions will be below the social optimum.

New and small firms may also face internal barriers to their development. For instance Scase and Goffee (1987, pp. 162–3) found a number of internal constraints which inhibit the expansion of firms:

- at the start the proprietor develops personal relationships with customers, but as the client base expands staff take over direct customer relations and the business can be jeopardized, hence staying small can be safer;
- lack of confidence in their ability to manage and lack of management skills;
- worry about changing relations with staff as the firm develops (for example, as the firm expands, relationships with staff may become more formal);
- desire not to hire new employees due to fear of employment law prohibiting dismissal of unsuitable staff, and the limits on personal

independence and freedom (for example, due to the necessity for seeking higher sales turnover to pay staff);

- difficulty in recruiting good staff, especially if the employee is measured against the entrepreneur's own more highly motivated performance. This can partly be dealt with by increasing use of profit or share price-related pay and bonuses for all staff in the organization.

At different stages in the development of the business, different types of support are required. People starting up businesses who have wide experience in the industry are not likely to need general business advice and are more likely to get advice and support from specialist private firms. Hence many of the general public policies are aimed at those with more limited experience and where market failure is greatest.

The existence of market failure may, in itself, not necessarily justify government intervention. Governments may try to overcome these market failures, although some economists argue that these attempts will often not actually improve the allocation of resources. This is because, first, the costs of the intervention may be greater than the benefits, so policies need to be efficient and effective.

Second, intervention can lead to further market distortion. For instance, a government scheme which provides cheap credit to people with low incomes wishing to start a business, might result in commercial lenders withdrawing from that market as they are no longer willing to lend at such low interest rates. Hence this could reduce the total amount of credit available to firms. However, on the other hand the current commercial interest rates may reflect the international market for capital within which the lenders operate and not the market conditions within which the local firms operate.

Third, while the negative externalities such as the effects of a firm closing may be easy to see (unemployment, lower incomes, knock on multiplier effects, etc.) the benefits of such closures may be less clear (opening new opportunities to others, reducing inefficiency and so on). Pressure to prevent the negative aspects may be greater than pressure to promote the benefits, so unwarranted intervention may result. These reasons do not mean that governments should not intervene, indeed for some forms of market failure they must, but this intervention must be clearly thought out and evaluated.

Public policies can broadly be considered at the macro and the micro levels. Broadly the former seek to influence the macroeconomic environment in which entrepreneurs operate. Microeconomic policies and programmes are broadly targeted at directly supporting individual entrepreneurs. For instance, the European Union (CEC, 1998) seeks to foster entrepreneurship through creating a supportive macroeconomic environment and through encouraging and helping individuals to get the necessary skills to become entrepreneurs. There are many such policies (see for instance, OECD, 1998) and some major ones are now considered.

Macroeconomic policies and the economic environment

In the United States, the 1953 Small Business Act states that 'It is the declared policy of the Congress that the Government should aid, counsel, assist and protect, insofar as possible, the interests of small business concerns in order to preserve free competitive enterprise.' The Act argued that small businesses should be supported to maintain competition and a balance between established, large enterprises and new, growing ones. It also suggested that there were linked political and social benefits so the motives were not purely economic. The Act set up a government agency, the Small Business Administration, which developed its mission as being 'to serve America's small businesses to (1) help preserve free competition, (2) contribute to the strengthening of the Nation's economy, and (3) assist disaster-ravaged communities recover from their losses.'

In Japan 'The Fundamental Law of Small-Medium Enterprises' in 1963 has been called a constitution for small and medium sized enterprises, as it set a broad policy framework covering a variety of legislation. A prime aim of the law was to eliminate the 'barriers associated with smallness' and to modernize the sector. Other countries such as Germany also had strong policies to reduce the barriers to setting-up and growing small enterprises in order to improve competition, innovation and efficiency of production and to preserve social balance.

Governments have an important role in supporting the basic economic infrastructure of the country, such as communication networks, an educated workforce, research and development, and supporting the diffusion of knowledge. In addition the specific 'macroeconomic' policies that are now discussed are macroeconomic stability, taxation, regulation, access to public sector markets, culture and legal and other factors.

(i) Macroeconomic stability

Providing a stable macroeconomic environment has been seen as being crucial to support entrepreneurship and the development of small businesses. Low inflation is seen as important, as it reduces distortions in market signals (which can result in inefficiencies) and also reduces uncertainties associated with unforeseen changes in prices, exchange rates or interest rates. For example, the UK government has argued that its support for entrepreneurship has included trying to achieve low and stable inflation (in a range around 1–4 per cent), altering the taxation system and making it easier for small firms to sell their products to the government (DTI, 1995, 1998).

The European Union (EU) argue that policies of stable exchange rates, low inflation, and a low interest rate environment together with 'sound' public finances will lead to a virtuous 'crowding in' effect, whereby short-term investment and employment is encouraged due to improved confidence in the private sector and a reduction on the risk-premium and interest rates (CEC, 1995). The Single European Currency used by many EU countries further reduces exchange rate risks and transactions costs for trading within the EU.

Such stability should allow entrepreneurs to better appraise opportunities and their associated risks and so encourage greater entrepreneurial activity. On the other hand, a turbulent macroeconomy can also create opportunities for some, a prime example being George Soros (see the Illustration in Chapter 4), who apparently made over a billion dollars in a few weeks by speculating in currency.

(ii) Taxation

Simplifying and reducing the burden of taxation on new enterprises is claimed by many to reduce costs, encourage investment and increase incentives. A high level of taxation may act as a disincentive to entrepreneurs (or an incentive to move elsewhere), although the taxation system also influences the comparative advantages of different business strategies. The taxation systems in Europe have generally been claimed to provide incentives to restructure existing small firms rather than start new ones from scratch, as new firms need large cash flows in early years and the tax regulations are expensive and time-consuming.

The taxation structure in many countries has shifted from high marginal rates on personal income toward indirect taxes. In the decade of the 1980s personal income tax rates fell, from as high as a marginal rate of 98 per cent in the 1960s. However to compensate taxes were shifted to indirect taxes such as Value Added Tax (VAT) with this sales tax rising from 8 per cent to 17.5 per cent. Hence this was largely a redistribution of taxes as the total tax collected as the share of GDP did not generally fall. Marginal tax rates continued to be reduced for small firms (from 42 per cent in the 1980s to 25 per cent in the 1990s for firms earning under £300 000 in profits). A further taxation change designed to help small firms was to increase the turnover threshold below which a firm need not charge VAT, hence many small firms do not need to charge it or have the complex accounting systems involved in operating it. Changes were also made to the timing of payments of the VAT collected by firms to the tax authorities, so as to improve the cash flow of small firms.

Inheritance tax was also changed to allow greater relief on business property so it can be passed from generation to generation free of tax in most cases. Similarly capital gains tax relief was changed (in the November 1993 budget) specifically to encourage investment in unquoted trading companies, hence improving finance for entrepreneurial firms. Taxation regulations were also simplified so as to reduce the costs of compliance by small firms. For instance self-assessment (as used in the US and other countries) was introduced in the UK and quarterly rather than monthly payments brought in for employer collected income taxes, such as PAYE and National Insurance payments for some small firms.

(iii) Regulation

Reducing or streamlining regulations and bureaucracy is also seen as encouraging entrepreneurship and small firms. For instance, some small firms in the UK were exempt from industrial tribunals and the need to reinstate staff after maternity leave. Policies to increase labour market flexibility (such as making it easier to hire and fire staff) have been claimed by some to encourage entrepreneurship and the hiring of staff to try out perceived opportunities, in the knowledge that if the opportunity failed then the firm would not necessarily have high, long-term labour cost commitments.

Administrative regulations have also been reduced in many countries. For example, the Enterprise Deregulation Unit was set up in 1986 in the UK, within the Department of Trade and Industry, explicitly to reduce the administrative burden faced by small firms. This was followed by an independent Better Regulation Task Force in 1998 to further reduce the burdens of regulation or business. These provide mechanisms to try to balance such administrative costs for firms against the benefits gained for society from safety, consumer protection and other regulations.

Increasingly regulations affecting businesses are originating at the European Union level. Here there is usually an attempt to explicitly recognize their potential impacts upon small and medium-sized enterprises and there is a deliberate policy to reduce the costs of regulation for new and small firms. For instance, the EU has tried to reduce the burden of regulation and to simplify the financial environment for entrepreneurs (CEC, 1998). Ironically there may be problems with policies of reducing regulation compliance costs for small firms, as Sengeberger *et al.* (1990) point out. If employee protection and so on is increased, this may make it easier for small firms in the short term, but in the longer term it may be harder to attract and retain skilled labour as staff will be inclined to leave for better conditions and wages. Deregulation may also encourage small firms to be complacent and compete on the basis of cost rather than higher value added products and services.

(iv) Access to public sector markets

Now turning to the role of government as a source of demand for firms, it is useful to note that the public sector is one of the largest customers of industry in most countries. However the sizes of their contracts are usually far larger than a small firm could supply and government tendering processes are often difficult and expensive. The reasons for the long tendering process include the need to obtain best value and to avoid unfair competition among suppliers. In the EU there is also the need to follow tendering procedures for large contracts to ensure firms in other EU countries get a fair chance to obtain contracts. Such factors can make it difficult for small or new firms to gain government contracts.

The Small Business Administration and other departments in the US Government have a long tradition of trying to overcome these barriers and to support small firms get larger shares of government contracts, including the huge Department of Defense contracts. In the UK similar policies to encourage procurement from small firms by government have included: splitting contracts into smaller components; developing promotional videos, booklets and other information on tendering; offering advice to small firms; involving representatives from small firm organizations in reviews to simplify the tendering process; and creating 'best practice' guides for government departments to encourage such procurement (DTI, 1995). In addition (as is dicussed below) governments have sought to help small firms find foreign markets through advice, information, credit guarantees and more general opening of trade, such as through GATT and World Trade Organization agreements. The Department of Trade and Industry also set up a network of ten Regional Supply Offices throughout England to help purchasers find more competitive suppliers and to help suppliers expand their customer base. This assistance is then linked to local business development agencies.

(v) Culture

From a more sociological perspective some countries or regions are said to have an 'enterprising culture'. In these cultures many people's attitudes encourage forward looking perspectives, innovation, calculated risk-taking, and individuals actively participating in creating prosperity through developing the organization they work in or through starting one up. They also support continuous learning so as to be able to respond effectively to the opportunities presented by change and by the future. 'Self help' by individuals and communities is seen as important, rather than people seeing the solution to problems or the taking of opportunities as someone else's responsibility. While in countries such as the US the term 'entrepreneur' generally has positive connotations, in other countries considerable efforts have been made to link it with the significant contributions to economic development and positive cultural values. For instance, in Scotland the main economic development agency has had a series of policies to encourage people to have a more positive perspective on the contribution of entrepreneurs to society and to encourage people to start their own business (Scottish Enterprise, 1993, 1996).

Other policies to promote a more entrepreneurial culture have included altering the tax system, providing start-up grant support (such as the Enterprise Allowance Scheme in the UK), sponsoring awards for innovation and entrepreneurship (such as the Queen's Award for Industry) and publicity campaigns (DTI, 1998). In less supportive cultures business failure can lead to considerable loss of social status and may often mean that future businesses or initiatives by that individual will not be supported by banks or others, hence a fear of failure stifles innovation and entrepreneurship.

Less entrepreneurial economies may also concentrate upon short-term tactical decisions rather than long-term strategic issues, for instance treating employees as disposable commodities rather than investments when human capital is increasingly seen as being fundamental to longer term success in most industries.

(vi) Legal and other factors in the economic environment

In some cases there may be a lack of fundamental business infrastructure, as was the case in East-Central Europe immediately after the fall of communism. This generated particular problems for governments and entrepreneurs, such as people trying to rent an office when no one was sure who owned it. Unlike most developed countries there was an absence of appropriate commercial law, property rights, accounting standards and procedures, as well as capital markets, which are all required for a market orientated economy. During their transition to more market based economies this business infrastructure had to be created and entrepreneurs had to learn how to use them efficiently.

In developing countries the level of self-employment is often extremely high, with many people living at subsistence levels. There are particular problems for small firms seeking significant growth potential due to lack of market size, funding sources, skilled labour and so on. In such countries (and many developed countries) the macroeconomic environment often needs to change to reduce subsidies to larger firms and the associated discrimination against small enterprises, enhancing inputs (including credit, other finance and labour) needed by small enterprises, and increasing the range of domestic and international market opportunities.

The above examples broadly show how governments seek to provide a general macroeconomic environment that is supportive of entrepreneurship. We will next discuss specific direct assistance to entrepreneurs and small firms.

Illustration – integrating small businesses support in the European Union

The European Commission sought to ensure that EU initiatives and measures which have been developed to assist small businesses are consistent with, and did not overlap, those of the member states (that is, countries). The Commission published an Integrated Programme for Small Medium Sized Enterprises (SMEs) which aimed to ensure a closer partnership between all those involved whether at regional, national or European level.

The programme identified priorities and objectives for actions which were designed to support SMEs. These included:

- simplifying and improving the administrative and regulatory business environment, for example, through simplifying the Internal Market legislation which allowed easier trade between countries in the EU;
- improving the financial and fiscal environment for enterprises, for instance, through loan guarantee schemes;

- helping small businesses to 'Europeanize' and internationalize their strategies, in particular through better information services;
- improving SME competitiveness and ensure that they have access to research, innovation, information technologies and training; and
- promoting entrepreneurship and supporting select groups, such as women or young people.

Microeconomic policies to support entrepreneurship

Policies to directly assist new and small firms are usually put in place where there is evidence of market failure. Many national, regional or local agencies have such policies to directly support entrepreneurs, so as to increase the number of businesses or aid the competitiveness and expansion of existing small firms. Such policies are generally aimed at assisting new and small firms to develop necessary skills, identifying opportunities and assemble resources. A strong and healthy business structure in terms of the supply of private sector support services, such as accountants, financiers, patent agents and so on, is also crucial for entrepreneurs. Hence public policies usually focus upon complementing these private services. Support for entrepreneurship within government and non-profit orientated organizations have already been considered in Chapter 8. The 'microeconomic' policies discussed below are: access to advice and training; finance; technology; markets; physical infrastructure; and the characteristics of the locality.

(i) Training, information, advice and the promotion of entrepreneurship

In most developed countries there are agencies funded by the public or private sectors or public–private sector partnerships which operate at national, regional and/or local levels and which provide a range of training, information and advice to assist potential or existing entrepreneurs. These promote the learning and development of business skills and the assessing and taking of opportunities. They also often run basic and advanced courses on issues such as taxation, regulations, business practices, opportunity identification, motivation and technical training, as well as business skills in areas such as bookkeeping, marketing or generating business or product ideas. Some of these policies are further considered below.

In the education system other skills considered useful to entrepreneurship in any type of organization, such as team working, adaptability, presentation skills and so on are also often explicitly developed within schools, colleges and universities. Some policies have particularly targeted business start-up skills for school children, such as the 'Young Enterprise' programme where school students set-up their own small company. Common examples of these include selling school tea towels or small items, with the 'company' being 'wound-up' at the end of the school year. These types of programme seek to improve the students' knowledge of businesses generally, and specifically, increase knowledge of how to set-up and run a small business. The programmes help develop a variety of useful business and general skills, from marketing to team building. The programmes are often seen as attempts to increase awareness of entrepreneurship and to change attitudes of people, at a relatively young age, towards being more positive about setting up their own businesses in the future or towards entrepreneurs in general. However, such educational programmes may have a high opportunity cost and some argue that it may be better for students to spend their time on basic numeracy and literacy skills instead, unless the entrepreneurship education is clearly used to develop and apply these basic skills.

Support for businesses also includes general business training, especially for those starting their first business. The type and levels of support may vary according to the experience of the entrepreneur (Birley and Westhead, 1993) with less experienced entrepreneurs requiring more basic marketing and financial advice. These services may be organized or run by public bodies, such as regional development agencies or local government, or by private sector organizations, such as some Chambers of Commerce in the US or France, or by joint private–public activities. In the case of France these bodies are largely funded through employer taxes. Following the passing of the North American Free Trade Agreement (NAFTA, P.L. 103–182), Section 507 of the implementing bill authorized states to establish assistance programmes to help unemployed workers train for self-employment and to be paid a self-employment allowance in lieu of unemployment compensation.

In the UK many joint private–public initiatives such as the Enterprise Trusts were specifically set up to provide support to start-up firms and carry out other related activities such as offering small office or industrial accommodation. Generally evidence suggests that firms receiving advice from such Trusts have a better survival rate than firms not receiving such support. Failure rates also appear to be lower in firms receiving management training. Trusts and other agencies have also often acted as catalysts to set-up (but not operate or fund) 'small business' clubs where owners can meet to discuss and exchange ideas or issues and learn from one another (McQuaid, 1996).

During the 1990s in the UK there was a shift from the provision of small firm policies by central government towards more localized publicly funded development and delivery of policies. In England and Wales networks of Training and Enterprise Councils (TECs) and Local Enterprise Companies (LECs) in Scotland were set up to provide business support and training for those running small firms, as well as other local economic development support. These TECs and LECs were originally set-up with a private sector majority on their board, although with funding almost entirely from the public sector. This was hoped to bring in more entrepreneurial and private sector expertise to their strategies and activities.

Their policies are usually carried out in partnership with other local bodies such as local enterprise agency, Chamber of Commerce and the local authorities. Once a business has started, further advice and training of technical and management staff may be provided, especially as expansion is often hindered by management capacity, finance and weakness in sales and marketing (see the discussion on Scase and Goffee above). It is important that such support is specifically adapted to the firm's needs. One of the most important issues for policymakers is to improve our understanding of how entrepreneurs learn and develop their skills and abilities, so that these processes can be improved.

The actual provision of the training or advice is often carried out by private sector firms with the public funder acting as an enabling organization, that is, they fund or ensure that the service is provided, but do not actually provide the service themselves (see Chapter 8). However there is a danger that the sub-contracted supplier may become so embedded in working on behalf of the public agency and trying to access the grants that are available, that they no longer efficiently meet the market demand of the businesses being assisted. There is also the possibility that funding such services limits the creation of an efficient market for the services if the grants push up the cost of services without an associated increase in their quality.

One example was where people thinking of starting a business in a rural area were given grants of 65 per cent of the cost of having a business plan prepared for them, up to a maximum grant of £650. This was to encourage more business ideas to be tested, some of which might come to fruition and so lead to employment and wealth creation. However, in the local area the consultants who wrote the plans suddenly raised their average prices from £500 to £1000. The potential entrepreneurs were still happy as before they paid £500 for a plan but now it only cost them £350 after the grant, although its full cost had actually doubled. The main impact then was that most of the grant was captured by the intermediary with the potential entrepreneur only getting a relatively small share, so less new business plans were generated than expected. So the grant was primarily subsidizing the consultants who received double the fee for an equivalent amount of work, claiming £1000 was the new market price. This illustrates a general problem with some grant and subsidy programmes of having very high transactions costs in terms of administration and economic 'capture' by the intermediaries.

(ii) Finance

There are a number of reasons why obtaining finance can be difficult for new firms. First it may be due to their lack of a 'track record'. This results in uncertainty for investors as there is little historical information to base the investment decision on and the person setting up the business may not have had direct experience of starting such a business. Second, there may be difficulties in obtaining funding due to economies of scale making the cost of agreeing finance for relatively small amounts extremely high. The cost for an investor of analysing a business plan and making and realizing an investment has large fixed components, so the cost associated with investing $50 000 will be proportionally much higher than an investment of $5 000 000.

Third, there may be a higher real or perceived risk in investing in new or small firms. This is a particular problem for small innovative firms who need funding to develop a prototype of a product to show that it is marketable. There is a high risk that the prototype may not work well, or customers may not fully accept the product and the final market size may be difficult to calculate. Also any returns are not likely to be received for some years (particularly for products such as biotechnology or pharmaceuticals) and the market may change during that period. So it is often difficult to get funding, unless the people involved have an excellent track record of starting or running similar businesses.

Hence, it has often been argued that a capital 'gap' exists which makes it difficult to fund relatively small amounts for start-up or expansion, as reported in the 1979 Wilson Report on financing for small firms and many subsequent reports. There have been a number of initiatives to improve capital accessibility and bridge the capital 'gap', such as government investment grants, loans or Loan Guarantee Schemes, common in Europe and also the US through its Small Business Administration. In 1996 the SBA assisted 52 700 businesses with loans, to a value of $10.2 billion. Of these 19 per cent were to minority businesses who often in the past had difficulty obtaining finance due to the lack of track records, limited personal capital or discrimination. The EU and others have helped part-funded venture capital funds to focus on new and small firms, such as their 'Joint Venture Action' programmes, often as part of a wider regional development strategy.

A main source of funding for small firms is from entrepreneurs themselves. Various studies have suggested a link between new firm formation, and income savings per head and the level of housing ownership. One reason for this may be the way in which funders such as banks seek security: the house can be used as security against the loan and so banks are more willing to lend to entrepreneurs who already have such assets. In those parts of the country where house prices have risen greatly the potential entrepreneur has a greater gap between their house loan or mortgage and the house value to act as security for any business loan, so getting funding will be relatively easier.

Access to finance (including equity and loans) for businesses is normally through bodies such as banks, venture capitalists and private investors. Such investors can be entrepreneurs themselves and can be of value to the economy by efficiently bringing together entrepreneurs and finance, providing non-financial advice and guidance (often through taking a place on the Board of Directors), and sometimes by using their wider experience to make better decisions than those starting-up or operating the business.

Investment from private venture capitalists is extremely important for many businesses, as it offers not only finance but often also specialist advice. However much of the money invested by venture capitalists is in established businesses, including management buy-outs, rather than to finance the early stages of start-up businesses. There are clear advantages for new businesses in getting such equity funding rather than borrowing, as no interest has to be paid each month, so the gearing of the company's funding is better. However getting funding through raising equity means the owner must in return give up a substantial share of the company's ownership to the venture capitalists, and so lose some control and a share of future profits. Most venture capitalists will wish to withdraw their investment after between three and seven years, by which time the company should be financially stable. However, if the firm has inadequate capital then, after a few years it may get into a weak financial position and be forced to seek further funding from venture capitalists. The original founder may then have to give up a majority of their shares in return for this extra funding, so it is important that the original business plan and funding package is well thought out (see Appendix). Sometimes individuals, termed 'business angels', invest their own individual venture capital into high-risk ventures and may become involved in the operation of the business along side the original entrepreneur.

(iii) Technology

Not surprisingly, given the links between entrepreneurship, innovations and opportunities offered by new technologies, many government policies seek to improve access to and support for developing new technology. These policies can be particularly crucial given the importance of new technology for competitiveness and the rapid growth of some new technology firms, such as Microsoft or Sun Microsystems, from being a start-up to being huge employers within a decade or so. Various policies have been used to improve the access of new and small firms to technology. One set of policies has been to encourage the commercializing and disseminating of research carried out in universities, government and defence research establishments. Grants or other support to firms to develop new products or production processes have also often been provided by agencies. Some policies have sought to improve technologies transfer and access to information and advice on new technology, such as through the network of business innovation centres part funded by the European Commission.

Many agencies have targeted assistance for new 'high tech' and biotechnology firms, through direct support or sometimes through providing defence or other contracts to develop new technologies (Hall *et al.*, 1987). The EU's 'Growth and Employment Initiative' also seeks to support high tech start-up businesses. The issue of new technologies, or the new application of existing technologies, is often fundamental to entrepreneurship and is discussed more fully elsewhere in the book.

(iv) Demand factors

Product demand and access to markets is crucial for entrepreneurial firms. A number of studies have indicated that demand deficiency is the greatest hindrance to small firm growth. For example, Smallbone (1992) found the most common problem facing firms after their first two-and-a-half years, and the most common cause of failure, was lack of demand.

There have been many policies to help firms increase sales such as training, marketing initiatives, forming joint or co-operative marketing bodies, improving means of joint bidding for large contracts, market intelligence, trade fairs, trade directories, and 'marriage brokering' services with foreign firms. For instance, the EU has a network of over 232 European Information Centres originally established in 1987 which provide information on public contracts, potential business partners in all parts of the EU, taxation and other issues specially geared towards helping small firms increase trade and form links across Europe. However, it is sometimes claimed that small firms still fail to see opportunities for their products in different uses due to lack of innovative thinking, although those firms showing entrepreneurial behaviour should not normally miss them.

Exporting by small firms has often received considerable government support. Such support needs to be easily accessible, well targeted, linked to specific sectors with particular strengths and where opportunities are not being exploited, and responsive to the needs of users of the support. Generally firms follow a sequential process during which the firm gradually increases its commitment to exporting, starting with the local area, then the wider region, the rest of the country and finally abroad. The most important variables about whether a firm will export appear to be the characteristics and perceptions of the decisionmaker and not the characteristics of the product and markets.

(v) Physical infrastructure

The lack of physical infrastructure can significantly hinder entrepreneurs. The availability, flexibility, cost and letting terms of suitable premises is often cited as a problem, especially for new firms. Landlords demanding long leases may deter start-ups and prevent growing firms moving to more efficient premises. This is often because a new firm hoping to expand does not want to sign a 25 year lease for a property which may not be large enough for it in a few years, after it expands. Also a long lease increases the risks for the entrepreneur, because if the business contracts or closes then they will often have to personally guarantee the lease for the remaining period. More recently landlords have developed much shorter and more flexible leases for new and small firms, due partly to competition from development agencies and other private providers who were willing to offer more flexible leases.

Many public agencies have provided small factory or office units for rent where there has been a lack of private provision. In other cases subsidies have been offered to private property developers to build units for small firms where they would not have done so otherwise. Such property provision may be linked to general business advice and specialist services. Developments of groups of small manufacturing or office units also can help small firms gain agglomeration economies by being close to similar firms. For instance, specialist property developers such as science parks or small business incubators form tenant meetings or other mechanisms for exchange and discussions among local firms.

A number of Enterprise Zones were set up in the US, UK and other countries. These are areas zoned for industrial and/or commercial development, usually with generous tax allowances or subsidies. They often have few land use planning regulations. Some were successful in generating construction and employment in the zones. However, the cost in lost taxes was often extremely high and many of the developments had simply moved from other areas just outside the zones so little was added to the local economy. Also many zones introduced strict land use requirements, so as to protect the value of properties from being reduced if a 'noxious' neighbouring development occurred (such as a glue factory being sited beside an office complex), hence public land use as zoning regulations may be just replaced by legal requirements in the lease.

Access to information technology networks, such as the Internet, is important for entrepreneurs. When a town is connected to any new optic fibre or wiring system for the Internet, many US cities insist that all businesses in any part of a city must be connected, so as to avoid those installing the new optic fibre systems only picking the most profitable locations to connect and ignoring more remote businesses. In rural areas 'tele-cottages' are sometimes provided where small firms can access 'state-of-the-art' information technology connections for an hourly or daily charge. This is a way of providing small firms who could not afford their own information technology equipment and connections to effectively share costs and have access to the latest technology.

(vi) Characteristics of the locality

The local characteristics and industrial structure of a location have an important impact upon entrepreneurs. In the US, parts of Europe and East Asia certain regions and countries appear to have had an 'entrepreneurial engine'. This is where there is a diversified economy with many firms at different stages of their life-cycle (from birth to declining, or dying) and across a range of industries. So resources such as entrepreneurial skill, skilled workers, market knowledge and networks can move from declining to growing firms (OECD, 1997) within the same region.

The fermentation within the economy can help sustain it and avoid stagnation, particularly where demand for the products of industry as a whole are rising. Other factors that may support entrepreneurship in a location include the levels of scientific and technical expertise, the business culture, networks of firms, successful role models, quality of life, access to government contracts and research and, development activities in universities or public or private bodies, skilled and well educated labour (with good education and retraining facilities), venture capital and other finance, access to technology transfer and access to markets as discussed above. A relatively high density of firms and population may also aid growth and development through agglomeration economies.

These and the other factors considered earlier need to be available and accessible to entrepreneurs, although they need not all be located in the particular place. Their presence can assist entrepreneurship but they cannot, of course, guarantee it. In general local policies that reflect local characteristics and circumstances, are flexible in their design and delivery and which adopt a partnership approved between the various key public and private actors appear to be most likely to succeed (OECD, 1996).

While a general policy thrust of creating an economic and business regulatory environment conducive to the development of an enterprise culture is in line with a general adherence to supply-side policies, there are ideological limits to the extent of government intervention, given the belief that market forces are the means of developing a competitive and responsive economy. Thus, intervention in markets such as the specific policy initiatives outlined above, have been made consistent with the principal of limited intervention by claiming that they represent measures aimed at ironing out market imperfections which prevent small firms operating effectively (Curran, 1990).

Storey *et al.* (1987), however, argue that business failure is central to the efficient operation of a market economy. A policy of intervening to prevent markets from determining the most efficient uses of resources through natural selection may serve to subsidise inefficiency rather than to promote efficiency. There are also difficulties with the concept of failure. Storey *et al.* differentiate between the concepts of business failure and entrepreneurial failure. The former reflects the closure of a business unit for whatever reason, but this may not correspond to the failure of the owner-manager, who may own other successful businesses, or go on to develop successful businesses.

Illustration – UK government policies

Some of these specific policies of the UK government aim at redressing instances of market failure. In the case of the supply of finance these relate to: (a) the provision of equity and loan capital, and (b) the provision of tax allowances and grants (DTI, 1995). The key UK policies implemented included:

(1) The Business Expansion Scheme – aimed at encouraging 'business angels' to invest in new unquoted companies; the Loan Guarantee Scheme – aimed at reducing the risk to the lender and thus increasing the supply of debt finance by guaranteeing 70 per cent of a bank loan to a small firm; the Unlisted Securities Market – aimed at increasing supply of equity capital to small firms without the costs or administrative restrictions of a full stock exchange listing.

(2) The provision of tax allowances and grants: for example, the reduction in corporation tax for small firms; the Enterprise Allowance Scheme, which provided weekly financial assistance for unemployed individuals entering self-employment for a specified period of time; the Enterprise Initiative, which provided grants for small firms which qualify in Development Areas under the Regional Enterprise Grant Scheme, and grants specifically aimed at helping with the cost of capital in investment projects and innovation projects; the Small Firms Merit Award for Research and Technology (SMART), which offers phased financial support for the development of new technology in small firms which qualify.

(3) In an attempt to redress market failure in the supply of information and business consultancy, the government introduced regional agencies such as the Scottish Enterprise and a network of Local Enterprise Companies in Scotland (although they succeeded earlier agencies), and Training and Enterprise Councils in England. A primary remit of these initiatives is to ensure provision of advice and training for small firms, as many surveys have identified a lack of marketing, sales and management skills as significant barriers to growth.

Some further issues in analysing policies

When considering policies of public bodies developing initiatives factors that need to be considered include: what it is trying to achieve (the objectives of the policy); the options of how to achieve it and the costs and benefits of each option; an analysis of these options and choosing between them; and how they are to be achieved (the way the policy is to be implemented). The impacts of the policy and the efficiency and effectiveness in attaining the aims are crucial, and this requires a clear policy framework and criteria for judging the success, or lack of success, of the policies. When trying to measure the benefits of a policy, policy-makers also need to compare all the direct and indirect effects, including multipliers, displacement and 'deadweight' effects (see below). Different types of firms will have different direct and indirect impacts on the local economy. When the full effects of the policy are estimated, then it should be possible to decide if a policy justifies its cost.

A number of indicators are commonly used to identify types of firms for support. For example: employment generation; value added and change in value added per employee; change in wages per employee; new capital expenditure per employee; and supplier, customer and other links to the local area. Looking at these criteria more closely, the employment likely to be generated directly is a major criteria. This needs to be considered in terms of both full-time and part-time posts, the characteristics of the jobs (are they seasonal, do they provide opportunities for promotion to higher skill levels and so on) and factors such as investment in training (which may be a partial estimate for investment in human capital by the firm). The wage levels of employees and likely changes in wage are important for the individuals and for the impact of their purchasing power on the local economy. Value added per employee gives some measure of labour productivity for firms and higher levels should increase longer-term competitiveness and permit higher wages. Capital expenditure per employee is a measure of investment by firms and their capacity to generate new investments.

In addition the indirect impact of policies elsewhere in the economy need to be considered, particularly the multiplier effects and displacement. Considering multiplier effects first, when a firm expands or increases its employment then, aside from the direct jobs created in the firm, there will usually be 'supplier' multiplier effects associated with increased jobs or income created in supplier firms. There will also be 'income' multiplier effects as the extra income of the firm's workers is spent in local shops and services. Workers in-migrating to take the new jobs also increase the demand for public and other services, such as schools. This extra income for suppliers or shops and services will itself be spent generating a further smaller 'multiplier' or induced effect and so on.

The size of the multiplier effects will depend on the characteristics of the firms and industry, inter-industry links, and on whether the effects of increased employment, income or of output are being considered. For example, new high-technology firms often have a higher multiplier effect than other sectors due to their higher proportion of professional management, scientific and technical staff than in the small firm sector as a whole. These are likely to be well-paid people generating high demand in the local community. In addition, such firms create a demand for high value-added services in the local economy, and they were found to have a lower propensity to import; they sub-contract locally to a higher degree. The importance of each of these factors will depend upon the specific local economy and characteristics of the firms involved.

Displacement effects are a major issue that policies to support new firm formation need to consider. These result when an increase in economic activity occurs as a result of the policy but this 'displaces' other activity in the local economy. For example, if a new firm is helped to start-up, for instance by a subsidy, then another local competitor may contract and shed jobs or close because they have lost market share to the new firm. Hence any extra income or employment generated by the new firm may have a similar negative impact on the competitors and the local economy overall may experience little benefit. Storey (1994) has argued that demand deficiency is the greatest problem for the small firm sector and that most start-up firms should not be aided as they will primarily cause displacement among other local firms. Other evidence also suggests that the level of displacement by start-ups is large. For example, a study of the Enterprise Scheme, which was to help unemployed people start-up firms in Ireland, found 90 per cent of all their business was taken from other firms and hence did not increase the size of the economy. Hence many policies focus upon traditional export-base theory stressing the need for bringing income into the area through exports from the region of manufactured goods or 'exportable' services.

This is the basic reason for public policies preferring firms that 'export' from the area or substitute for goods or services that would otherwise be 'imported' in the area. Hence, most hotels and the tourism industry can generally be termed 'export' as they sell their services to those outside the area. These exports lead to further multiplier impacts upon the local economy through the links with local suppliers and services. Innovative, manufacturing and higher growth firms generally have a larger geographical market and a higher rate of internationalization, so their displacement effect should be relatively low. However, shops are usually not aided as they would displace trade from other local shops.

Such displacement may not be totally negative as the reduction in market share of the existing firm may be due to better or more efficient services or products of the new firm. Indeed in any dynamic market economy there will be some displacement among firms. However, if policies just keep inefficient firms operating at the expense of efficient local ones, or one subsidized firm after another simply replaces other firms, then it can damage the local or regional economy.

Another form of displacement is where large parts of government budgets are used to employ consultants, for instance, to give advice or other support to businesses or to the government funded business development agencies. These consultants might spend a large part of their time and other resources working on such publicly funded contracts, or seeking the contracts, when it may be more efficient for the economy for them to be working directly for, and being paid by, private businesses instead. The publicly funded contracts may present such an opportunity cost for the consultants that they no longer act as entrepreneurially and seek business outside the region, so not directly expanding the region's economy. The consultants may however, help expand the region indirectly through the effects of their advice on businesses.

A final issue when analysing policies is the need to consider what would have happened in the local economy anyway. Activity that was supported by the policy but that would have taken place anyway without the policy is called 'deadweight'. For example, a firm may have been given support to start-up, but would have done so even without the grant. So this support did not actually lead to the firm starting and so is 'deadweight'. In the Enterprise Scheme cited above the 'deadweight' effect was found to be between 40 and 50 per cent, that is, almost half of the people would have started the business anyway. However, the policy may be justified if it helped sufficient firms expand more or faster than otherwise would have happened, or reduced failures, as these benefits should not be termed 'deadweight'.

Hence the real benefits of a policy is its 'additionality'. This is the output from the policy as compared to what would have occurred without the government intervention – that is, the net sum of the direct and indirect impacts, less any 'deadweight'. Good evaluation of the full effects of policies is crucial to greater understanding of the underlying processes behind changes in the economy and in entrepreneurship and how policies might influence them in different circumstances.

Illustration – Regional initiative to support entrepreneurship

A government economic development agency in Northern Ireland (Local Economic Development Unit, LEDU) set out its policy to support entrepreneurship and competitiveness among small firms according to the industrial sector and the stage of business development. In each main business life-cycle stage they had a number of initiatives.

Creation of enterprise culture awareness

This was done through seeking to:

- build positive attitudes to enterprise among the population;
- work with educational bodies, such as schools, so young people are taught its importance;
- expose individuals and small firms to role models of successful businesses and to opportunities for growth.

Pre-start-up stage

Policies focused upon:

- targeting those people most usefully attracted into business, especially those suffering constraints that prevent them from starting-up.

Start-up stage

Support for those starting-up was provided through:

- seeking to improve their skills by offering counselling and training;
- the development of suitable premises;
- providing finance and grants;
- assisting with marketing and research and development support.

Existing businesses

Support for existing businesses was provided through:

- developing initiatives based on knowledge of specific industrial sectors, for example, identify changes in markets, technology legislation, or prompt exploration of growth opportunities;
- supporting the development of operating plans and future growth strategies and plans;
- providing assistance for product/process innovation, and the design of quality projects (especially for exports);

- encouraging private professional advisers to support the policies;
- encouraging widening of horizons and skills within existing firms and professional advisers;
- taking initiatives to encourage improved private-sector financial support.

Growth opportunities

Specific high growth firms (for example, those with an expected 25 percent per annum increase in profitable turnover for three years) were targeted for additional support through:

- clearly identified and defined policies and approaches for specific industrial sectors;
- supporting companies to carry out evaluation, planning and implementation;
- ensuring increased management and skills development within the targeted firms;
- encouraging the development of a larger venture capital market;
- supporting the development of projects, especially those improving competitiveness and management skills.

This initiative follows a clear sequential pattern following the various stages through which an entrepreneur and their firm may develop.

Targeting policies

A further aspect of policies is the decision on where to target the policymaker's limited resources. How should the policies be targeted so as to achieve maximum impact and efficiency? Let us clarify two meanings of the word 'targeting' in this context. First it may mean prioritizing the allocation of resources to certain areas of support at a sectoral or strategic level, for example, deciding to aid existing firms in general rather than start-ups. Second, it can mean identifying and supporting specific individual businesses or potential businesses.

There are a number of arguments for and against targeting. First, targeting can help focus support agencies on strategic issues, increase effectiveness of support and respond to the diverse needs of firms. Strategic targeting of resources to different kinds of policies or support must depend on a full understanding of an economy and the role different kinds of firms are likely to play in its development. They need to decide if they should focus on policies to aid wealth creation or job creation or both and allocate resources accordingly. Hence targeting should lead to a clearer, explicit focus by the agencies developing the policies.

Second, as discussed in Chapter 2, the broad evidence suggests that a relatively few expanding firms are likely to account for most economic impact. They also have larger geographical markets and so less local displacement. Storey (1994) and Storey *et al.* (1987) similarly argue that 50 per cent of the employment gains attributed to start-up and small firms comes from only 4 per cent of the initial stock of the previous ten years and most growth comes from a few 'high-flyer' businesses. Also a general increase in the number of small self-employed businesses may not lead to more employment as there is little relationship between change in self-employment and change in national employment (OECD, 1992). Hence in terms of economic impact and cost effectiveness there appears to be a case for greater targeting of specific types of new and existing firms with significant growth potential. This is difficult to implement as there are problems with trying to 'pick winners' (see below).

Generally high growth small firms concentrate on quality, service levels or innovation. They identify new markets for existing (or slightly modified) products and increase the proportion of higher value added products (Smallbone *et al.*, 1995). Other less high growth small firms often concentrate upon price or credit as key competitive advantages. Growing firms encounter more obstacles in terms of finance, skilled labour, exporting, premises and so on than other firms and therefore may need more assistance from public and/or private bodies. In fact some go so far as to argue that no public assistance should go to start-up firms in general and support should only be given to those with a good track record or good prospects. This, however, tends to ignore market failure in terms of information for start-ups and assumes that growth firms will have this information through experience or private-sector professional advisers. Others argue that high growth firms have few problems and subsequently need little public assistance, and that growth firms will seek out sources of support themselves and so do not need to be targeted.

A third area of argument about targeting is that it may be difficult as public officials are not usually close enough to the technologies and markets to decide which has most growth potential and it may not be technically feasible to identify key distinguishing features of fast-growth firms. There may also be a lack of information due to the scale at which policy is planned. However, while it may be difficult, or near impossible, to identify specific firms or individuals which will succeed, it may be possible to identify types of firms whose success will greatly benefit the local economy. Support mechanisms (such as subsidized technical consultancies) can be made available to firms meeting relevant criteria. These firms may then be 'self-selected', (for example, only those responding to advertisements or other promotion of the schemes or those with a track record of high growth), that is, the firm approaches the support agency.

Fourth, it can be argued on the grounds of equity that it is unfair for the public sector to aid only certain types of firms, unless a clear case for doing so is provided. However, this will depend also on the degree of other support available to those who do not receive assistance and the criteria for targeted support. A fifth issue further concerns targeting, in that it has been argued that targeted support might be expensive to administer, although it should have less 'wastage' than general support. It has also been argued that market forces will allocate resources more efficiently than government agencies, and public agencies may deter private firms providing these services commercially, although the case of possible market failure and social benefits and costs has previously been mentioned.

Sixth, what if the wrong target is chosen? For instance, attention may be focused upon small firms, while key changes are occurring elsewhere, for example at the global level. At this level global firms with access to global production and markets are dominant. They may not increase their employment size due to sub-contracting, but they should increase their value added over time. Hence access by small growing firms to global companies, and so to global markets, may be an important focus for policies.

However, it should be noted that most economic development agencies have a range of policies covering such issues as support for inward investment, new business start-ups, existing small firms, disadvantaged communities and training for individuals. In summary, the development of policies must take careful consideration of their displacement, multiplier and deadweight effects, and the pros and cons of targeting.

Conclusion

There are a number of circumstances when economic welfare could be improved through international, national and local policies to support entrepreneurship and the creation of new firms. However, such policies need to be carefully designed and be based upon a thorough understanding of the economy and entrepreneurship. Otherwise the implementation of such policies may have negative displacement effects elsewhere in the economy, or have significant 'deadweight' and so adding little to what would have happened anyway. The national economic and social environment is important for entrepreneurship to flourish in all parts of the economy. Policies to support entrepreneurship are wide-ranging and include those to stimulate demand for new and small firms, to improve attitudes towards entrepreneurship, to aid access to research and development, technology, advice, finance, including venture capital, education, training and other infrastructure. These may all assist to increase entrepreneurship in the form of business startups and expansion; so too might reductions in unnecessary burdens of regulation and inappropriate taxation, although there must be a balance between taxation levels and the necessary human and physical infrastructure it supports.

There is a debate on whether support should be targeted upon the small number of high growth firms that supply most new jobs or rather upon helping to generate a large number of new firms. Supporters of the latter view stress the difficulty of identifying fast growth firms, the possibility of more fast growth firms arising from a larger pool of new starts (even if the proportion of fast growth firms in the pool is low), and most fast-growth firms might grow even without public support. Supporters of the former stress greater impacts, effectiveness and efficiency of a targeted policy, the displacement effects of large numbers of low growth start-ups and the low impact if limited resources are spread too thinly.

In addition, as was considered in Chapters 2 and 8, there are also many other ways in which policies can support entrepreneurship in the economy, such as encouraging it in large firms, or in government, albeit with suitable safeguards, or among other organizations such as 'not-for profit' organizations.

References and further reading

Birley, S. and P. Westhead (1993) 'A comparison of new businesses established by "novice" and "habitual" founders in Great Britain', *International Small Business Journal*, Vol. 12, pp. 38–60.

Blair, J.P. (1996) *Local Economic Development*, Thousand Oaks, Calif., Sage Publications.

CEC (Commission of the European Communities) (1995) *The European Employment Strategy: Recent Progress and Prospects for the Future*, COM (95) 465 Final, Luxembourg, OOPEC.

CEC (1996) *Enterprises in Europe*, 4th report, Luxembourg, Office for Official Publications of the European Communities.

CEC (1998) *Fostering Entrepreneurship in Europe: Priorities for the Future*, COM (198) 222 Final, Luxembourg, OOPEC.

Coase, R.H. (1960) 'The problem of social cost', *Journal of Law and Economics*, Vol. 3, pp. 1–44.

Curran, J. (1990) *Bolton Twenty Years On*, London, Small Business Research Trust.

Curran, J. and R. Blackburn (1994) *Small Firms and Local Economic Networks: The Death of the Local Economy*, London, Chapman Paul.

DTI Department of Trade and Industry (1995) *Small Firms in Britain 1995*, London, HMSO.

DTI (1998) *Our Competitive Future: Building the Knowledge Driven Economy*, Cmnd 4176, London, HMSO.

Hall, P., M. Breheny, R. McQuaid and D. Hart (1987) *Western Sunrise: Britain's High-Tech Corridor*, London, Routledge.

Harrison, J., B. Taylor, A. Todd and M. Tampoe (1986) *Supergrowth Companies – Entrepreneurs in Action*, London, Butterworth Heinemann.

Keeble, D., P. Tyler, G. Broom and J. Lewis, (1992) *Business Success in the Countryside: The Performance of Rural Enterprise*, London, HMSO.

McQuaid, R.W. (1996) 'Social Networks, Entrepreneurship and Regional Development', in M. Danson (ed.), *Small Firm Formation and Regional Economic Development*, pp. 118–31, London, Routledge.

OECD (1992) *Employment Outlook*, July 1992.

OECD (1996) *SMEs and Employment Creation: Overview of Selected Quantitative Studies in OECD Member Countries*, OECD Working Paper IV, Paris, OECD.

OECD (1997) *New Directions for Industrial Policy*, Policy Brief No. 3, Paris, OECD.

OECD (1998) *Fostering Entrepreneurship: A Thematic Review*, Paris, OECD.

Saxenian, A. (1994) *Regional Advantage: Culture and Competition in Silicon Valley and Route*, 128, Cambridge, Harvard University Press.

Scase, R. and R. Goffee, (1987) *The Real World of the Small Business Owner*, 2nd edn, London, Croom Helm.

Scottish Enterprise (1993) *Improving the Business Birthrate – A Strategy for Scotland*, Glasgow, Scottish Enterprise.

Scottish Enterprise (1996) *The Business Birthrate Strategy – Update*, Glasgow, Scottish Enterprise.

Sengenberger, W., G.W. Loveman and M.J. Piore (1990) *The Re-emergence of Small Enterprises: Industrial Restructuring in Industrial Countries*, Geneva, International Institute for Labour Studies.

Smallbone, D. (1995) 'Targeting established SMEs: Does Age Matter', *International Small Business Journal*, Vol. 13, pp. 47–64.

Smallbone, D., D. North and R. Leigh (1995) 'Characteristics and Strategies of Groups of High Growth SMEs in the UK 1979–1990', *International Journal of Entrepreneurial Behaviour and Research*, Vol. 1, pp. 44–62.

Storey, D.J. (1990) 'Entrepreneurship and the New Firm', in J. Curran, M.J.K. Stanworth and D. Watkins (eds), *The Survival of the Small firm: The Economics of Survival and Entrepreneurship*, Vol. 1, Aldershot, Gower.

Storey, D.J. (1994) *Understanding the Small Business Sector*, London, Routledge.

Storey, D.J., K. Keasey, R. Watson and P. Wynarczyk (1987) *The Performance of Small Firms: Profits, Jobs and Failures*, London, Croom Helm.

UK Treasury (1997) *Appraisal and Evaluation in Central Government*, London, HMSO.

Wilson Committee (1979) *The Financing of Small Firms: Interim Report of the Committee to Review the Functioning of Financial Institutions*, London, HMSO.

Part IV
Conclusions

10
Conclusions and Summary

Introduction

The previous chapters have shown the wide variety of ways in which economists and economic theory have considered entrepreneurs and entrepreneurship. By explicitly taking account of entrepreneurship these theories have helped improve our understanding of change in the economy. The field of entrepreneurship is rich in its variety of perspectives, often using different assumptions and providing different insights. The current chapter briefly pulls together a summary of the various ideas and concepts covered in earlier chapters.

What is entrepreneurship – revisited

The term entrepreneurship has been used to mean different things by different writers and there are various approaches to explaining its meaning. Five broad overlapping perspectives for considering entrepreneurs and entrepreneurship were described in Chapter 1. First entrepreneurship as an economic function was considered and the various roles of an entrepreneur within the economy, especially those of risk taking, resource allocation, innovation and as 'middleman'. Second, entrepreneurship was viewed as a form of behaviour which can be learned. Third, entrepreneurship was discussed in terms of the individual characteristics or personality of entrepreneurs. Fourth, entrepreneurship was viewed as an event, such as the creation of a new firm or organization. Finally, entrepreneurship is sometimes considered to be synonymous with owning and managing a (usually) small firm, although this was considered to inadequately capture the full behaviour and roles of entrepreneurs.

The entrepreneur has an important role in helping the economy to deal with the effective diffusion and use of knowledge, innovation and change, and the associated risks and uncertainty. Whether they cause or just respond to these changes is debated by various researchers. Another key element is that entrepreneurs assemble and combine resources to achieve things. Whether or not the entrepreneur actually needs to own these resources, or even to the level to which an entrepreneur is constrained by the level of existing resources are also issues of debate. However, fundamental to entrepreneurship is concrete achievement – actually making things happen.

The effective response to change and opportunity of all individuals and organizations (for example, large or small) is crucial to the success of a society and its economy. An entrepreneurial response is likely to be strategic rather than 'changing for the sake of change', or simply following the flow of others. Of particular importance in helping many economies to adapt to fundamental changes is the role of new business formation and particularly the development of fast growth businesses.

Entrepreneurship can be seen to encompass all parts of society, private, public or 'not-for-profit' sectors as well as those who are self-employed or owning, developing or running a business. However, the focus of the book is primarily on the role of private businesses in creating wealth and adding value to society through developing and building new business ventures. A broader perspective including social entrepreneurs who are primarily seeking to add value to society in other ways and non-traditional business organizations, such as community businesses and co-operatives is also considered in Chapter 8.

Entrepreneurship results from a combination of: the socio-economic environment such as the opportunities in the economy and the social context they live in (are entrepreneurs encouraged or frowned upon in society?); the personality of the entrepreneur; experience and how they learn necessary skills and attitudes and strategic thinking; and the use of purposeful insights to identify and take the opportunities identified. So the interaction between the entrepreneur and the environment within which they operate is important, and many disciplines (such as economics, management, psychology and sociology) can better help us to understand their role and behaviour.

Various definitions of firm size were discussed in Chapter 2. The vast majority of businesses in most economies are very small (which corresponds to the owner-manager or creator of a firm perspectives of entrepreneurs), although they are usually less important than medium and large-sized firms in employment terms. However, they have been important for job generation in most developed countries and have generally increased their share of total employment although small firms also suffer high job loss or death rates. Most new jobs and wealth have come from a tiny minority of very rapid growth new or small firms which reflects the innovative, risk taking and behavioural perspectives of entrepreneurship. The relative growth in numbers of new firms has been significant, although this has varied according to time and place.

The growing importance of small and new firms has been the result of a number of inter-related sets of factors, such as changes in the general socio-economic environment leading to greater opportunities for new firms, a greater supply of potential business creators together with a more supportive environment for entrepreneurship. How these factors may change in the future is, as always, uncertain.

Theories of entrepreneurship

Part II of the book considered a number of different theories and approaches to entrepreneurship. The various theories are shown to have different methodologies, basic assumptions and to be trying to do different things. However, with the possible exception of earlier neoclassical theories, all the approaches which were considered regard entrepreneurship as a specific and vital economic function. In each theory, entrepreneurship might be perceived overall as a key force within economies which allows them to develop and function efficiently.

Neoclassical versus market dynamics approaches

In early neoclassical general equilibrium models, there was no explicit entrepreneurial role identified. Although later neoclassical theorists have attempted to incorporate a specific entrepreneurial function, their attempts to do so are rather limited in their outlook and generally do not differentiate between entrepreneurs and business managers (see Chapter 3).

A main concern of neoclassical approaches is with the achievement of a final equilibrium at a point in time, rather than the process through which that equilibrium is achieved. In this relatively static analysis, there is limited scope for analysing entrepreneurship beyond narrow parameters that are laid down by the need to specify the rational behaviour of economic actors within the economic system, the type of behaviour they implement and the impact of their behaviour on the system. Thus entrepreneurs are a component in the system, with their behaviour being directed by exogenous forces. In this respect, this approach has difficulties in incorporating aspects of reality such as dynamic and purposeful human behaviour and the causes of change in the economic environment. Even in later general equilibrium models which do identify a specific function for entrepreneurship in equilibrium, this function is normally narrowly defined in terms of the management of a production process in some respect, and the prime or sole motivation for undertaking entrepreneurial activity is income, generated from residual profits.

Within the more 'realistic' Marshallian partial equilibrium approach, there is still limited scope for analysing entrepreneurship. While all business managers have to be 'enterprising' in order to survive and develop, there is no specific group of economic actors who may be defined as entrepreneurs rather than business managers. An important aspect of Marshall's analysis, however, is the concern with economic evolution and time rather than the more static approach of general equilibrium theory. Knight makes a clear distinction between entrepreneurs and managers, with entrepreneurs possessing the ability to make judgmental, strategic decisions which generate profits for their firms. Purely administrative managers do not do this as it is argued that they have insufficient foresight, and thus they are not entrepreneurs. In all of these approaches, however, there is insufficient scope for the type of purposeful, proactive and dynamic behaviour which is typically associated with successful, 'real world' entrepreneurship, and there is the assumption that perfect knowledge can in some way exist in the economic system which entails that optimal resource allocation is possible at a point in time. Neoclassical economics does serve as a solid basis against which to judge the theoretical and practical value of the other approaches to analysing entrepreneurship. However, some question the appropriateness of using static neoclassical models and analysing changes at the margin when trying to understand and model the dynamic world inhabited by entrepreneurs.

There are a number of alternative economic approaches, central to which are differing conceptions of the nature of knowledge in the economic system and the ways in which decisionmakers acquire and use knowledge. They see entrepreneurship as an essential function in the process of market change and adjustment. Kirzner and Schumpeter, in contrast to most static neoclassical analysis, both relate entrepreneurship explicitly to their dynamic operations. However their approaches are each based on different assumptions (refer to Chapter 4).

Kirzner viewed entrepreneurs as individuals who exploit price differentials, created by ignorance on the part of others, in return for profit. In the process, entrepreneurs signal information to other market participants and help to restore markets to equilibrium. This view of entrepreneurship as a stabilizing force in market economies is in contrast to Schumpeter's view of the entrepreneur as a creator of disequilibrium, through innovation and new ideas, in return for profit. In both of these theories, as in Knight's, in order to carry out the entrepreneurial function entrepreneurs, as individuals, must possess particular abilities. In these theories the most important aspect of entrepreneurship relates to the ability to create or adapt to change and to exploit new ideas and opportunities in the pursuit of profit. Schumpeter emphasizes entrepreneurs as creators of change.

Towards a comprehensive theory

Casson attempts to synthesize elements from different theoretical approaches into a comprehensive theory of entrepreneurs and their activities – see Chapter 5. Fundamental to Casson's theory is the notion that entrepreneurs must also be good business managers in order to manage the expansion of their firms so as to exploit profit opportunities. It may be questioned whether entrepreneurs can also be business managers given the contrast in the skills and abilities it takes to perform each function. Casson's theory also recognizes socio-economic influences on entrepreneurial activity, in particular, in determining the entrepreneur's ability to gain access to resources.

The impact of social influences, rather than purely economic influences, on entrepreneurial activity was further developed in the work of Etzioni. While Etzioni did not perceive entrepreneurship as the cause of change, he still defined the central role of entrepreneurship as the cause of economic evolution, in that only entrepreneurs test out new ideas and ensure that the best survive. The organizational theory of economic evolution developed by Nelson and Winter also finds a role for entrepreneurs as the promoters of new and better ideas, and as the decisionmakers who can determine the best organizational forms through which change can be implemented efficiently.

A common feature of the theories considered so far is that they concentrate primarily on the 'function' of entrepreneurship, whether the emphasis is purely economic as in Knight and Kirzner, or within a wider social and institutional environment as in Schumpeter, Etzioni or Casson. There is some conflict, however, with regard to whether entrepreneurial activity is best undertaken at an individual or a collective level.

Underlying this conflict are differing views of human decisionmaking in the face of imperfect knowledge.

The Austrian school's view of individuals making 'incorrect' rational choices because they are ignorant of some information, conflicts with that of the socio-economic and organizational view that imperfect knowledge leads to bounded rationality, which suggests that collective decisions should be consistently better than those of individuals. This debate illustrates the importance of the problem of 'knowledge' in economic theory, in terms of how it is created, accessed and used in decisions concerning resource allocation.

The concept of economic evolution (considered by Marshall as far back as the late nineteenth century and which is central to the theories of both Schumpeter and Etzioni) is developed further in Chapter 6. This considers the qualities required to act entrepreneurially, and related entrepreneurship to market dynamics and economic evolution, as well as equilibrium. In addressing the issue of the nature and impact of entrepreneurship in determining patterns and modes of production a range of economic approaches were brought together. It is argued that social and cultural factors are fundamentally important in determining economic performance.

Non-economic approaches to entrepreneurship

'Non-economic' perspectives on entrepreneurship have, in general, placed greater emphasis on the sociological and psychological determinants of entrepreneurial activity and on management issues (Chapter 7). Such non-economic perspectives pay greater attention to entrepreneurs as people, with personal attributes, needs and ambitions, or to entrepreneurship as a form of behaviour which is associated with successful businesses, rather than entrepreneurship as an economic function. Of course, all of these factors can be included in a wider definition of economic approaches to entrepreneurship and are not necessarily mutually exclusive.

A review of these perspectives identifies that the broad concern in sociology is with the types of people who are entrepreneurs in terms of their social backgrounds and influences, while psychologists have generally focused on the intrinsic cognitive factors which predispose some people towards becoming entrepreneurs. Management theorists, on the other hand, are shown to have displayed a greater interest in the manifestations of entrepreneurship as forms of managerial behaviour adopted in developing successful businesses. It is felt that such analyses of entrepreneurial management behaviour have helped to advance management science. Combining more interdisciplinary economics and non-economic perspectives may lead to a more 'holistic' emerging 'entrepreneurship paradigm' which tries to combine the subtle influences of the individual entrepreneur with the wider economic and social environment within which they operate.

The main economic implications which arise from incorporating non-economic factors influencing entrepreneurial activity are considered in terms of the reasons why individuals decide to undertake entrepreneurial activity, and the subsequent performance of their firms. Two broad sets of factors which determine entrepreneurial activity are identified, they are 'push' factors, and 'pull' factors. Only the latter corresponds to the perception of entrepreneurship in economic theory of opportunistic and innovative activity.

People who are 'pushed' into entrepreneurial activity due, for instance, to the loss of their previous job, will generally not run growth-potential firms. This is not to say that this will always be the case. A review of dynamic generalist theories of entrepreneurial development suggests that some of these entrepreneurs may develop into more 'businesslike' entrepreneurs pursuing profits and growth, and implementing strategic managerial practices to achieve those goals. The evidence, however, is that the majority will not, and their firms will remain small and they will not add much value to the economy individually. It is important, however, to look at the issue of entrepreneurship in the small firm sector at an aggregate level, taking account of wider network relationships.

Entrepreneurship in the wider society

The book also considers some of the links between the role of entrepreneurship and the wider society and public policies. In particular it considered non-traditional businesses with social as well as economic aims and social or civic entrepreneurship in third-sector and public bodies. Social entrepreneurship was considered important throughout the economy, especially in the development of the growing third- or 'not-for-profit' sector of the economy, in Chapter 8. Hence it influences the dynamism of the economy and its ability to deal with crucial social, environmental and other issues. It shares many of the characteristics of entrepreneurship within the private sector, with the main exception of aiming for social benefit rather than profit and arguably focusing relatively more upon different stakeholders (such as the clients rather than owners of the organization). Many social entrepreneurs still seek to obtain profits, although these profits may not be distributed to share-holders, but rather used to further the purposes of the organization or to ensure its survival. While attempts have been made to bridge social and commercial objectives through business organizations such as community businesses or co-operatives, evidence of success is generally mixed.

A number of reasons are discussed whereby economic welfare could be improved through supra-national, national and local policies to support entrepreneurship and the creation of start-up firms (see Chapter 9). However, if they are applied inappropriately or not designed carefully such policies could also have negative displacement effects elsewhere in the economy, or have significant 'deadweight' by adding little to what would have happened anyway. Some policy factors affect primarily the national economic and social environment, such as tax structures, open trade, a supportive culture, and stable monetary and fiscal policies. These are important for assisting entrepreneurship to flourish in all parts of the economy, including new start-up businesses, as well as in small, medium and large-sized firms.

A variety of generally more local or microeconomic policies have been developed in many places. Different policies appear to be based upon each of the definitions of entrepreneurship – some focus upon the event of starting a new business, others on economic functions such as innovation, others as a form of behaviour in various types of organizations. Psychological or sociological perspective have also been used to understand, develop and target policies among different groups of the population. Such policies, generally based upon ameliorating market failure, include providing business support infrastructure, assisting potential entrepreneurs by providing advice and training to develop necessary skills and competencies. They also assist small firms to overcome barriers due to market failures in areas such as access to finance, technology, markets and physical infrastructure. A strong and healthy supply of private sector support services, such as accountants, financiers, patent agents and so on is also crucial for the successful development of firms in an area.

A tiny percentage of the most entrepreneurial new firms create most new jobs in that sector. There is therefore a debate on whether support should be targeted upon the small number of high growth firms that supply most new jobs or rather upon generating a large number of new firms. Supporters of the latter view stress the difficulty of identifying fast growth firms, the possibility of more fast growth firms arising from a larger pool of new starts (even if the proportion of fast growth firms in the pool fell) and the possibility that most fast growth firms might grow even without public support. Supporters of the latter stress the greater impact, effectiveness and efficiency of targeted policies and the displacement effects of large numbers of low growth start-ups, together with the lowering of impact if limited resources are spread too thinly. Often a combination of some targeted and some less targeted policies is adopted. Generally, however, policies rarely explicitly state their theoretical basis.

Finally, the appendix briefly discussed business planning in order to identify some of the key practical issues facing potential entrepreneurs in developing his or her ideas and gaining the necessary resources to carry them out. It is stressed that the business planning process is part of a wider strategic decisionmaking process. It illustrates generally how both the internal characteristics of the business and its external environment both profoundly affect the entrepreneur's decisionmaking process. So it shows how the individual and the external environment may come together as discussed in the 'emerging entrepreneurship paradigm' above.

Final comments

In conclusion, the role of entrepreneurship in all parts of the economy is too important to be relegated to a footnote in economic theory. However, there remains no standard theoretical approach to the study of entrepreneurship. In this book a wide range of contrasting perspectives has been considered, each shedding some light upon the role of entrepreneurship in the economy and in economic theory. The theories seem to be moving towards more 'holistic' approaches which try to understand both the unique motives and actions of individual entrepreneurs, together with the two-way influence of the dynamic external social and economic environment upon the entrepreneur.

This has important implications for empirical methodologies and the process of theory construction in the study of entrepreneurship. Emphasis needs to be placed on developing conceptual models which help to 'ground' theory in reality. The knowledge base has been built up across a diverse range of contexts.

Emphasis needs to be placed upon the dynamic process of entrepreneurship and more research on the performance of small entrepreneurial firms and entrepreneurship in other types of organisations, using techniques such as in-depth empirical analysis observation, is required. This is in order to generate theory which is grounded in reality and which can provide the building blocks for the development of a body of higher level theory for an 'entrepreneurship science'.

Appendix: Business Planning – a Guide to Developing a Business Plan

Introduction

In the main chapters of this book we considered a number of theories of entrepreneurship. Whether the entrepreneur decides to go ahead with a new business or project will depend upon many factors, including the characteristics of the business and the likely impacts of the external environment. This appendix considers some of these practical issues faced by potential entrepreneurs as they seek to identify and consider whether to take the opportunities available to them. As discussed in earlier chapters, some of the key aspects of entrepreneurship are: searching for and analysing opportunities; testing out these ideas; having clear goals and timescales to achieve them; assembling and organizing resources; implementing the plans; growing and developing the business; and finally for some entrepreneurs realizing the value created through the business. Careful, honest and well thoughtout strategies and plans, plus perhaps luck, are essential components of realizing the opportunities identified by the entrepreneur. Hence analysing the business plan process will help to achieve a deeper understanding of entrepreneurs' actions.

A business plan is a written statement of what the business or organization expects to achieve and the resources and actions required to achieve it. It is part of the wider strategic decisionmaking process of the organization. A traditional rational model of the strategic decision-making model involves an interactive process of: analysis of the external environment; consideration of internal resources; analysis of strengths, weaknesses, opportunities and threats (SWOT); determination of the expectations of stakeholders (owners, staff, customers, suppliers and others with a stake in the organization) and of the organization's mission, goals and objectives; identifying and choosing between the strategic choices; implementation; and monitoring and evaluation of the strategy. So the business plan results from the strategic decisionmaking process and is used for external and internal management purposes particularly in fast-growth firms (Baker *et al.*, 1993).

The role of a business plan

A business plan tests the viability of an idea and sets out what the business or organization expects to achieve together with the resources and actions required to do so. Once developed it acts as a map for the operation of the business showing what is expected to be done and when. Hence it also allows monitoring of actual progress against the plan. Of course, as the business develops so will the business plan.

There is no single particular form that a business plan should take. Its form will depend on factors such as the specific people and products involved, whether the plan is for setting up a new venture or expanding an existing one, whether the organization is profit or not-for-profit orientated and so on. In this appendix the main focus is upon business plans for setting up new businesses. However, what is important is the process of developing, clearly setting out and implementing the best, practical plan.

Business plans have different roles in different circumstances. The process of creating a new business helps to establish the goals, strategies and tactics for start-up and operation of the new venture. The creation process goes through a number of phases: identification of the opportunities; commercial and technical feasibility analysis; business planning; resource acquisition (what resources are needed, how are they acquired and assembled, or control gained over them?); implementation; and monitoring and evaluation.

The first role of the business plan is to check the commercial and technical viability of the idea. Will the business be financially viable and give an adequate return? Can the goods or services be produced to the desired specification within the costs. Is there a realistic market for the proposed product and will the plan lead to a viable level of sales in the market?

Second, the plan will: establish goals, strategies and tactics, for starting-up the business and then operating it; and to show that the goals are achievable and what the results of achieving them are. In other words it sets out and analyses what the objectives of the business are, what needs to be done to achieve them. In so doing it also helps identify the skills of the team that will be needed to fulfil the ideas (as no entrepreneur is likely to have all the necessary skills themselves). Some of the key skills for entrepreneurs that are essential in developing and implementing a good business plan include building an effective team, picking good advisers, product development and marketing skills, obtaining finance and usually, preferably, prior experience of a new start-up situation.

A third role is to use the plan to convince external organizations to provide the necessary resources for implementation. Indeed, most banks, investors or even grant giving agencies will demand a business plan before agreeing to provide any funds, as a good plan should show that the business idea has been fully considered and is viable. Jerry Kaplan's 1995 book 'Startup: A Silicon Valley Adventure' gives an interesting account of the difficulties of financing a small high-tech start-up company.

Fourth, the plan has an internal role acting as an operational plan for the venture. Such an operational plan is likely to be longer than one aimed at an external audience. A fifth role is for the plan to act as part of a monitoring system. So if actual performance of the business varies from that identified in the plan, then the reasons for this and the implications for the future need to be considered and any remedial action taken at an early stage.

Why is a business plan useful?

A business plan takes considerable resources and effort to develop, but in return it provides a number of benefits. These benefits include:

(1) It provides a logical framework to develop a well thought-out plan of action and identifies objectives to be achieved during the period covered by the plan.
(2) It identifies and analyses existing and future strengths and weaknesses of the proposed business and shows that opportunities, for example, for high sales growth, have been identified.
(3) It pulls together the various plans and tasks that need to be carried out and relates them together; that is, marketing, production, finance and human resources plans. This may be particularly important where an entrepreneur has perhaps worked in the industry and has knowledge of the product, but limited expertise in other areas of running the business.

(4) It ensures that the plan is viable – technically and financially – and that necessary analysis, such as a marketing plan, has been carried out fully (see above).

(5) It defines key aspects of the business environment in which the business operates, how these affect the business and how the business can adapt to potential changes in the environment.

(6) It considers realistically the constraints on the operation and development of the business and sets out ways that these will be overcome.

(7) It provides a framework for viewing the future and helps set out well thoughtout contingency plans to meet potential constraints or changes in the environment.

(8) It allows an assessment of risk and uncertainty, and sensitivity to different variables (for example, if sales forecasts are over optimistic) and how these are to be dealt with.

(9) It allows monitoring of expected and actual performance by providing a benchmark or targets, and so aids early alteration in direction if targets are not being met or if performance is likely to lead to future problems, or if there are unexpected future occurrences.

(10) It serves as a basis for gaining the commitment of others including employees, other stakeholders or funders.

Hence the business plan improves our understanding of the business and the internal connections between its various components, such as marketing and production, and the external connections with the wider economic and social environment, as well as setting out a clear way forward for all those involved to follow.

There are also some potential problems with using business plans. The quality of analysis may be poor or weaknesses not fully considered. For instance, demand projections are often overestimated and so a plan that may appear to be viable may in practice be unprofitable. Hence sensitivity analysis is usually included, where the sensitivity of the results to variations in key assumptions or estimates (such as sales) is determined. For example, what are the implications of sales being 10 per cent or 20 per cent below expectations, or of labour costs being 5 per cent higher?

Another problem is that the plan may be used as a means to gain funding, but once this happens the plan often gets ignored. Conversely, the plan could act as a 'straightjacket' as people follow it and miss out on other opportunities that arise during its implementation. The plan must be flexible and adapt to, and show the impacts of, changing circumstances and proposals. Otherwise it will become primarily a control mechanism possibly limiting or constraining the action of the organization.

Components of business plans

There is no single format or type of business plan. For instance, different types of business will seek different balances of funding between loans and shares. A business seeking a loan from a bank may emphasize the assets owned and the steady, long-term sales, as these provide security to the lender and demonstrate an ability to repay the loan and interest.

On the other hand a business seeking funding from a venture capitalist or private investor may emphasize the high sales growth potential, the financial projections, the experience of key staff in high growth businesses and the opportunities for the investors to realize their investment within a short time scale (for example, through a stock market listing, management buyout or selling business to a larger firm). These investors may be looking for an annual compounded return of 25–50 per cent or more over a three to seven year period. This high return is partly justified by the high risk and the need for high returns on the successful firms in the investor's portfolio to compensate for other investments which fail. Hence the business plan must be adapted to meet the needs of its intended audience.

Figure A1 outlines an example of a business plan format and each component is now discussed in turn.

Executive summary

This concisely covers all the main points in the plan and must convince the reader that it is worth reading the remainder of the plan.

Description of the business

This will include a description of the business and its current and proposed future legal status (for example, a franchise, or independent producer and whether it is a private corporation, partnership, proprietorship/sole traders and so on), the management team and any strategic alliances (proposed or existing) with other businesses (details and letters of agreement are likely to be attached in an appendix). Also included may be a review of the organization's mission, short- and long-term goals, objectives and strategy, and identification of the key personnel involved in implementing the strategy.

One key question will be 'what business are we in?' One example was a bus company who along with their passengers carried considerable

Figure A1 Example Format of a Business Plan

Executive Summary	
Description of the business	– description – objectives/strategy
Markets and competition	– proposed market – analysis of competition
Product/service offered	– product/service specification
Marketing	– pricing strategy – sales and promotion – distribution – sales projections
Operation and production	– equipment requirements – production planning – production control and quality – location/premises
Human resources	– ownership/management – people requirements – key skills required – recruitment and training programme
Financial data	– historical performance – capital expenditure – proposed funding – product costing – projected balance sheet – projected cash flows – projected profit and loss – sensitivity analysis – break-even analysis – return on investment – main risks
Company structure	– organization and responsibilities – ownership
Appendices	

Note: Business plans for specific audiences such as venture capitalists may stress aspects such as human resources (particularly the management team), growth potential and the corporate structure near the start of the plan.

volumes of goods in their buses. They redefined their business from being a bus company moving people to that of being a passenger and goods transport company. This then led them to purchase aircraft to meet the needs of customers wanting their goods transported faster than buses allowed.

Markets and competition

The existing and proposed markets for the business need thoughtful analysis. Key questions include a careful definition of what the market is (who will buy the product and how their decision is made) its size, trends, how the market is segmented, its elasticity of demand, and the influence of macroeconomic, demographic and social changes. In the case of foreign trade, access to markets may also be critical and issues such as patents, regulations, legal factors, quotas or tariffs, local acceptance of the product and the political environment need to be considered. How the business proposes to position itself (for example, high quality and high priced, market leader, or as a cheaper supplier) needs to be decided and justified.

Finally, the direct and indirect competition need to be analysed, possibly in terms of the general market and the specific market niche involved. Lessons can be learned from the operation and the products/services of competitors and their strengths and weaknesses. This will help determine likely responses of potential competitors and so impact upon the proposed marketing plan and other factors. You may have seen interviewers with clipboards asking people in the street about their attitudes to new or existing products. This is part of a market analysis. Market analysis and reports usually need to include going out and talking to and listening to potential customers and seeing what is happening in the marketplace.

Product/service offered

The characteristics of the product or service need to be specified and the product differentiated from competitors. This may cover the full service or product including, for instance, whether the product is to be sold through direct sales or mail order and how after sales service will be provided. Any further design or development work required has to be identified. The product may be differentiated from competitors in a number of ways, such as technology, product or service quality, speed of delivery, location and so on and use of e-commerce.

Marketing

After analysing the market a marketing strategy will need to be developed. This may include the product characteristics and product support services (see above), as well as pricing, promotion/selling and distribution plans. These and the market analysis are used to estimate sales forecasts or projections. Issues to consider include promotion through advertising, public relations, training and support for sales staff and the cost and effectiveness of different options. For example, the Tesco supermarket used to 'stack them high and sell them cheap' when it came to tins of baked beans and other food but then moved more 'upmarket' with greater choice and quality of some products. When looking at new products or businesses created by Virgin, it is common to see the entrepreneur Richard Branson's face prominently displayed, as part of their marketing strategy.

Marketing is a crucial part of the plan, because if estimated sales are not achieved then the entire financial viability of the project is affected. Similarly an over-optimistic sales forecast can make almost any business plan appear financially viable. The level of activity of the business, for example, in terms of production levels, is also determined by actual sales, so these estimates and plans are usually sensitive to sales forecasts. However, sales projections are often the part of the business plan with the greatest uncertainty, as the costs of production and so on can often be estimated fairly accurately for given levels of output, but sales will depend on many uncertainties such as customer and competitor responses.

Operation and production

A major innovation in production and operation was made by Direct Line Insurance: they were the first major UK company to sell car and house insurance cover over the telephone. Before that most companies had expensive offices in towns across the country, or operated through brokers who were paid commission. Many customers found the new telephone based production method more convenient as well as being cheaper. Since then telephone, and then internet and e-commerce, banking, travel, insurance and other companies have sprung up.

This section of the business plan describes how the goods or services will be manufactured or provided, identifying any potential problems with new technology or new production locations, and the alternative supplies of key inputs. In the case of services the exact location of the service (especially for retailing) will be especially critical. For instance questions may include what kind of location and building is needed, how accessible are the proposed locations and will demographic or market shifts affect its attractiveness. Also described in the plan may be the systems needed to maintain product quality, ensure environmental compliance and reduce environmental impacts, the use of sub-contractors and the lead times for getting up and running, and changing production levels. The way in which the business operates and how operations are controlled may also be considered.

Human resources

Crucial to the success of organizations are the people working for them and how well these people are motivated and managed. Except in a very small business, there will be a management team with differing, but complementary, skills. The perceived quality of this team is often the most important factor in an investor deciding to support the business. Hence describing the management team and its strengths and weaknesses is a crucial part of the plan. Required skills and training of staff, recruitment plans, incentives, how two-way communication between staff and management will be promoted, and salaries and benefits all require consideration and need to be summarized in the plan.

Financial data

This section includes a number of financial forecasts, shown in cash flow statements, incomes statements/profit and loss accounts and balance sheets for the next five years or so. Each of these must be consistent with the rest of the plan and with each other, and should show existing and future financial needs. All types of expenditure and income need to be accounted for. These include sales, cost of sales (variable costs such as material, labour and a fixed cost or overhead element), plus marketing, research and development, interest, administration costs, stocks/ inventory, debtors/accounts receivable and creditors/ accounts payable, capital investments (e.g. equipment), cash holding, loans and equity or other investments in the business, depreciation, bad debts and taxes.

If external funding is being sought then the amount required, its form (e.g. equity or loan), why it is required, and the way in which it is to be used will also need to be stated. As discussed above, different potential funders may focus on different points such as security provided by assets (to cover a bank loan and interest), or growth and level of returns for the equity investors. If the firm is already in existence, the impact of new funding on its capital structure needs to be identified. The investors are likely to also consider the operating margins (gross profit), marketing, R & D and other expenses as a percentage of sales and compare them to industry norms or other experience. The financial ratios from the balance sheet will be important as they will show asset management (for example, managing cash or debtors) and financial investors are usually more likely to understand these than the product or operation of the business. Also they will carry out a valuation of the business often based on earnings after a few years together with an industry specific factor, so they can estimate the value of the business and their investment in it at that future date.

The forecasts need sensitivity analysis to be carried out on them. In particular the risks, key assumptions and variables need to be tested in order to see the effect of changes in them upon the overall forecasts. For instance, what if sales grow at 25 per cent less than forecast, or if material costs are 10 per cent higher than expected? Sensitivity in terms of time may be important also. What if the opening date is delayed, or a main customer demands an extra month's credit? These may all affect the viability of the project, but also the amount of investment or loan facility required and the size of the contingency budget. It is better to ask for a larger loan facility early on, rather than wait until a cash flow crisis has been reached by the business before approaching the bank.

Company structure

As mentioned previously the managerial organization, the structure of the company and the responsibilities of key managers need to be identified. In addition, the current ownership of the business and changes in the ownership due to implementing the plan need to be shown. Other future potential ownership changes, such as an exit route for investors (for example, a stockmarket listing), will depend upon the exact ownership structure of the business and are often also shown.

Conclusion

This appendix has outlined some of the wide range of factors facing an entrepreneur when decided on whether to proceed with a new business opportunity and how they can be combined in the logical framework of a business plan. These show some of the practical influences upon an entrepreneur's decision. What is important to note is that the plan will vary according to the type of business and the use that is to be made of the plan – in particular whether the audience for the plan is internal or external to the organization. In the end, however, it is the drive of those involved, rather than the plan itself, that determines if success is achieved.

References and further reading

Baker, W.H., H.L. Adams and B. Davis (1993) 'Business Planning in Successful Small Firms,' *Long Range Planning*, Vol. 26, pp. 82–8.

Grant, R. (1993) *Planning for Growth – How to Expand your Business Profitably*, Hemel Hempstead, Director Books.

Kaplan, J. (1995) *Startup: A Silicon Valley Adventure*, New York, Penguin.

Index